THE SECOND CENTURY OF CINEMA

THE **SUNY** SERIES

CULTURAL STUDIES IN CINEMA/VIDEO

WHEELER WINSTON DIXON | EDITOR

THE SECOND CENTURY OF CINEMA

The Past and Future of the Moving Image

WHEELER
WINSTON
DIXON

STATE UNIVERSITY OF NEW YORK PRESS

Published by
State University of New York Press, Albany

© 2000 State University of New York

Printed in the United States of America

For information, address State University of New York Press,
State University Plaza, Albany, N.Y., 12246

Production by Marilyn P. Semerad
Marketing by Dana Yanulavich

Library of Congress Cataloging-in-Publication Data

Dixon, Wheeler W., 1950–
    The second century of cinema : the past and future of the moving image /
Wheeler Winston Dixon.
        p.   cm. — (The SUNY series, cultural studies in cinema/video)
    Includes bibliographical references and index.
    ISBN 0-7914-4515-1 (hardcover : alk. paper). — ISBN 0-7914-4516-X
(pbk. : alk. paper)
    1. Motion pictures. I. Title. II. Series.
PN1994.D545 2000
791.43—dc21   99-29900
                                                                          CIP

10 9 8 7 6 5 4 3 2 1

For Dana Miller

Listen carefully to first criticisms made of your work. Note just what it is about your work that the critics don't like—then cultivate it. That's the only part of your work that's individual and worth keeping.

—Jean Cocteau to a young artist

CONTENTS

ACKNOWLEDGMENTS

Writing a book of this sort is a very difficult task, because in it I want not only to explore the future of cinematic representationalism in the coming century, but also to examine how key works in various dominant and marginal cinemas will help to shape the visions to come. As I will argue, the filmic medium itself is about to undergo a complete transformation. Video imagery is becoming cheaper and more pervasive, increasing the ease of both production and exhibition. At the same time, the portability and flexibility of low-cost video production gives new voice to those ignored by the mainstream cinema; yet, paradoxically, the increased costs of distribution make it ever more difficult for alternative cinema/video works to reach an international audience. As a production medium, 16mm film is dead; 35mm may well follow within the next ten to fifteen years, signaling a significant shift in the production and reception process of that which we call the cinema. Editing of film is no longer done on film itself; that vanished in the 1970s. For ease, for cost-effectiveness, for its multiple capabilities, the AVID system, among others, has become the new standard for film editing. Indeed, many new films are being shot entirely on digital video, such as Thomas Vinterberg's brilliant film *Celebration* and Bennett Miller's *The Cruise* (both 1998), and then blown up to 35mm for theatrical distribution. Soon 35mm projection may well become obsolete, leading to an entirely new digital video era of image production and exhibition, almost precisely one hundred years after the birth of cinema.

In the early years of the twenty-first century, I argue, we will finally do away with film altogether, replacing it with a high-definition matrix of dots and pixels laser-projected onto a conventional theater screen, and audiences will overwhelmingly accept this transformation without comment. The cinematograph, after all, is essentially an exclusion of the Magic Lantern apparatus—light thrown on a screen—and it has had dominion over the entire twentieth century. Now, in the new millennium, different images of image storage and retrieval will replace the allure of film as surely as magnetic tape replaced optical soundtracks as a vehicle of cinema production. We will be witnessing a silent revolution of images, in which the digital creations of a new breed of "directors" will be as real and substantial to us as Humphrey Bogart, Leonardo DiCaprio, Bela Lugosi, and Jean Harlow are to twentieth-century audiences and archivists. How will this transformation be effected? What will we look for? What new visions will we witness? These are some of the questions I hope to address in this volume.

Earlier versions of some of the chapters and materials in this book appeared in the following publications: my interview with Jonathan Miller, along with my article on Philip Glass's new digital opera, *Monsters of Grace*, both appeared in *Popular Culture Review*; my thanks to Felicia Campbell, editor. A version of my comments on the cinematic adaptations of the works of H. P. Lovecraft originally appeared as "Cinematic Interpretations of the Works of H. P. Lovecraft," in *Lovecraft Studies* 22/23 (Fall 1990): 3–9, Mark A. Michaud, publisher. "H. P. Lovecraft: A Critical Reevaluation," appeared in a different form in *West Virginia University Philological Papers* 34 (Fall 1988): 102–110, Armand E. Singer, editor-in-chief. My comments on the prescience of the "B," or independent film were first presented at the conference National Traditions in Motion Pictures at Kent State University in Ohio, in the spring of 1985, and were published as part of the proceedings of that event; my thanks to Rick Newton, Chair, Department of Modern and Classical Language Studies. My interview with Roger Corman originally appeared in *Post Script* 8.1 (Fall 1988); my thanks to Gerald Duchovnay, editor. My interview with Bryan Forbes originally appeared in *Classic Images* 270 (December 1997), and my interview with Brian Clemens appeared in issue 287 (May 1999) of the same journal; my thanks to Robert King, editor. My thoughts on the films of Paul Robeson, originally titled "The Films of Paul Robeson: Compromise and Triumph," were presented as a paper at the 1998 MLA National Convention, chaired by Mark Reid, and will soon be published in the journal *Classic Images*; my thanks again to Robert King, editor. Finally, an earlier draft of my thoughts on the cinematic adaptations of Shakespeare's plays appeared under the title "The

Performing Self in Filmed Shakespearean Drama" in *Shakespeare Bulletin* 5.4 (July/August 1987); my thanks to James P. Lusardi, co-editor. The cover photo for this volume is a scene from Jane and Louise Wilson's video piece *Stasi City*, courtesy of the 303 Gallery, New York.

For their continuing support of my work, I want to sincerely thank Mark Reid, John Tibbets, Marcia Landy, Tom Conley, Tony Williams, David Desser, Brian Foster, Michael Steinman, Thomas Elsaesser, Wendy Everett, Jim Welsh, Renèe de Graaf, Mark Baker, Venetria Patton, Frank Tomasulo, Steven Shaviro, Lloyd Michaels, James Welsh, Linda Pratt, David Brinkerhoff, Laurence Kardish, Joshua Siegel, and numerous other colleagues who have offered both assistance and valuable insights to me during the long work of writing this volume. I also want to express my sincere gratitude to my colleagues in the Department of English at the University of Nebraska, Lincoln, and particularly to the UNL Research Council for a Summer Research Fellowship in 1999, which allowed me to visit the New Zealand Film Archive, where I was graciously assisted in my research for chapter 3 of this volume by Frank Stark and Virginia Callanan, ably assisted by staff members, Bronwyn Taylor, Diane Pivac, Sarah Davy, and Miranda Kaye. My sincere thanks to them. In addition, I was able to do research on the films of New Zealand at the Studiecentrum Bibliotheek of the Nederlands Filmmuseum in Amsterdam, with help from Jasper Koedam, Michel Bonset, Bastiaan Anink, and Jan-Hein Bal, also during the summer of 1995. Finally, I presented a paper on digital cinema at the Millennium Film Conference at the University of Bath in July 1999, and delivered a series of six guest lectures on digital production theory at the University of Amsterdam as part of my research in that city. I wish to sincerely thank Donald W. Helmuth, Associate Vice Chancellor for Research, and Chancellor Rick Edwards of UNL for making this research activity possible. Most of all, I want to thank Gwendolyn Audrey Foster, who is a continuing inspiration to me always, and whose intelligence and keen insight I rely upon throughout all my work. Dana Miller, who has typed my books for the past several years, did her usual excellent job on this manuscript, working from my often hard-to-read handwritten originals; it is only fitting that this book is dedicated to her, as a person who has facilitated my writing in film for the past decade.

The future of the cinematograph is not in doubt, although what form the cinematographic apparatus itself will take in the coming century is another matter altogether. As I'll detail in the opening pages of this book, there already exist a number of video imaging systems where reso-lution and image quality genuinely rival that of 35mm film, and with the general introduction of video imaging instead of photographic image cap-ture, the motion picture industry will be taking a giant leap forward into the future. Nearly all films are now subjected to a digital "clean up" pro-cess on their route to final distribution; the original photographic images are transformed into a series of dots and pixels, manipulated in a variety of methods, and then re-transferred on to 35mm. The total digitization of the moving image cannot be that far off, nor will it be an apocalyptic event that utterly changes the face of image storage and reproduction in a noticeable fashion. Rather, as video imaging increases in ease, portabil-ity, and image quality, the already blurred line between cinema and video will vanish altogether, just as digital compositing has replaced traditional "mattes" in motion picture special effects. With more films, videos, tele-vision programs, and Internet films being produced now than ever before, and with international image boundaries crumbling thanks to the perva-sive influence of the world wide web (a technology still in its infancy), we will see in the coming years an explosion of voices from around the globe, in a new and more democratic process that allows a voice to even the most marginalized factions of society.

Although, as I will argue, Hollywood will seek to retain its domi-nance over the global presentation of fictive entertainment constructs, a new vision of international access, and a democracy of images, will finally inform the future structure of cinematographic camera in the twenty-first century. Many of the stories told will remain familiar; genres are most comfortable when they are repeated with minor variations. But as the pro-duction and exhibition of the moving image moves resolutely into the digital age, audiences will have even greater access to a plethora of visual constructs from every corner of the earth. It is to this new proliferation of public images, unfettered by commerce and distributed through the low cost means of the web and the Internet that this volume is ultimately ded-icated. We are now in the digital age where we were one hundred years ago in the era of the cinematograph: at the beginning. What happens next will be wondrous to see.

CHAPTER ONE

❖

Voices from the Margins, and the New Digital Cinema

As the end of the first century of the cinema becomes an accomplished fact, film critics and historians are busy compiling lists of the most influential or important films of the past one hundred years. The American Film Institute (AFI) famously announced its list of the one hundred best American films, including such rather dubious honorees as *E. T., The Extra-Terrestrial* (1982), *Raiders of the Lost Ark* (1981), *Fargo* (1996), *Tootsie* (1982), *Forrest Gump* (1994), *Close Encounters of the Third Kind* (1977), and *Rocky* (1976). Superb entertainment films perhaps, but as exemplars of the finest that the cinema has to offer? The AFI list of one hundred final choices was created from a master list of four hundred possible entries, compiled by the AFI curatorial staff. Subsequently, the list was sent to a range of industry professionals; "actors, directors, producers, cinematographers, studio executives, exhibitors, critics—and to a few outsiders, including President and Mrs. Clinton and Vice President and Mrs. Gore" (Watson and Brown 20). The entire enterprise is, of course, tied into a promotional tour, in which Blockbuster video and the AFI team up to present a memorabilia road show of cinematic detritus to publicize the selection of the "top one hundred films," and concomitantly into numerous home video promotions from the various companies who stand to benefit handsomely from the re-release of these certified crowd pleasers.

Simultaneously, the British Film Institute (BFI) has compiled their own list of the three hundred and sixty most influential films of all time, on an international scale, or one film for nearly every day of the year. The BFI list, curated by archivist David Meeker, offers a much wider selection of titles (partially, of course, because it is a much larger number of films), but it includes a wide variety of international cinema, including Louis Feuillade's *Les Vampires* (1916), Teinosuke Kinugasa's *Kurutta Ippeiji* (*A Page of Madness*, 1926), Jean Renoir's *La Chienne* (1931), and Luis Buñuel's *El* (1952) along with more mainstream choices such as Raoul Walsh's *White Heat* (1949), Michael Curtiz's *Casablanca* (1942), and Martin Scorsese's *Raging Bull* (1980). While more eclectic and certainly more balanced than the AFI list, the 360 feature films chosen by the BFI also manage to marginalize both women filmmakers and entire national cinemas, as filmmaker Stig Björkman pointed out when asked (in all fairness, by the BFI itself) to comment on their list.

> Dorothy Arzner, Jane Campion, Ida Lupino, Kathryn Bigelow, Lina Wertmüller, Liliana Cavani, Astrid Henning-Jensen, Julia Solntseva, Mai Zetterling, Marguerite Duras (*India Song*, 1975): a female perspective is almost completely omitted. African directors such as Youssef Chahine or Ousmane Sembene: a whole continent is omitted. [Other omissions might include] Tod Browning (*Freaks*, 1932), Bo Widerberg (Kvarteret Korpen, 1963), Blake Edwards (*The Party*, 1968), Bob Fosse (*Cabaret*, 1972), Werner Herzog (*Kaspar Hauser*, 1974), Otar Iosseliani, Abbas Kiarostami, Ken Loach (*Kes*, 1969), Sergei Paradzhanov, Glauber Rocha (*Antonio das Mortes*, 1969), Peter Watkins (*Edward Munch*, 1974), Maurice Pialat, Ettore Scola (*C'eravamo tanto amati*, 1974), the Taviani brothers, Mike Nichols (*Carnal Knowledge*, 1971). (James, *360 Classic* 28)

Other critics invited to comment on the BFI list noted that it contained no less than eleven films by John Ford, and, as Ed Buscombe noticed, "if you take out Satjajit Ray (over-represented here) there isn't much from outside America, Europe and Japan/China" (James, *360 Classic* 28). Critic Jim Hoberman notes that "the simple most egregious omission is Chantal Akerman, by any standard one of the most important European filmmakers of the post-'68 era" (James 30), while Philip Kemp deplores the absence of Ousmane Sembene, Edgar G. Ulmer, Eric Rohmer, and Ritwik Ghatak, among others (James 30). Colin MacCabe "regret[s] . . . the relentless good taste [of the list]: surely one of Terence Fisher's Hammer movies and at least one of Gerald Thomas' *Carry On* films" could easily have been on the list (James 30). David Thomson asks, "Do we really think *Marnie* or *The Birds* are better than *Rear Window* (1954)? Or that *MASH* is superior to *The Long Goodbye* (1973), *McCabe & Mrs. Miller* (1971), or *Nashville* (1975)? Do we all want to take *The Ghost and Mrs. Muir* over *All About Eve* (1952)? And is *Judex* in the same class as *Les yeux sans visage*?" (James 41), while Amy Taubin notes that at least ten "essential" titles are missing from the BFI list:

> *Jeanne Dielman* (Chantal Akerman, 1975); *Prise de pouvoir par Louis XIV* (Roberto Rossellini, 1966); *The Chelsea Girls* (Andy Warhol, 1966); *Dance, Girl, Dance* (Dorothy Arzner, 1940); *A Woman under the Influence* (John Cassavetes, 1974); *India Song* (Marguerite Duras, 1975); *Xala* (Ousmane Sembene, 1974); *Killer of Sheep* (Charles Burnett, 1977); *2 ou 3 choses que je sais d'elle* (Jean-Luc Godard, 1966); *Il gattopardo* (Visconti, 1962). (James 33)

Perhaps Colin MacCabe sums up the list's limitations best when he comments that:

> All canons are organised from a particular history: Meeker's list places him as a son of Henri Langlois, from the first audiences to be brought to cinema past and present, in a systematic way, and an initial canon composed of D. W. Griffith, German Expressionism and Soviet cinema. The *nouvelle vague* articulated its next stage of the canon, with the best of Hollywood leavened by the best of world cinema. Godard's list wouldn't look so different, except for more Mizoguchi or Rossellini. It *is* Eurocentric—but that simply means we should encourage such lists from Asian, African and Latin American perspectives. (James, *360 Classics* 39)

All in all, the BFI list has a greater claim to our attention despite these caveats, because at least it makes a sincere attempt to be as inclusive as it can within the confines of any closed set. Both the AFI and BFI lists, however, represent extensions of the same strategy that Jonas Mekas first propounded in the early 1970s, with the creation of his Essential Cinema list for Anthology Film Archives, which was (at first) a closed set of cinema classics projected quarterly at Joseph Papp's Public Shakespeare Theatre. Since that time, Anthology has moved to its new home on 2nd Street and 2nd Avenue in Manhattan, where it continues to project the Essential Cinema series, but now in conjunction with a wide range of new and classic films culled from archival collections around the world. All attempts at canon, it seems, must ultimately fail for the rather simple yet evanescent reasons: superb new films keep getting made, thereby calling into qualification all of cinema history by the very fact of their freshness and originality; and secondly, that cinema history is writ largest at the margins. Those films not included in any of these lists become all the more important by the mere act of their exclusion. With the proliferation of video technology, more and more classic films are available to the public at large, both on VHS tape and DVD disc, but also through such cable outlets as Turner Classic Movies, Bravo, and American Movie Classics.

Everyday, classic films of the past once thought lost are being found and restored to find new audiences, although it is still true that nearly *half* of all films made throughout the world before 1950 have been irretrievably lost through the twin exigencies of neglect and nitrate decomposition. And even re-mastered films will eventually need to be re-mastered again. As the producer Val Lewton once commented, making films is like "writing on water"—perhaps no other creative medium is as ephemeral as the cinema.

What fuels these lists of classic films is, of course, the fact that one hundred years of cinema have now passed us by, and as the new century dawns, all of us seek to make some sense out of the multitude of images we've collectively absorbed in our lifetimes, and with the death of such cinematic icons as Jimmy Stewart, Robert Mitchum, and Maureen O'Sullivan, we seek to hold onto the past as the century mark approaches. The movies are, above all, a zone of fantasy and audience participation in which all of us, sharing only the common bond of the price of admission, share an experience which is at once fixed and yet indeterminate, different for every viewer in the theatre audience. Reception theory holds that there are as many interpretations of a film as there are viewers, as many different stories within the confines of one celluloid construct as there are audience members who view a specific film.

THE CINEMA AS SPECTACLE

As we crest the wave of the new century, it is interesting to note how our shared perceptions of what a film is have changed, and how differently we view the film-going experience now than we did, say, at the mid-century mark, in the 1950s. Invited to comment on changing tastes and values in the cinema in the last days of the 1990s, former *New Yorker* critic Pauline Kael observed that,

> There's an enthusiasm for the young moguls, the new, sleek Sammy Glicks. They've become heroes. Although there is a fear on the part of some people in the press that movies are dying, the medium itself is still exciting to school kids—maybe more exciting than ever. It's the art of film as we used to talk about it that is probably metamorphosing into something else—into the show, which is what it started as. (Sawhill 93)

Cinema as spectacle. But how long can spectacle sustain us? What resonance does a film like the 1998 *Godzilla* have, or James Cameron's *Titanic* (1997), as they evaporate from our collective consciousness in a trail of tie-ins, manufactured memorabilia, promotional gimmicks, home video cassettes, and signature T-shirts? What lies beyond the horizons of the spectacle film, a genre which is so costly as to be open to only a few practitioners, in direct contrast to the relative democracy of the cinema during the period between 1900 and 1970? Now, budgets of one hundred million dollars and over for a film are not uncommon, with additional promotional expenditures of twenty to thirty million dollars to bring the film before the public. Major features now routinely open in several thousand theaters; this makes only the most exploitable, pre-sold films likely candidates for production and/or widespread theatrical release.

In an interview with Corie Brown and Joshua Hammer, four major motion picture producers (Joe Roth, John Calley, Laura Ziskin, and Michael De Luca) reflected on the influence of rising budgets and promotional expenses on the films they make. John Calley, at age sixty-eight a veteran of the Hollywood production wars (he worked at Warner Brothers as head of production in the 1970s, and now serves as the president of Sony Pictures), noted that,

> In the old days the amount you risked was infinitesimal. I was fighting with [Stanley] Kubrick on the 'Clockwork' ['Orange'] budget. He wanted $1.3 million. I wanted $1.282 million. I ruptured our friendship for months over $18,000, which today is lunch. It's grotesque the way it's changed. Last year we released 38 movies, and much of it was s___. And we had a huge year. (Brown and Hammer 117)

Laura Ziskin of 20th Century Fox admits that the current cinema "audience is not particularly demanding. If you give them something really good, they are really happy. But if you give them something not very good, they sort of don't care. They go anyway, if the movie has these other things . . . like thrills" (Brown and Hammer 117). Joe Roth, Chairman of Walt Disney Studios, notes that "It's [about] visual effects. That's the key to reaching someone in under five seconds in a cluttered world." He nevertheless remains optimistic about the future of the medium as a viable art form. "In 10 years, all these countries will emerge as markets, and this generation coming up will be incredibly potent" (Brown and Hammer 118). But what sort of films will this new generation of filmmakers create, and will they follow the same mold as contemporary Hollywood products? While some younger filmmakers embrace the model of the dominant cinema (as Joe Roth recounts,

> I walked on the set of one of my movies where the 32–year-old director and the 29-year-old cameraman were standing there staring at the *Variety* weekend grosses. And I'm saying, 'Hey, I'm the head of the studio and I can't be seen doing this. What are you guys doing?' [Brown and Hammer 117–118]),

many others are choosing to create films on a much smaller scale: films which are ambitious in content, but not in budgetary requirements. Aiding this shift to widespread low-budget commercial feature film production are a number of factors, but perhaps the most important is the shift from film to videotape as the primary production medium for many new projects.

A decade ago, this would have been unthinkable. Feature films originated on 35mm film (or in 16mm or Super 16mm film for riskier projects, such as *Leaving Las Vegas* [1996], which was shot in Super 16mm and then blown up to 35mm to reduce initial production costs), and were presented in theaters in 35mm film format. Video editing, first introduced in the early 1980s, has now entirely replaced conventional Steenbeck flatbed editing (which, in turn, replaced the use of the old upright Moviola as the primary tool of the film editor), and the AVID system has become the new industry standard (although other video editing systems are also employed). Yet while feature films pass through a digital video stage on their way to the final print, 35mm film remains, for the moment, the primary medium for original image capture.

This may be changing. Television programs—even those shot on 35mm film—long ago abandoned 35mm release prints as their final stage of post-production. Such teleseries as *The X-Files* and *Xena—Warrior Princess* are shot on 35mm film, then converted into digital video editing elements (both for editing and the creation of computer-generated special effects), and finished on videotape for final televisual distribution. No final film print is ever made. Similarly, when Turner Classic Movies makes a new print of one of the many classic feature films or short subjects in their vast library, they have no need to strike a new film print. They simply make a positive video image from the original film negative and optical soundtrack, and use the videotape for television and home video sales. Productions *originating* on videotape lacked the image definition, visual resonance, and depth of 35mm film, and when transferred *to* 35mm film from videotape, the video feature films of an earlier era looked washed-out, with poor color balance and image quality. (One example of this is George Schlatter's 1976 feature film *Norman. . . . Is That You?*, which was shot on videotape, but released to theaters on conventional 35mm film, with abysmal results.)

DIGITIZING THE MOVING IMAGE

A new generation of video cameras may make conventional 35mm cinematography, if not obsolescent, at least a luxury, or perhaps an aesthetic choice for the filmmakers of the twenty-first century. Sony has introduced a new line of video cameras specifically designed to produce images for transfer to 35mm film with a nearly undetectable difference in image quality. Just as the process of blowing up 16mm to 35mm has greatly improved over the past ten years, such as using new "T-grain" stocks and the wider Super 16mm format to increase original image quality, now Sony has produced a series of cameras for the new era of Digital Electronic Cinematography. As a technical brochure from the Sony Corporation notes,

> Digital Electronic Cinematography has a great deal to offer the independent film producer. The extraordinary strides of recent years in electronic imaging now allow superb images to be captured on compact digital cassettes. Sony's novel EBR Transfer System will transfer these digital images and sound directly to 35mm film, producing a high quality release print.

The DVW-700WS camcorder produces widescreen images of extraordinary clarity. When transferred to 35mm film, the results often exceed those of an equivalent Super 16mm origination that is enlarged to a 35mm film release print. And now, Sony has the world's first digital High Definition television camcorder—the HDW-700. When this tape is transferred to film its quality ranks with that of a direct 35mm film origination.

For the important and extensive low-budget independent sector, digital camcorders can bring very cost-effective solutions to cinematography. Sony's DCR-VX1000 camcorder will produce a film transfer that ranks with the best 16mm origination that is enlarged to a 35mm release print. The professional digital DVCAM version, utilizing the DSR-200 camcorder can produce even higher quality. ("Digital Cinematography" 5)

These cameras are lightweight and easy to use when balanced on the cameraperson's shoulder. As noted, they shoot "wide screen" images which can then be transferred, after final video editing, into a 35mm composite release print for theatrical screenings at a fraction of the cost of conventional filmmaking. Videotape requires no developing, workprints, sound transfers, or other viewing/editing preparations; immediately after shooting it can be played back.

Jerry Lewis first used videotape as a "video tap" on a conventional 35mm film camera to offer an instant replay of a take to see if it was usable. Today, the video tap is in nearly universal use on all theatrical and television film productions, both to save time (the director need not look through the viewfinder of the camera as often to line up a shot) and to improve the overall visual look of the production. 35mm film projection survives for the moment as a theatrical institution, ironically, because it is (for the moment) the cheapest method of producing a large, high-quality image on a conventional theatre screen. The moment that video projection advances to the level of conventional film projection in terms of image quality, sound, brightness and definition, 35mm film will be unceremoniously abandoned—perhaps within the next ten years. No doubt revival houses, museums, and specialized theaters will continue to present feature films in *film* format, but when one realizes that the cost of a DVD or DVT copy of a feature film is but a fraction of the cost of making a 35mm film print (perhaps twenty dollars versus fifteen hundred dollars per copy), one can see why the dominant Hollywood cinema would welcome the conversion to all-video production/exhibition purely on a bottom-line basis.

Nor does Hollywood's embrace of digital imaging stop with the complete digitization of the theatre image production process. Much has been written on the ramifications of computer generated imagery to conflate the "real" with the "cooked" in contemporary cinema. Such hyperdigital extravaganzas as *Titanic* (1997), *Starship Troopers* (1997), and *Armageddon* (1998) leave little doubt that the age of fully realized digital special effects is upon us, creating a fictive world so seamlessly seductive that the viewer can no longer discern where traditional image capture ends and the computer takes over, to create a final series of hyperreal glyphs which are then sequentially projected on the cinema screen. It has now become commonplace to see the images of long dead Hollywood icons—John Wayne, Fred Astaire, and others—lifted from their past films and plunked down in advertisements or feature films, brought back to flickering half-life like so many members of the fraternity of the undead. As far back as 1981, the prescient Michael Crichton posited the possibility of creating computer generated models of human actors to sell both merchandise and promote political candidates in his underrated film *Looker*. Now, that time may soon be upon us, as John Calley of Sony Pictures notes,

> I don't think I will be around to see it, but it will be really interesting when we start creating characters. When you get a [special-effects guy] who creates Julia Roberts and Brad Pitt, these irresistible leading men and women, and they don't really exist and the world falls in love with them . . . I've been talking to Sean Connery about doing it in a small film. I said, 'Listen, if there is a flashback, you know you are going to look like s___ with some terrible hairpiece and makeup and you're 15 pounds overweight. How would you feel if we do a 35–year-old Connery?' He's open to it. (Brown and Hammer 118)

CINEMA AT THE MARGINS

At the other end of the spectrum, Marc Levin created his cinema verité–style fiction feature *Slam* by shooting on location at a jail in Washington, D.C., in a mere twelve days, using a handheld 16mm camera to shoot much of the work. The film, a testament to a raw and unsparing vision of humanity in crisis, captured with a minimum of technical legerdemain, went on to win the Grand Jury Prize for Best Dramatic Film at the 1998 Sundance Film Festival. And Darren Aronofsky, shooting on 16mm black and white reversal film (one of the most non-commercial production mediums imaginable), created *Pi*, his first feature film, for a grand total (including 35mm blowup) of $134,815. Of this amount, the single biggest expenditure during production was film purchase and processing: $5,414 for the raw film stock and $18,000 for developing. The 35mm blowup cost $25,571, and the final optical soundtrack cost $3,000. Film editing was done on an AVID, but the "negative" cutting (or "master" cutting, since this film was shot entirely on positive-image film) cost $9,915. This runs to a total of $61,900. The actual production of the film itself, aside from these bare-bones figures for physical production materials, was thus completed for a mere $72,915 ("Pieces of Pi" 82). This is still a long way from the $1,200 production cost of Andy Warhol's *Chelsea Girls* (1966), or the $1,000 Ron Rice spent to create his epic romantic feature *The Flower Thief* (1960). But in terms of production costs by Hollywood standards, $134,815 is a pittance, what a major film would spend on "craft services" (food for cast and crew) in less than a week. In an interview with Scott McCaulay, Darren Aronofsky and his producer Eric Watson described how they accomplished this astonishing feat.

Using borrowed, begged, and scavenged equipment, Aronofsky shot 53,000 feet of 16mm film—some twenty-three hours—over a twenty-eight-day shoot. The major location for the filming was an apartment set created in a desolate warehouse in Bushwick, which Aronofsky acknowledged is "a pretty grim area . . . we found this back room there, gutted it, and built the set. It was cold. It wasn't the best situation in the world, but at the same time, for no money, it allowed us to have a set" ("Pieces of *Pi*" 27). As for location filming in New York's subway system, Aronofsky and his crew simply walked in and shot. They had no money for permits. "We just hung out on the platform from 10 PM to 6 AM for about a week" (30). *Pi* emerges as a paranoid masterpiece, fueled by the desire to simply make a movie with the materials and facilities at one's disposal, in the face of all possible obstacles. Hyperedited, filled with grainy close-ups of the protagonist's anguished countenance, this mathematical conspiracy thriller won the Director's Award at the Sundance Film Festival, and went on to successful and critically acclaimed commercial release, perhaps the first black and white 16mm "no-budget" feature to break out into mainstream distribution since Kevin Smith's $27,000 debut film *Clerks* (1994).

Aronofsky is not alone. For as the cinema enters its second century of imagistic production/exhibition, both alternative syntactical structures and production methodologies will continue to come to the fore. Spurred on by an all-consuming personal vision, and in many cases disinterested in following the traditional Hollywood route, Aronofsky joins such film-makers as John Waters, Kevin Smith, and Lisa Cholodenko (who made an impressive debut with her 1998 feature *High Art*). These filmmakers work outside the mainstream, but manage to get their films noticed by the discerning public in major metropolitan centers, while simultaneously solidifying their future professional careers.

Whether or not they will continue to seek out their personal vision is another matter; after the stunning success of his first feature *Sex, Lies and Videotape* (1989), Steven Soderbergh went on to direct *Kafka* (1991) and *King of the Hill* (1993), both commercial failures, though superb films from a purely critical viewpoint. However, Soderbergh found himself increasingly on the margins of employment in the commercial cinema until he directed the routine Elmore Leonard crime programmer *Out of Sight* (1998), designed primarily as a vehicle for George Clooney. Similarly, Roberto Rodriguez directed his breakthrough color 16mm feature *El Mariachi* (1992) in two weeks for a mere $7,000, substituting (as Aronofsky did in *Pi*) arresting visual setups and kinetic camera movement for action or facilities greater funding would have provided. Rodriguez photographed, edited, directed, wrote, and co-produced the film with one of its principal actors, Carlos Gallardo. When the film was blown up to 35mm and released with a re-mixed soundtrack, it attracted both critical and box-office attention, but Rodriguez's subsequent work has been decidedly less arresting, and as of this writing, he seems to have been absorbed by the Hollywood machine.

The most inventive and original cinema continues to be produced at the periphery of the commercial marketplace. Along with a new wave of video art, live performance pieces (many of them one-person shows), and new directions in painting and sculpture, the cinema of the next millennium will continue to find its greatest inspiration in those who operate outside the system, creating works of originality and brilliance beyond the zones of corporate financial risk.

Lisa Cholodenko's *High Art* (which Cholodenko scripted and directed) is another interesting example of the new wave of low-budget independent filmmaking. Syd (Radha Mitchell) is an assistant editor at a trendy fashion/photography magazine, who meets by happenstance Lucy (Ally Sheedy), a once popular photographer who has seemingly abandoned her career for a life of drugs and aimless drifting through life with her lover, Greta (Patricia Clarkson), a hopelessly stoned junkie who once acted in the films of Rainer Werner Fassbinder. The film is photographed in a deceptively low key manner, playing off the youthful ambition of Syd against the world-weary cynicism of Lucy and her heroin addicted companions. Greta is justifiably suspicious of Syd's attention to Lucy; Syd sees cajoling Lucy back into the world of art photography as her entrée to a better job at the magazine where she works, but Syd is also fascinated by Lucy's lifestyle, and gradually falls in love with the older woman. Greta, whose slurred speech and theatrical presence recall Tallulah Bankhead at her most self-indulgent, seems powerless to affect the relationship, until she induces Lucy to do one last fix of heroin with her as a gesture of farewell. This gesture proves fatal for Lucy, who dies of an accidental overdose at the end of the film's narrative.

As Syd persuades Lucy to meet with her superiors at the magazine during a series of high-power lunches, during which Syd's bosses offer Lucy free artistic reign for a photo essay to be featured on the cover of the next issue, Lucy continually resists the urge to be pulled back into the avant-garde "mainstream." Finally, desperate to have Lucy fulfill the commission (and thus save her job, which is contingent upon Lucy's successful completion of the photo essay), Syd agrees to serve as Lucy's model and lover, during an informal road-trip photo shoot for the magazine. At first intimidated by the gaze of Lucy's camera, Syd succumbs to her visual and physical advances, and the two women have sex in the idyllic Victorian bedroom of a country bed and breakfast resort. Feeling personally compromised by these highly intimate images (Lucy has gone so far as to photograph their lovemaking), Syd initially submits some of Lucy's old work for publication. But her editors reject the earlier photos as dated and unusable, forcing Syd to hand in the photos Lucy has taken of the two women together. Syd's editors, while surprised that Syd has agreed to model for Lucy, are impressed by the photos, and agree to run the entire series of images as a photo essay, putting Syd's face on the cover of the magazine. Shortly after the issue is published, however, Syd learns of Lucy's death as a result of the heroin binge with Greta, thus leaving Syd's ascendance at the magazine highly compromised.

While a number of New York critics found *High Art* to be simplistic or overdrawn, it seems to me that the film captures the tone of desperation and empty chic which pervades much of the edgier manifestations of throwaway pop culture. Ally Sheedy's burnt out, world-weary performance as Lucy perfectly fits the tenor of her character, and Sheedy herself welcomed the film as a significant change of pace from her earlier work. Best known for her films as a relative youngster (1983's *War Games*, and 1985's *The Breakfast Club* and *St. Elmo's Fire*), Sheedy had grown weary of her fresh-scrubbed ingénue image, and dropped out of films for almost a decade. *High Art* gave Ally Sheedy a chance to reinvent herself, to come back in an independent project which would allow her more latitude than the mainstream roles she had previously been chosen for. Speaking of her dissatisfaction with the manufactured images created by the dominant cinema, Sheedy stated:

> It was frustrating. I thought, Oh, my God, this is so backwards. Hollywood is the definition of sexual discrimination. So I figured, I'll do something that pays me well once a year, and with the salary my husband [David Lansbury] makes from acting in the theater, we'll get by from job to job. I'm very happy with the work that I do, and I have a lot of time for my daughter, and really, I don't want to be a superstar because it takes a great deal of effort to maintain that kind of life once you've created it. The pursuit of fame becomes your career, and you have to spend all your time trying to look good. You have to have a real love for that particular game. I have the desire to work as an actress, but I have no ambition to be a star. (Weitzman 73)

A concrete example of the difference between Cholodenko's *High Art* and some of Sheedy's previous Hollywood films came during the filming of the climactic lovemaking scenes between Syd and Lucy. Compared to previous sex scenes Sheedy had been required to appear in, her lesbian scenes with Radha Mitchell as Syd were

> more comfortable than doing a love scene with a guy. Usually sex scenes are completely geared toward making the man look good: You're waiting underneath him, burning with passion or whatever, the accessory to his great sexuality. *Always*. It's so boring! But for this one, I didn't have to feel like, 'OK, now they're lighting him to show his muscles and sweat, and I need to get into some seductive curve on the bed here, ready for him.' (Weitzman 73)

The naturalness of this sequence, combined with trancelike music from the techno-pop group Shudder to Think and Cholodenko's cool, contemplative visuals, create in *High Art* a world which is both seductive and dangerous to know and experience.

Katja Von Garnier's *Bandits* (1998) offers an example of the new wave of post-feminist German independent cinema. The plot of *Bandits* is simple: four women in prison unite to form a rock and roll band, and then escape from confinement when they are allowed to play outside the prison at a policeman's benefit. Hoping to escape to South America, they become cult heroines on the radio, as their songs generate excitement in the Hamburg underground. Von Garnier reacts violently when some critics describe her film as primarily a feminist tract:

> If a film is about a bunch of men, no one asks if it's a men's movie. A film is just a film. Men and women differ in that women are allowed to show their emotional wounds but not their anger, whereas men show anger but conceal their emotional pain. All this does is make it difficult for everyone. (Adams 34)

Having just gotten a deal with Columbia Tri-Star, Von Garnier will now have a chance to bring her outlaw vision (exhibited both in *Bandits* and her 1993 film *Makin' Up*) before a wider audience.

Vincent Gallo's *Buffalo 66* (1998) is another uncompromising film, but in a different fashion: the audience is asked to root for Gallo playing a perpetual loser named Billy Brown, a pathetic, motor-mouthed failure who has just been released from prison. To impress his spectacularly dysfunctional family, Gallo kidnaps a young girl named Layla (Christina Ricci, late of the *Addams Family* movies, but now grown up into a curiously mature and yet innocent teenager) and forces her to pose as his wife for his crazed and lecherous father Jimmy (Ben Gazzara) and his sports obsessed mother Janet (Anjelica Huston). Shot in a flat, Jim Jarmusch-styled series of opposing masters on 35mm color reversal film (a major departure from conventional feature cinematography) by Lance Acord, *Buffalo 66* proceeds as a triumphal domestic nightmare, with brutal and deadpan assurance. Nevertheless, the film manages to make audience members care deeply about Billy as a seriously conflicted protagonist, and Layla's confused but persistent affection for him, even as the drab contours of their lives threaten to devour them at every turn. Set in a bleak universe of shabby hotel rooms, donut shops, and strip joints—a zone in

which even one's childhood home is a location of unremitting anguish—
Buffalo 66 is a film made entirely on its own terms both visually and nar-
ratologically. In this, Gallo's film recalls Peter Emmanuel Goldman's
Wheel of Ashes (1968), a film about the torment of a young man living a
marginal existence in 1960s Paris, starring Pierre Clementi, Katinka Bo,
and Pierre Besançon. Shot on a shoestring, *Wheel of Ashes* effectively con-
veys Clementi's despair and loneliness as he threads through the fragments of mainstream society hoping desperately to find a foothold which
constantly eludes him.

THE VISUAL ARTIST AS SOCIAL CRITIC

Many of today's independent features are indebted, stylistically or spiri-
tually, to the independent feature films of the 1960s, films that tested the
boundaries of accepted audience discourse during that era, and often
were marginalized as a result. Andy Warhol's *I, A Man* (1967) is a ninety-
nine-minute 16mm feature starring Tom Baker, Ivy Nicholson, Nico,
and most notoriously, Valerie Solanas (who would unsuccessfully
attempt to assassinate Warhol the following year). It is a nearly plotless
film in which Baker roams restlessly through a series of cluttered apartments in search of sex, momentary satisfaction, and perhaps a fleeting
human connection. Like Vincent Gallo's insistently verbal protagonist in
Buffalo 66, Tom Baker in *I, A Man* never shuts up, although his dialogue
is less engaging, and his rapacious persona almost totally devoid of audience empathy. Rather than seeking a relationship with one partner (and
finding it, for, against all odds, *Buffalo 66* ends on a triumphant note of
heterotopic bliss), Baker is, at the end of *I, A Man*, as frustrated and
unfulfilled as he was at the start of the film, always on the prowl for some
new conquest.

Compare this vision of macho dystopia to Mai Zetterling's rarely
seen *Flickorna* (*The Girls*) (1968), in which a troupe of women led by Bibi
Andersson set out to perform the play *Lysistrata* in the provinces of Swe-
den, only to find both incomprehension and hostility from their rural
audiences. *The Girls* (the title itself is now something of a cultural
"marker") effectively demonstrates why the culture in the 1960s had to
change, buckling as it was under the Vietnam War, the continued threat
of patriarchal interference in the arts, and a pervasive double standard
which made any real relationship between women and men a near impos-

sibility. As the leader of her theatrical troupe, Andersson is both resolute and hopeful that creating a dialogue with the audience will bring about real changes in social relationships. At one point, she even steps out of character at the end of a performance to ask the audience to comment on what they have just seen, but her entreaties are met with strong silence. What seemed an unbridgeable gulf then now seems more easily traversed, thanks in large measure to the large number of women who are turning to film and video in the late 1990s as a means of expression and communication.

Susan Skoog's *Whatever* (1998), for example, chronicles a young woman named Anna (Liza Weil) whose disastrous home life leaves her ill-prepared for the perils of young adulthood. Set in New Jersey in the early 1980s, *Whatever* joins Richard Linklater's *Dazed and Confused* (1993) as one of the key films about the pleasures and dangers of adolescence in pre-AIDS heterotopic America. This movie, however, presents Anna's situation against a backdrop of dysfunctional and/or abusive domestic spheres; Anna's best friend, Brenda (Chad Morgan) has clearly been damaged by her supposedly wholesome suburban upbringing.

Skoog is a native of Red Bank, New Jersey, who worked her way through a series of menial jobs at VH-1 before moving to Los Angeles to break into the film business. After one short film, *A Dry Heat*, was successfully screened at Cannes, Skoog decided to spend her savings on her first feature film—as with Aronofsky's *Pi* and so many other independent features, no other financing was directly forthcoming. As Skoog told Sarah Jacobson, "I had a big hunk of money I had been working like crazy to save. What was I going to do with it? Buy a house and have no movie?" (44, 47). As with so many other independent cineastes, what finally drove Skoog to make the film was the dearth of films that dealt honestly with the rites of passage of being a heterosexual teenager. Says Skoog, "I really hadn't seen a movie that realistically portrayed what it's like to be a teenage girl in this country" (47). Following the now time-honored route of using her savings, credit cards, friends, family and, in time, outside investors, Skoog created in *Whatever* an authentic vision of the misery and splendor of teenage angst, and the film was picked up by Sony Pictures Classics for distribution, and opened to a commercially and critically successful reception.

Yet the boundaries which once constrained women in the arts in the 1960s have not altogether vanished. Indeed, the performance pieces presented in Manhattan bring the need for artistic license into sharp focus, and remind us that the threat of censorship is never far from work that operates on the cutting edge of the social fabric we so tenuously share. Karen Finley became something of a *cause célèbre* with her mid-1990s performance piece *We Keep Our Victims Ready*, in which she smeared herself with chocolate and tinsel as part of a ritualistic depiction of the plight of the socially and sexually marginalized within American society. Finley presented her piece *The Return of the Chocolate Smeared Woman* in the face of a Supreme Court decision upholding a "decency test" as part of the process for awarding federal arts grants. Finley has an MFA from the San Francisco Art Institute, and has received numerous grants and awards throughout her career, including a Guggenheim Fellowship, a grant from the National Endowment on the Arts, an Obie, two Bessie awards, and a grant from the New York State Council on the Arts.

The Return of the Chocolate Smeared Woman, which was presented in the summer of 1998 in a small performance space in Manhattan's Chinatown called the Flea, is an attempt to deconstruct *We Keep Our Victims Ready*. It signals Finley's move from this provocative performance piece which defined so much of her early work to new and fertile ground. As part of *The Return of the Chocolate Smeared Woman*, Finley, rather than covering herself with ritualistically daubed chocolate and streamers, instead appears on stage already covered in full performance regalia and accompanied by a troupe of scantily clad go-go boys and girls named the Furballs. To an endlessly looped version of the old disco dance hit "The Hustle," Finley and the Furballs gyrate down a makeshift runway in front of the audience, simultaneously critiquing the entire act of body display for a commercial audience and reveling in it. After an introductory "chorus line" greeting to the audience, the Furballs abruptly depart, and Finley takes to the stage alone. Accompanied by only the most minimal lighting designs and video projections, Finley spends the bulk of her time on stage reprising updated sections of her earlier work in *We Keep Our Victims Ready*, offering a scathing analysis of the social, sexual, and political mechanics behind the censorship process in the United States, and then ritualistically cleaning her body of the chocolate and tinsel with two large buckets of water. She drapes herself in a shawl, and concludes her performance with an invocation and prayer for the homeless, for those who are HIV positive, and for those who come from abusive families. The depth of her sincerity and commitment throughout the performance is evident in her piercing gaze, her curiously confrontational and yet engaging manner with the members of the audience, and her willingness to demystify the performance process by including several theatergoers as a peripheral part of the staging of her presentation. From time to time, Finley improvises new sections of the piece during the performance, and directly addresses the technical crew to give them new lighting and/or sound directions; at other points she breaks out of character momentarily to ask for the audience's help in moving props, rearranging the seating, or adjusting the staging area.

I witnessed the July 3, 1998, performance of *The Return of the Chocolate Smeared Woman*, managing to get into the door at the last minute despite the fact that the performance was sold out (apparently, a number of people had made reservations, and then simply failed to appear). The performance space itself was minimal in the extreme. In a bare loft with four large, painted-over windows (reminiscent of the loft made famous in Michael Snow's 1968 film *Wavelength*), using only the simplest of staging areas (a catwalk constructed on the right side of the loft, which then continued around the room at the front), and a few props (a director's chair, some plastic buckets, and water), Finley mesmerized the audience with an eighty-minute display of ferocious virtuosity that effectively interrogated the dark heart of the American dream. Appropriately, the seating arrangements for the audience were extremely primitive. Large plastic buckets turned upside-down, the kind used on industrial construction sites to hold large quantities of caulking, for example, were used for the majority of seats; a few folding chairs were brought in at the last moment to accommodate latecomers. Having seen several of Finley's earlier performances dating back to the early 1990s, I was to some extent prepared for the spectacle I was about to witness. But this time, the atmosphere was tinged with new anger and sadness. Not only had the Supreme Court ruled against Finley and three other performance artists during the previous week, declaring that the National Endowment on the Arts had the right to impose a vaguely constructed "decency" standard on those whom it funded, but Finley also announced from the stage (to a resounding chorus of disapproval) that her upcoming show, *The Great American Nude*, which was to have been presented at the Whitney Museum for American Art in December of 1998, had been abruptly and somewhat inexplicably canceled.

"There's going to be a piece in the *New York Times* tomorrow about this," Finley told the crowd, more in resignation than anger, but it was clear to me that she was in a state of shock from this latent assault on her works. The article, which ironically appeared in the July 4, 1998, issue of the *New York Times*, quoted a spokesperson for the Whitney as stating that the cancellation of Finley's show "was not just a financial decision, but finances had something to do with it" (Gussow B12). While the Whitney denied that its decision had any connection to the Supreme Court ruling or the content of Ms. Finley's proposed show at the Whitney, others were less sanguine. As Mel Gussow, author of the *New York Times'* article noted in his commentary on the cancellation, "artists have suggested that institutions like galleries and theaters might use the [Supreme Court] decision as a means of limiting their artistic freedom" (B12). And Thomas Healy, Ms. Finley's gallery representative, was even more forthright. As Healy told Gussow, "this would have been a good time to mount an exhibition in defiance of the ruling," and added that the cancellation was "a little too bizarre to be a coincidence" (B12). Gussow then went on to detail the proposed presentation that the Whitney had decided to cancel.

> At the center of 'The Great American Nude' exhibition would have been Ms. Finley's 'Go Figure,' an installation of a class in life drawing. Continuing through museum hours, the life class would have been led by Ms. Finley, who would herself have been one of the artists' models.
>
> Any member of the public visiting the museum would have been eligible to take part as an artist in the class and Ms. Finely would have been available to criticize the work. This part of the exhibition was to be a re-creation of a show that Ms. Finley had presented last year at the Museum of Contemporary Art in Los Angeles. (B12)

Finley herself was understandably furious at the decision, which the Whitney insisted was brought about as much by financial exigencies (the need to raise the "$300,000 to $400,000" [Gussow B12] needed to mount the show) as other mitigating factors. "It's astonishing the way the decision was made," Finley commented. "The Whitney is the leading museum for American art in this country and the world. By not having my show, the museum is saying, 'She can't be funded, and our board can't fund her'" (as quoted in Gussow B12). This cancellation is made all the more curious by the fact that the Whitney was presenting, at the same time, an exhibition of sculptures by Charles Ray, including his massive sculpture (so large that it fills an entire room by itself) "Oh! Charley,

Charley, Charley . . ." (1992), which, as described by Calvin Tomkins, "presents us with eight nude replicas of the artist engaged in mutual masturbation" (73), in complete anatomically correct detail. Describing Ray's sculpture correctly as "an orgy for one," Tomkins also notes that "Ray himself has described the piece as asexual and 'kind of sad' . . ." (73), a totemic exercise in isolated autoerotic self-delusion. Yet the work's visual splendor and supposed shock value remains both fixed and transfixing, inviting the viewer to investigate its tangle of mannequin-perfect bodies without risk of personal involvement.

As part of Finley's proposed show at the Whitney, the artist had hoped to perform an homage to Marcel Duchamp's once-scandalous "Nude Descending a Staircase," in which Finley would replicate the movements captured in Duchamp's painting in a live performance piece on a stairway at the museum. That, of course, would confront the viewer with the image of a *living*, not safely plasticine, human body—apparently the figurative line that contemporary culture seems unwilling to cross. Curiously, the Whitney was also presenting, at the same time as the Charles Ray retrospective, a rather staid show of landscapes by the late Andrew Wyeth. As Tomkins noted of the disparity between the two exhibitions, "What is there to love or to hate [in Wyeth's paintings], after all? . . . In spite of Wyeth's virtuoso technique, his range is too limited to involve the viewer on an active level, and it asks no questions. His arrow hits the target every time, but it's always the same target. [Wyeth's] art is not just pre-modern; it's stone dead" (73). Which seems to me to be precisely what the American public wants at the end of this century, just as we did in the late-Victorian era: postcard-perfect visions of a safely encapsulated world, presented to us without risk or engagement. Finley's show was finally presented, as she had originally envisioned it, at the Aldrich Museum of Contemporary Art in Ridgefield, Connecticut in late 1999.

As a complementary vision to Karen Finley's ongoing fight to present her work, *An Evening with Quentin Crisp* offered New York audiences in the summer of 1998 the spectacle of the ninety-year-old performance artist, writer, and social critic still engaged in a vigorous dialogue with his audience despite his advancing age. Since Crisp's life story was made into a superb telefilm starring John Hurt as Crisp in 1974 (*The Naked Civil Servant*), Crisp has appeared in a variety of stage and film presentations, including Sally Potter's widely praised film *Orlando* (1993), in which the openly and flamboyantly gay performer appeared in full drag as Queen Elizabeth I. In addition, he has authored several volumes of aphorisms and social commentary, including *The Wit and Wisdom of Quentin Crisp, How to Have a Lifestyle,* and *Resident Alien.* But the best of Quentin Crisp can arguably be found in his work as a solo performance artist, in which he effortlessly takes the stage to deliver an hour-long monologue on his eventful life as a "self-evident" homosexual, who made his early living by serving as a live model for art classes (as Karen Finley had proposed to do in her aborted performance piece at the Whitney), while simultaneously drifting in and out of a series of affairs and living arrangements that were both risky and adventurous. After an intermission, during which audience members are asked to write out their questions on cards for Crisp to respond to, the author/activist spends the second hour of his time on the stage responding to these written queries, and then taking general questions from the audience as a whole. In all of this, Crisp is modest, self-effacing, and gentle. Yet he projects an undeniable air of steely authority in his presentation that suggests, despite his intentionally foppish behavior and dress, that he is not a person to be trifled with. Indeed, how else could Crisp have survived for so long in a world manifestly hostile to the central fabric of his being?

Born in England in 1908, Crisp endured the homophobia of British mainstream society with a flamboyance and regal bearing that saw him, somewhat perilously, through two world wars, the Great Depression, and the advent of swinging London before he emigrated to America in 1980 at the age of seventy-two. Despite his stubborn insistence on matters of employment and/or long-term relationships—Crisp feels that one should make a career out of "being" one's self rather than "doing" any specific task—Quentin Crisp has become both prolific and notorious as a performance artist and social commentator. "I'm more brazen than I've ever been," Crisp told Aaron Hamburger in the early summer of 1998. As Hamburger noted,

> Crisp realized at an early age that he was not like other boys . . . his life-long project, almost a kind of performance art, of portraying a "self-evident homosexual" through manner and dress has ticked off many observers. Why heterosexuals might be startled by the sight of this man seems fairly evident. Surprisingly, though, Crisp has drawn fire from gays, not only for his persona, which many feel reinforces effeminate stereotypes about gay men, but also for his unorthodox views on gay rights. (25)

Given some of his pronouncements on the subject, this is not surprising. "I think the gay community has gotten worse," Crisp told Hamburger. "It has gotten louder, crueler, cruder, shriller, more belligerent. But I can't explain it to them. It makes them angry." Continuing on, Crisp avers that "sex is a mistake . . . men are not homosexual or heterosexual. They're just sexual." Freely admitting that he writes "to make money . . . I only write the books I'm told to write," Crisp notes that "that's why I say in my show, 'am I saying the words you wish to hear?' My whole wish is to please America. Since I'm allowed to live here, where everyone talks to you—you know, in England, no one talks to you—what can I give in return?" And for his younger admirers, Crisp offers this commentary and advice:

> I like them, but I never understand them because they seem to want to break with all the rules without any reason or system. They dress in any old thing. And I say, "It looks marvelous, but what does it mean?" It hasn't occurred to them they must say who they are through their appearance. (25)

In another interview from the same period with Liesa Goins, Crisp expanded upon his observation that people "must say who they are through their appearance." "Your identity is like your fingerprints," Crisp told Goins. "They are your very own, but if discovered can be used against you" (15). Certainly Quentin Crisp has undergone more than his share of personal hardship, and continues to survive despite a Spartan personal lifestyle that depends almost wholly upon "the kindness of strangers." Each day, Crisp wakes up in his small apartment on the Lower East Side of Manhattan, and decides whether he will spend the day entirely indoors, dressed only in an old robe as he moves about his apartment, or whether he will get dressed (for Crisp, a laborious process involving several hours' work) and venture forth into the outside world. If he does so, Crisp will usually make his way to his favorite restaurant, where he will sit for hours in a booth sipping coffee, until, as he put it during a performance of his latest show that I attended, "some kind stranger approaches me with the offer of paying for a meal." His social commentary is as razor-sharp as it's ever been. As Goins comments,

> Part Dorothy Parker, part Oscar Wilde and part Cosmo Kramer, Crisp cuts life experiences to the quick with acerbic aphorisms. His charm is difficult to pinpoint. It may be because his observations are

as funny as they are true ("Art objects are like washing machines, only not so useful"). Or perhaps, because they are topical ("Mr. Clinton behaved perfectly, he didn't say a word about the whole affair"). (15)

Yet, at age ninety, Crisp has clear intimations of his own mortality. As he told Goins, he still lives in a small room which hasn't been cleaned in eighteen years ("After four years, the dust doesn't get any worse"), and feels that it seems senseless to make any real plans for his personal future. Notes Crisp, "I think I've done everything I can do, because I have little capacity to do anything. I think what little I can do has been done. I expect to die at any time" (15). Yet if Quentin Crisp's career is undeniably in its final years, Crisp has created a compelling work of art of his own life, using minimal materials, and his own sense of style, to transform what could have been an ordinary, or "shadow," existence into a triumphal act of crossgendered cultural resistance. Sadly, Quentin Crisp died on November 21, 1999.

PERFORMANCE RITUAL IN THE PUBLIC SPHERE

Another performer whose career is currently in ascendance, after a long, self-imposed exile, is Yayoi Kusama, the Japanese artist who was once notorious in the 1960s for her performance art, most notably her piece *Grand Orgy to Awaken the Dead* which she performed at the Museum of Modern Art in August, 1969. Under Kusama's direction, eight naked performers stood in the pool of the sculpture garden of the museum, striking poses which parodied the sculptures that surrounded them. As Lynn Zelevansky notes, "Kusama's performances were notorious. Even her most consistent supporters had, as one critic put it, 'the lurking sense that there is absolutely nothing she would not do for publicity'" (27). Yet Kusama was, in fact, one of the originators of the "happening" or "performance piece," and her influence can be seen in the later works of Yoko Ono, Carolee Schneemann, and other artists. After a series of solo exhibitions in her native country, Kusama left for the United States in 1957, settling first in Seattle but inevitably gravitating to New York. Kusama had her first solo show in Manhattan in 1959 at the Brata Gallery, but it was in the 1960s that she hit her stride. She appeared in Jud Yalkut's film *Self-Obliteration* (1967), performing her "dot painting" on leaves, flowers, horses, and finally on a group of nude performers, who copulate with ritualistic frenzy as Kusama covers them with dots from her paintbrush.

The *Self-Obliteration* performance piece was in fact an ongoing project of Kusama's. She followed this documented performance with a series of "happenings" at The Electric Circus, the Cheetah Club, a 1968 protest in front of the New York Stock Exchange entitled *Naked Demonstration/Anatomic Explosion* (during which Kusama distributed a flyer proclaiming, "STOCK IS A FRAUD! STOCK MEANS NOTHING TO THE WORKING MAN. STOCK IS A LOT OF CAPITALIST BULLSHIT . . . OBLITERATE WALL STREET MEN WITH POLKA DOTS" [Zelevansky 26]), a nude "happening" on the Alan Burke talk show, a performance piece entitled *Homosexual Wedding*, and numerous other exhibitions, presentations, and public appearances.

Simultaneously serious and playful, Kusama's work in the 1960s recalls the publicity seeking of Andy Warhol. Kusama was always the first to alert the media to her forthcoming presentations, and her *Grand Orgy to Awaken the Dead* attracted enough notoriety to be featured on the front page of the New York *Daily News*. Yet behind all the self-publicizing, Kusama, like Warhol, was absolutely sincere in her work, creating a prodigious number of paintings, sculptures, and environmental spaces, such as "Kusama's Peep Show," a mirror-infinity environment chamber the artist created in 1966. From the first, Kusama was obsessed with what she termed "infinity net" paintings, in which a series of intricately intertwining nets are painted on canvas, cloth, or sculptures (as in her new "Venus de Milo" statues, produced in serial repetition in full-scale copies of the original, covered with dots and each painted a different iridescent color). Kusama also created a group of "food obsession" suitcases and other objects, which are covered with uncooked macaroni; and a series of sculptures in which hand-sewn phallic-shaped cloth objects are affixed to tables, ladders, and chairs. Kusama has also turned her attention to novellas and poetry, with *Hustler's Grotto* and *Violet Obsession* having been published.

Many of these works have not survived; Kusama's career has been marked by a strange mixture of frenzied creation and paradoxically uneven preservation of her works, both by the artist herself and others. After a decade and a half of unceasing creative activity, Kusama returned to Japan in 1973, and voluntarily checked herself into a Tokyo psychiatric hospital, where she resides to this day (Gomez 29). For much of the 1970s and '80s, Kusama's work and influence were largely forgotten by the public, but not by the artists with whom Kusama had come in contact. In

1989, Kusama organized her first New York solo exhibition in more than a decade, at the Center for International Contemporary Arts. This retrospective of Kusama's early work helped to propel her back into the forefront of public consciousness, and led to a full-scale retrospective at the Los Angeles County Museum of Art. This retrospective later traveled to the Museum of Modern Art, the Walker Art Center, and the Museum of Contemporary Art in Tokyo in 1998–1999. Kusama's work, both fetishistic and obsessive, perfectly mirrors the artist's own personality. In the catalogue for her 1996 show at the Robert Miller Gallery, Kusama noted, "Meshes of a net and polka dots painted by me are a fundamental manifestation of stereotyped repetition caused by the disease. My art and nothing other is a representation in which I had it sublimated as extremely as possible. . . . More than once or twice I had thought of suicide. Why was I saved? Because there was art for me" (n.p.). In working out her private obsessions in the public sphere, Yayoi Kusama's creates a portion of the hitherto "invisible" legacy of feminist and post-feminist art, out of a need to cleanse herself of what she terms "negative" energy. Notes Kusama, "if my sculpture and performance are a positive, my visionary and apocalyptic paintings, which I have produced in large quantities, are a negative. They spring up from the bottom of my negative soul to heal it" (Gomez 31). Kusama's work, at once liberating and troubling, forms a major body of artistic achievement which is accessible and still mysterious.

If Kusama's and Crisp's autobiographical performance work is both deeply personal and yet intricately self-contained, other performance artists working in fin de siècle American society choose a variety of alternative, differing approaches, ranging from raucous and confrontational to measured and introspective. John Leguizamo's one-man performance piece, *Freak*, was a sensation during its 1998 run at the Cort Theatre in New York. Written and performed by Leguizamo, and directed and developed by David Bar Katz, Leguizamo's *Freak* centers on the author's tempestuous upbringing in Manhattan during the 1960s, and especially on Leguizamo's tortured relationship with his father. As portrayed in the performance piece, the father is by turns abusive and tender. The father dominates family life in the small tenement apartment where the author grew up. He drifts through a series of abortive get-rich-quick schemes and menial jobs, all the while bullying Leguizamo's mother, until, inevitably, the family revolts. When Leguizamo's father is hired as a dishwasher in a posh Manhattan restaurant, he lies to his family that he has landed a job as a waiter in the establishment, and is hobnobbing with the likes of Elizabeth Taylor on a daily basis. When John and his brother go to the restaurant to proudly see their father at work, they are crushed when a door to the kitchen swings open, and they see their father bending over a huge sink full of dirty dishes. Ashamed, they leave the restaurant in silence. Leguizamo's father keeps up the deception at home, but becomes even more abusive towards his wife and children, correctly suspecting they know the truth. When John Leguizamo finally gets his first stage acting gig in an off-off Broadway play with the unlikely name of *Junkie Christ*, however, his father visits him backstage and awkwardly congratulates him on his performance, and the two men share a fleeting moment of cathartic intimacy. In between these major defining moments, Leguizamo weaves a heartbreaking and compassionate tale of his youthful rites of passage: his first sexual encounter (with a prostitute who works at a Kentucky Fried Chicken restaurant, and pretty much rapes Leguizamo in the back of the store during business hours—an assignation arranged by Leguizamo's father), his uncertain attempts at molding a professional career, and his personal battles against racism as a Latino.

Brilliantly using lighting cues, sound effects, and an amazingly athletic physical presence in the place of conventional props, John Leguizamo's *Freak* takes us deep into the author's childhood, into the heart of racial prejudice in America, and into the shattered soul of a tormented family trying to construct a familial existence against the longest of odds. Under David Bar Katz's direction, invisible "doors" audibly open when Leguizamo takes us into his one-room tenement family home; an elevated subway train screams by during one of Leguizamo's father's tirades, entirely obliterating the text of his stern admonitions; overhead lighting cues and slide projections evoke a series of discotheques, parking lots, and childhood memories that comprise the emotional terrain of Leguizamo's journey to adult consciousness.

Leguizamo's career is an enviable one, as he manages to bounce between mainstream projects (his role as a Latino drag queen named Chi Chi Rodriguez in *To Wong Foo, Thanks for Everything, Julie Newmar* [1996], and as Tybalt in the Leonardo DiCaprio version of *Romeo and Juliet* [1997]), and more personal ventures, particularly his series of one-person performance pieces that began with *Mambo Mouth* (1991), an off-Broadway play in which Leguizamo played seven different characters. This was followed by *Spic-O-Rama* (1995), which was so successful it was taped and aired on HBO, to resounding critical and audience acclaim. With *Freak*, Leguizamo consolidated his reputation as a performance artist of intense skill, depth, and technical virtuosity. He frankly admits that the process of creating *Freak* was an emotional and psychic roller coaster. In the program notes for the play, Leguizamo notes that "a one man show is anything but," and describes the process of creating the show as an "emotional enema" for his "inner child." Leguizamo continues, "Thanx to my family for letting me roast them—ouch! I know it hurt. Sorry" (Leguizamo 24), to which co-developer David Bar Katz adds, "[In co-creating this play, I offer] special thanks to everyone who's helped John and me during this long, painful, outrageous process, but of course, special thanks to John, for having the strength and bravery to let me strip-mine his past in search of laughter and misery" (26). And indeed, as with Kusama's and Crisp's work (although Leguizamo's is more directly confrontational), it is the artist's own personal inventory of life-experience that forms the raw material of his completed presentation. *Freak*, especially, went through a long development process, first appearing at the Goodman Theatre in Chicago in 1997, then at the Theatre on the Square in San Francisco in May through June 1997, and finally, before moving to the Cort Theatre, at P. S. 122 in New York in August of 1997 (21). During this long "work shopping" process, the piece went through substantial versions and editing, so that the final production is simultaneously raw and yet extremely polished. It is this intense process of raw strip mining and intense editorial invention that combine to create the searing emotional impact of the final piece.

THE MARGINALIZED VOICE
OF INTERNATIONAL CINEMA

In the work of Crisp, Kusama, and Leguizamo, marginalized voices move closer to the mainstream, bringing different cultural visions to contemporary audiences without compromising the integrity of each artist's individual vision. In the summer of 1998, the Walter Reade Theatre in Lincoln Center brought together a truly dazzling array of alternative cinematic visions as part of their 1998 Human Rights Watch International Film Festival, allowing viewers to see the works of filmmakers from a variety of social, political, and economic landscapes. The films ranged from documentaries to full-length fiction features and shorter works, and used 35mm film, 16mm film, and a wide variety of video formats to capture the images presented on the screen, but, in all cases, the depth of personal involvement and political engagement was both intense and highly personal. Tahani Rasched's 1997 video documentary *Four Women of Egypt*, for example, is a ninety-minute film in which four Egyptian intellectuals, bound together by their mutual desire for companionship and lively debate, discuss their status as women within Egyptian society, and how their roles and values have changed with the passage of time. One is a teacher, one a politician, one a writer, and one a political activist, and their views and personalities often clash.

Wedad, Amina, Shahenda, and Safynaz could not be, in many respects, more different individuals. One is a Christian, one a fundamentalist Muslim, one an atheist, but all of them share a common heritage of struggle within Egyptian society as a whole. One woman's life changed entirely when her political activist husband was assassinated; others have spent time in other countries, but have returned to Egypt to regain contact with their culture of origin. The women express their frustrations, fears, and often violently opposing positions in a series of individual interviews that culminate in a heated group exchange which threatens, at one point, to erupt into real acrimony: "Does your 'script' call for us to come to blows?" one of the women sardonically inquires of the filmmaker during one particularly contentious moment. Yet despite their differences, these women are united in a common struggle to change the face of Egyptian society, and the opportunities that it affords (and denies) its female citizens. Video is the ideal medium for this personal and contemplative film, which is simultaneously modest in physical execution but ambitious in scope and purpose.

Another film in the Festival which spotlights the plight of women in contemporary society is Prakash Jha's truly astonishing *Death Sentence*, a 1997 wide-screen epic, shot in 35mm CinemaScope, and running one hundred and nineteen minutes. In a series of dazzlingly designed tableaux, *Death Sentence* tells the story of Ketki, a young woman who marries a young man, Vinay, whom she first admires and then comes to despise because of his brutality and corrupt behavior. Set against a backdrop of a society in seeming collapse, *Death Sentence* portrays modern India as a cultural miasma, in which under-the-table deals and lecherous holy men conspire to dominate women both socially and economically, and all too often get away with it. When Vinay renounces his corrupt business partners, Ketki is delighted, until she sees him blown to bits on a booby-trapped motorcycle in an accident staged by his former colleagues. Enraged, Ketki embarks on a one-woman crusade to bring justice to the morally bankrupt Indian political landscape. She eventually murders her arch-nemesis at point blank range with a shotgun, and his mortally wounded body tumbles into the Ganges. Superbly photographed and wrenchingly acted, this post-feminist revenge fable is as compelling as it is visually striking. It signals a new direction in Indian cinema beyond the generic boundaries of the formulaic musicals which have for so long been the staple of both production and audience reception in India.

An equally compelling but culturally different vision is offered by David Pultz's *Eternal Memory: Voices from the Great Terror*, which Pultz completed in 16mm in 1997. Running eighty-one minutes, the film documents, in the words of the film's pressbook,

> the Stalinist purges and terror in the former USSR during the 1930's and 1940's. Centering on Ukraine, the film incorporates historical footage, interviews with witnesses and survivors, historians, and public officials. The historians interviewed include Robert Conquest of Stanford University and Roman Szporluk of Harvard University. Others interviewed include Zbigniew Brzezinski, former U.S. National Security Advisor, Leonid Kravchuk, former President of Ukraine, and Mykola Holushko, a former KGB official. The film is narrated by Meryl Streep. [Production of the film involved] two trips to Western Ukraine to interview witnesses, survivors and public officials. The first trip, in the fall of 1991, came just at the time of the breakup of the Soviet Union. It was a rare opportunity. Director David Pultz and his film crew were among the first from the West that had been given the chance to freely travel and talk with citizens of the newly independent Ukraine. The result is a film with riveting eye witness accounts to Stalinist terror, framed within an historical context by some of the most respected historians on the subject. (Pultz n.p.)

Born in Greensburg, Pennsylvania, Pultz graduated from Emerson College in Boston in 1976. Since that time, he has worked as a color timer for Du Art Laboratory in New York, one of the leading film and video-post-production facilities on the East Coast. At Du Art, Pultz worked with such respected documentarians as Frederick Wiseman, Albert Maysles, and Ken and Rick Burns as their various projects would pass through Du Art. During this time, Pultz also completed two short films, *Confessions on B Street* (1979) and a documentary, *Visiting Neighbors*

(1988). For *The Great Terror*, Pultz joined forces with the Canadian documentarists George Yemec and Marco Carynnyk to create a film which has been described by critic Adriana Leshko as "compulsively watchable" and "lyrical." As Leshko notes, the film

> addresses a difficult subject matter—the systematic arrests and executions of innocent Ukrainians (from the early 1920s through the late 1940s) under the Soviet regime—with a visual and stylistic grace that transcends assumptions about the mediums of both documentary and human rights film-making. Perhaps the most important thing that can be said about such a film is that it is an artistic achievement in its own right, a feat of old-fashioned storytelling that hooks the viewer from its opening moments forward. (6)

In an interview with Leshko, Pultz described how he went about constructing the film, creating a work that breaks away from many traditional models of "documentarist" discourse in which stock footage and "talking heads" are intercut to create a static text rather than a visually compelling and emotionally cathartic experience. Says Pultz,

> although the film begins with an exhumation, it quickly moves into the whole history of Stalinism and the purges. . . . We wanted to put that historical framework first, then [intertwine this material] with personal stories. The personal stories are most important to the emotional resonance of the film. That's where the real human interest of the film comes in. Without that, it's really cold history. The kind of film that really turns me off (sometimes you see it on television, for instance on World War II) is about 90 percent stock footage with a narrator and maybe a couple of historians and that's about it. That kind of film is like reading a textbook. (Leshko 6, 21)

In contrast to this reductive model, Pultz's film uses historical perspectives on the Stalinist purges, intercut with the personal recollections of the few who survived Stalin's reign of terror, to create a sinuous tapestry of image and memory in which all of us are implicated, if only by our silence. During this period, twenty million Ukrainian citizens were systematically killed by Stalin's secret police—the NKVD, headed by Nikolai Yezhov. Family members denounced each other in vain attempts to avoid arrest and torture, while the NKVD organized mass executions of Ukrainians and dumped thousands of bodies in unmarked mass graves. As Meryl Streep notes in her opening narration for *The Great Terror*,

In the Ukrainian village of Vovchkivtsi, residents are exhuming the remains of three victims of Stalinism, killed in 1945 by the Soviet secret police. In the 1930s and '40s, millions of people throughout the former Soviet Union were killed by the state. Their bodies still lie hidden in mass graves. Only since the break-up of the Soviet Union have people been able to search for these graves, exhume the remains, and give them a proper burial. In Ukraine this ritual of exhumation and reburial revives painful memories. The mass slaughter of those years reached all levels of society, and altered life in every Ukrainian town and village. (Pultz n.p.)

Pultz's film offers compelling evidence that such rampant inhumanity can easily be replicated in today's society, as indeed it is in various nations throughout Europe and Africa even today, so long as those who witness the carnage remain silent.

Anand Patwardhan's brief video short *We Are Not Your Monkeys* (India 1996, five minutes) deals with a more insidious form of social marginalization: India's rigid caste system, in which the "untouchables" are consigned by circumstances of birth to the very lowest rung of Indian society, and thus to a life of poverty, menial labor, and, quite often, early death. The catalogue for the Walter Reade Theater's Human Rights Watch International Film Festival describes the video as:

A lively Indian "call to arms," sung and drummed to an attentive audience of villagers seated in a circle on the ground. The song traces the mythological origins of the "untouchables," exploited folk at the very bottom of India's brutal caste system—explaining how the god Rama turned Hunuman into a monkey and then created a monkey army—"untouchables"—in order to preserve racial purity. Now, the singer promises, the tables will be turned: "We will make you human." (Burres 7)

Economical and direct, the video is further proof that through newer and cheaper means of production, even the poorest visual artists can potentially have access to mainstream audiences.

A more expensively produced but still cheerfully subversive film is Arturo Sotto's Amor Vertical (*Vertical Love*), released in 1997. This Cuban/French co-production deals effectively with issues of race, gender, and need for intimacy in the Kafkaesque, and often overwhelming, world of a crushing bureaucracy. *Amor Vertical* follows two young lovers, Ernesto (Jorge Perugorría) and Estela (Silvia Águila), who are desperately seeking a secluded location in which to consummate their relationship, to no avail. Ernesto works as a male nurse in a Havana psychiatric hospital, while Estela is a student who works part time for the government, assisting in the official crackdown on substandard living conditions. But Estela does not have the heart to preside over an endless series of evictions, and attempts suicide by slitting her wrists. Thus it is that Ernesto and Estela meet, and their romance blossoms. Ernesto, however, is ostensibly living with Lucia (Susana Pérez), a woman who works as a projectionist in one of Havana's crumbling movie palaces, and so Ernesto can find no privacy there. Estela lives with her outrageously puritanical father and his family, a ménage so twisted that it recalls the Luis Buñuel films *El* (1952) and *The Criminal Life of Archibaldo de la Cruz* (1955) in its depiction of a sexually frustrated, hypocritically repressed familial domain. Finally, the two lovers are accidentally stuck in an elevator in a large downtown apartment building, and while an assortment of grotesquely caricatured tenants impatiently wait for the elevator to free itself, Ernesto and Estela are finally able to make love with some degree of privacy.

Thwarted in their further attempts to find some time alone, Ernesto and Estela cobble together a ramshackle shanty from cast-off doors, walls, bits of fiberboard, and discarded packing crates and create a makeshift zone of domesticity in which to share their love. However, their idyll is short-lived as the government moves in, declares their new "home" unfit for human habitation, and summarily bulldozes the shack into the river. Estela and Ernesto have no choice but to return to the elevator where they first consummated their passion, and in doing so, they create a national trend. Radio Havana announces to the public that there seems to be an epidemic of elevator failures throughout the metropolis, and that the odor of "flowers and sweat" can be discerned wafting from the numerous stalled conveyances. And with this quietly disruptive triumph of human intimacy over government interference, *Amor Vertical* ends with a sweeping pan of Havana's decaying skyline. Although *Amor Vertical* is a comedy, it makes a number of serious points, most tellingly in the scenes involving Estela's plight while working for, and being manipulated by, the corrupt Cuban government. The offices of the Housing Administration where Estela works are seen as an endless landscape of rusty desks, idly swirling overhead fans, and indifferent employees, all eager for the day to come to an end, and indifferent to any notion of service to the public. "Comedy doesn't necessarily mean something light," noted director Arturo Sotto in an interview at the time of the film's release. "*Amor Vertical*, based on a short story I wrote some time ago, is a reminder of times when feelings and spiritual values were foremost in people's minds" (pressbook for *Amor Vertical* 2). As the pressbook for *Amor Vertical* notes,

> Arturo Sotto [is one of] a new generation of budding Cuban moviemakers. Born in 1967, Arturo Sotto has already established himself in [Cuba] as a promising young film director. Sotto, who graduated from the Escuela de Arte de La Habana and from the Escuela Internacional de Cine in San Antonio de Los Baños, wrote and directed his first play at age 20. After some busy years during which he wrote another play, made two shorts and two documentaries, and gained considerable experience as Director of Photography, he directed his first feature, Pon Tu Pensamiento En Mí, in 1995, one of the three Latin American films selected for the Tokyo Film Festival. (2)

With this impressive beginning, Sotto seems launched on a promising career, and in his choice of Silvia Águila and Jorge Perugorría as Estela and Ernesto, Sotto aligns himself firmly with two of the most influential young stars in the Cuban cinema. Perugorría, particularly, has made a considerable name for himself in Tomás Guittérez Alea and Juan Carlos Tabío's *Fresay Chocolate* (1993), which was a substantial hit in international art houses and proof that, just occasionally, an independent film from the non–Dominant Cinema can do well at the box office, providing that it is given adequate distribution and publicity. A popular star on Cuban television, Perugorría has also appeared in Octavio Cortázar's *Derecho de Asilo* (1994), Alea and Tabío's *Guantamera* (1995), and Bigas Luna's *Bambola*. For Silvia Águila, *Amor Vertical* marks her major screen breakthrough, and in her passion and intensity of performance she reminds one of a young Giulietta Masina in Fellini's *Nights of Cabiria* (1957) (a film, incidentally, that has now been restored to its original running time, in a newly subtitled version, by Canal Plus Distribution). *Armor Vertical* is thus a key film for the new Cuban cinema, and a further example of the vitality and originality of cinema forced to operate on the margins.

An equally compelling, yet much more serious vision of personal self-actualization, can be found in Chris Tashima's *Visas and Virtue* (1997), a twenty-six–minute 35mm short film which won the Academy Award in that same year for best short live action film, as well as placing first in the Fiction category of the USA Film Festival. Shot in a mere seven days in November of 1996 by a crew who, for the most part, donated their labors (including award-winning director of cinematography Hiro Narita, A.S.C., one of the most sought-after DPs in Hollywood), *Visas and Virtue* tells the story of a Japanese diplomat and his wife, stationed in Lithuania at the outbreak of World War II. The movie depicts Consul General Chiune "Sempo" Sugihara defying his government's orders and writing literally thousands of life-saving transit visas, allowing Lithuanian Jews sole passage out of the country, and out of the shadow of the coming Axis onslaught. In addition to directing and co-scripting *Visas and Virtue*, Chris Tashima also portrays Sugihara himself, taking on the lead role in a tightly budgeted production with ease and authority. For an added note of authenticity, Tashima sought out those whose lives had actually been saved by Chiune Sugihara's intervention, and found Hanni Vogelweid, still alive, and arranged for her to appear in the film. As Tashima noted, "Hanni Vogelweid is a 73 year-old woman who lives in Huntington Beach, California with her husband, Lloyd. When she was 17, a Sugihara visa saved her life. On November 13, 1996, Hanni Vogelweid came to the set of *Visas and Virtue* to offer her support and appear in the film." Noted Tashima, "her presence grounded the whole project in reality. She served as a vivid reminder of why we want to tell this story." Added Vogelweid, "very few people know about Sugihara . . . it was hidden, and he suffered . . . so you're doing a great thing" (Tashima n.p.).

From the first, the production of *Visas and Virtue* was a labor of love. Those involved were motivated by the desire to tell the story of Chiune Sugihara, to provide a new perspective on Asian involvement in World War II, and finally, to increase the visibility of members of the Asian creative community within the racially proscribed world of the Dominant Cinema. *Visas and Virtue* began its life as a one-act play written by Tim Toyama, which was presented in November, 1995, at the Road Theatre Company in North Hollywood. Chris Tashima jumped at the opportunity to play Sugihara on stage because, as he admitted during a talk at the Walter Reade Theatre in July, 1998, "you don't get many chances to play a leading role, let alone a heroic leading role, as an Asian actor" (author's notes). Tashima went on to explain that after appearing in the stage production, he was so taken with the project that, in concert with Tim Toyoma and Tom Donaldson, director of the stage production, Tashima conceived the idea of adapting the play for the screen. The first draft of the screenplay, which condensed the one-act play to a tight twenty-six-minute running time, was completed in a two-day marathon session that ended on February 26, 1996.

After this had been accomplished, Tashima and producer Chris Donahue set out to raise the funding to make the film from thousands of individual backers, who each contributed from one hundred to ten thousand dollars. Most donations were small, and the final production budget was modest. It was only with the help and participation of the many members of the Asian-American film community working in Hollywood that *Visas and Virtue* was able to make it to the screen. It is a film which is both modest and transcendent, a compact morality tale for the late 1990s. The play's original cast members all played the same roles in the film. Shizuko Hoslin serves as the off-screen voice of an elderly Yukiko Sugihara, Chiune Sugihara's wife, who narrates the story (which, for the most part, is presented in somber black and white) in flashbacks. In his remarks at the Walter Reade, Tashima admitted that much of the film had been fictionalized or "composited" for dramatic effect: The Rosens, a young couple who seek aid from Sugihara, are actually a composite of the many couples who sought the consul's help. Sugihara's wife, Yukiko, who actively assists the Rosens in their application ("answer 'yes' to all my husband's questions," she cautions them at the outset of their interview with Sugihara) in the film, in fact had little to do with the process, which usually took only a matter of minutes rather than being a lengthy interview.

Despite these instances of dramatic license, or perhaps because they aid in recreating Sugihara's story so vividly, *Visas and Virtue* emerges as a film with a genuine sense of both mission and verisimilitude. Chiune "Sempo" Sugihara's visas directly saved from two thousand to six thousand lives, since each visa guaranteed passage for an entire family. *Visas and Virtue* is a brief, epigrammatic tale in which humanity triumphs over the forces of destruction. What makes it all the more riveting is that it is, for all intents and purposes, entirely true. In 1984, Sugihara was recognized by Yad Vashem, the Holocaust Martyrs' and Heroes' Remembrance Authority, as being "Righteous among the nations" for his heroic act, in which he directly disobeyed the orders of his government to save the lives of thousands of innocent people. *Visas and Virtues* is a stirring testament to Chiune Sugihara's legacy, and a striking example of a story that could only be told on the screen by a cinema that operates outside the commercial constraints of the mainstream.

Another aspect of the Asian-American experience in World War II is explored in Terri de Bono and Steve Rosen's *Beyond Barbed Wire* (1997), a stunning documentary on the "Japanese-American soldiers who served in the U.S. Army's 100th Infantry Battalion and the 442nd Regiment—units that absorbed the highest casualties and became the most decorated during World War II" (Burres, Harding, and Masone 9). A mainstream Hollywood feature, Robert Pirosh's 1951 *Go for Broke!*, attempted to document the actions of the 442nd Regimental Combat unit but from the Eurocentric perspective of Van Johnson. Johnson is a racist commander who is unwillingly drafted to train the troops and lead them into combat. However, no film within the Dominant Cinema has accurately documented the saga of the Asian-American soldier. *Beyond Barbed Wire* effectively weaves together archival footage, contemporary interviews, and a superb narration spoken by Noriyuki "Pat" Morita into a multifaceted portrait of Asian-Americans on the home front and in the battlefield. Asian-Americans faced arbitrary deportation to internment camps at home (as well as the loss of their houses and possessions), while drawing the most dangerous and often suicidal assignments on the battle front. "Go for Broke!" was their slogan, and it aptly sums up the plight of Asian-Americans during World War II's climate of racist hysteria and unreason. Given a choice to either go to prison for being a "potential spy" or serve in the military, the veterans interviewed in *Beyond Barbed Wire* realized that they had little choice but to sign up, fight, and often die in a series of campaigns designed to test them beyond the limits of all human endurance. While their families languished in prison camps at home (hence the title of the film), young Asian-Americans had little choice but to fight and die in a war that would eventually cost the lives of millions of innocent civilians. By laying bare the racism of society in the United States during World War II, and sharing the marginalized vision of those who had to bear the brunt of that racism both at home and at war with contemporary audiences, *Beyond Barbed Wire* offers us a vision of an America divided by race, class, and social distinctions, seemingly unaware of the racism that informs its every political act. This extraordinary feature-length documentary deserves the widest possible audience; it is both reprehensible and pathetic that *Go for Broke!* remains, for the moment, the Dominant Cinema's last word on this simultaneously shameful and heroic episode in our nation's deeply conflicted past.

Other films of interest at the Human Rights Watch International Film Festival included Hillie Molencar and Joop Van Wijk's *Crossroads* (1997), an hour-long documentary on the Tutsi-Hutu violence that still plagues Rwanda to the present day. The film manages to truly humanize this conflict through the use of interviews, by focusing on a few key participants, and by using footage of the residents of Benaco, a small town where the refugees of the violent conflict sought to start a new life.

Balufu Bakupa-Kanyinda's *The Draughtsman Clash* (1996) is a forty-minute 35mm featurette from Gabon. In it, a despotic ruler forces a young man to play "draughts" (a variation on checkers) with him until late at night, threatening the young man with death if he wins (thus affronting the ruler) and death if he loses (proving unworthy of competition). Shot in black and white except for an opening and closing panshot of the countryside in appropriately washed-out color, *The Draughtsman Clash* is a funny, profane, and violent meditation on the capriciousness of rule by force alone.

The late Heiner Carow's *Coming Out* (1989) was made in East Germany just before the collapse of the Berlin Wall, and thus remains the only gang-themed film to emerge from the former Soviet satellite nation. In *Coming Out*, a young teacher comes to terms with the fact that he is gay, despite the general disapproval of the society around him. The journey is not an easy one, as the man faces discrimination and violent reprisals on all sides. Nor does *Coming Out* offer a typically pleasing ending to artificially satisfy the viewer. The protagonist, Philip Klahrmann, drifts through an ultimately unsatisfying relationship with a woman, and then shares a night of passion with a young man. He is ultimately rejected by both his lovers, and is left at the end of the film to face an official inquiry into his capabilities as a teacher, the results of which seem to favor his dismissal. Sumptuously photographed in color and inventively staged, *Coming Out* is all the more poignant because Carow never had the opportunity to work in the West, and died without knowing that *Coming Out* would ever receive a screening outside the Soviet bloc.

Carlos Siguion-Reyna's *The Man in Her Life* (1997) is a superb gay film from the Philippines, in which a young woman, Selya, has a brief and unhappy affair with Bobby, a footloose, unreliable traveling salesman. When Bobby quite expectedly vanishes after impregnating Selya, the young woman marries a local landowner and school principal, Ramon, to avoid scandal. After the wedding, Selya bears a son. But Selya has been tricked: as everyone in the village knows, Ramon is gay, and his behavior has been the source of local scandal for several years. No one believes for a moment that the child is Ramon's, and Selya, discovering Ramon's true orientation, recoils from the relationship in disgust. When Bobby returns, demanding that Selya leave Ramon and take her son with him, Selya faces a moment of truth. Should she go with the unreliable and mercurial Bobby, or stay with Ramon, and enjoy the security of a real home? Ultimately, Selya decides that Bobby is simply too immature to be trusted in a long-term relationship, and stays with Ramon, whom she finds to be "more of a man" than the macho, violence-prone Bobby. When *The Man in Her Life* was first released in the Philippines, it was heavily censored on the official grounds that "homosexuality does not exist in the Philippines." Only after extensive recutting was the film given an exhibition license in that country; in the United States, the uncensored version has been screened at several festivals to unanimous critical acclaim.

Lisa Lewenz's piquant *A Letter Without Words* offers a personalized vision of the Holocaust using home movies to uncover the horror of life in Nazi Germany. As Lewenz's notes for the release of the film state,

> All families have secrets. Ella Arnhold Lewenz tried to protect hers by asking her son to burn her personal letters and papers after she died. He did. What motivated this Jewish grandmother's request, when she also left behind dozens of reels of 16mm color and black/white films documenting a large family who had once been powerful figures in the history of Germany? Until this discovery in her family attic in 1981, director Lisa Lewenz had little idea about her family's silenced past.
>
> *A Letter Without Words* exposes a granddaughter's sixteen year quest to discover her grandmother's motives for having made films long after 1933, when independent filmmaking became illegal. Ella risked her life to chronicle an otherwise forgotten time. Her footage documents a carefree family; elaborate Nazi extravaganzas; and notable figures who soon would become exiles from Hitler's regime: such as Albert Einstein, Rabbi Leo Baeck, actress Brigitte Helm. Lisa retraced her grandmother's footsteps and invited her family to participate in the journey. This film chronicles an imagined correspondence between generations while questioning the role of the historical witness. The 1998 film, *A Letter Without Words*, explores

themes of racism, genocide and ongoing attempts to grapple with effects of political upheaval, while discovering a silent personal history. (Lewenz n.p.)

The stark immediacy and directness of Lewenz's documentary makes the overwhelming tragedy of the Holocaust a direct challenge to the viewer; these could be anyone's home movies, images of a shared life, but they document not only the personal odyssey of a family, but also the activities of one of the most brutal regimes in modern history.

THE HUMAN MACHINE

The films presented during the Human Rights Watch International Film Festival offer a cross section of cinematic practice on the margins of film and video production designed as a vehicle for personal expression, rather than as a means to generate box-office receipts. All of these films, even *Death Sentence* (which seems strikingly lavish in its execution), were modestly budgeted. Despite their appeal to local audiences, none of them will probably ever receive widespread distribution in the United States, with the aforementioned effect of "ghettoizing" foreign films on videotape in all but the most exceptional cases. Where the United States used to be a lucrative foreign market for many foreign productions, now Hollywood often buys the rights to a film and *remakes* it with American actors, a practice which strips the original film of both its artistic dignity and any potential market value. Having the opportunity to view these phantom projects, then, once again forcefully reminds us that in the age of *Saving Private Ryan* (1998), only the most carefully calculated, mainstream feature films will ever reach a substantial international audience. Outside of major metropolitan centers, the voice of cinematic independence has been all but silenced, in a wave of multi-million-dollar star vehicles backed by intensive, global, saturation booking campaigns. But if the images that we see are being stratified into the public and the private sphere of cinema/video reception, what is happening to film/video production is a minor affair compared to current developments on the side of "reception," namely, the re-engineering of the human body to adapt to the twenty-first century.

Advances in genetic engineering have made possible the cloning of animals, and probably within the next decade or so, the cloning of humans (despite whatever legislation may be passed to stop it). But perhaps more disturbing is the potential surgical modification of human beings into ultra-efficient weapons of battle, a project currently being seriously examined by military leaders both in the Untied States and abroad. As Tyler Schnoebelen reports in his unnerving essay "Be More Than You Can Be," the possibility of reconfiguring and modifying the human body into a super-efficient war machine is already the topic of serious debate in technological and military think tanks.

> "Today we strap on night-vision devices," Admiral David Jeremiah, a former member of the Joint Chiefs of Staff, announced in 1995, "but by 2025 we almost certainly will implant enhancements in the human body to deal with biological warfare, to enhance visibility [and] increase strength of the soldier." (43)

That was in 1995. In the summer of 1998, the army conducted a three-day conference, with more than two hundred scientists from government, the private sector, and research universities attending, on the subject of "Nanotechnology for the Soldier System" in Cambridge, Massachusetts. The symposium was organized by Soldiers Systems Command (SSCOM), a government agency charged with the care and feeding of men and women in uniform. But during this conference, it seems that SSCOM's agenda had expanded into new realms of inquiry. As Colonel Richard Ross told the convention attendees in his opening speech, as reported by Tyler Schnoebelen,

> "Using technology to our advantage, our soldiers are becoming more lethal, more survivable, and more mobile than ever before. . . . The individual soldier of 2025 will be as effective as a tank of 1995." (43)

Apparently, all that is stopping the army from introducing such technology on a widespread scale is the public's understandable misgivings about such an enterprise. But Philip Brandler, director of the army's Natick Research Development and Engineering Center, feels that such objections will eventually be overcome:

> "In general, our intentions and plans have not explored the use of invasive procedures not because we reject it, but because of the dif-

ficulty of introducing it. But if the medical community can get it through the FDA, then we'll embrace it . . . once it appears acceptable [to the general public], we will ask it of your sons and daughters who have chosen to wear the uniform" (Schnoebelen 43).

All of these "advances" are made possible by nanotechnology, the creation of intensely miniaturized and reassembled clusters of rearranged atomic and molecular structures, enabling everything from computers to surveillance devices to be scaled-down to the size of a pinprick. As Schnoebelen notes, while such uses can be beneficial in medicine, communications, and numerous other fields of human endeavor, it can also lead to more sinister applications. In his essay, he recounts that

> presenters at the conference predicted that, within 10 years, the army will use "biochips" to keep track of supplies and personnel. Within 20, nanorobots in the body could act as artificial blood cells to protect against biological and chemical warfare, while smart bullets could find their way to targets with perfect precision. (43)

Nanotechnology is also capable of creating frightfully panopticonic zones of perpetual hypersurveillance, in which miniaturized computers and surveillance cameras will track each person's every move twenty-four hours a day, often without the object of surveillance being aware of the intense scrutiny she/he is being exposed to. Already, the effects of fiber optic technology and the miniaturization of surveillance equipment are making it harder and harder to escape the "gaze that controls."

As veteran night-life observer Anthony Haden-Guest has reported, a hypersurveillance web site known as www.spy7.com features images of the rich and famous as they make their rounds of New York City's nightclubs, images captured by a miniaturized video camera using "a fibreoptic lens, itself the size of a grain of caviar" (27). Spy 7 calls this hypersurveillance project NiteLife Cam, and uses a group of young clubgoers who are wired up with these sub-miniaturized video cameras as its agents in the field. Interestingly, the visuals have no sound because under the current law, sound recording of one's voice without one's prior permission is legally prohibited as "bugging." However, using a concealed video transmitter to document the movements of total strangers is not, apparently, illegal as of this writing. Where all this will ultimately lead is anyone's guess. Haden-Guest suggests that celebrities will retreat into their own homes, and forswear venturing out into the public sphere, as they already are wont to do in Los Angeles (27). But aside from video documentation of the fashionable set, the average citizen has much to fear from the new zone of continual scrutiny being created by modern video cameras and their attendant technologies. In many major metropolitan centers, video surveillance cameras are now so ubiquitous that they cover virtually the entire city through an intricate network of television cameras perched atop buildings, on bridges or television towers, aimed at literally every sector of the surveilled metropolis. There are so many video surveillance cameras employed throughout Manhattan, each with the individual capability to pan, zoom and tilt as needed, that no one can walk the streets of Midtown without being the object of scrutiny. In London, even as far back as the early 1990s, remote cameras placed at traffic intersections and triggered by infrared radar guns, have snapped photos of the license plates of speeding automobiles. Although the driver is unaware of it at the time, s/he has just been "arrested" for speeding; a ticket arrives in the post a few days afterward. As insurance companies call out for greater supervision of public work and recreation areas, more and more video surveillance devices will undoubtedly be employed, until only the domestic sphere would remain relatively free of the constant, impersonal gaze of control, and even that zone of supposed personal privacy is fast becoming nonexistent. While the technological advances of sub-miniaturization, nanotechnology, and its attendant disciplines hold great promise for advancing medical technology and increasing the human lifespan, the potential for the abuse or misapplication of these ascendant processes is also a genuine threat.

In 1990, Julia Scher designed a home surveillance environment dubbed "the house that watches back," featuring surveillance

> restraint systems, quarantine blocks, multiple I.D. indexing, driver escorts, computerized mobile surveillance, closed circuit television and cameras, motion detection, essential vibration monitors, personal identification, time lapse recording, biometrics, risk assessment/private evaluation, continuous central station monitoring, access control, audio surveillance, man trap booths, [and] life support control systems. (Scher 116, 117)

In such a domestic environment, every movement of the inhabitants would be videotaped, timed, measured, recorded, and archived, much like the zone of hypersurveillance inhabited by Jim Carrey in *The Truman Show* (1998).

Another example of the phantom zone of hypersurveillance being transformed into the site of artistic endeavor is Jane and Louise Wilson's *Stasi City*. A 1997 video installation which was presented in New York in the 303 Gallery in the summer of 1998, *Stasi City* creates an atmosphere of sinister nuance out of the ruins of the former headquarters of the East Berlin secret police. Sisters Jane and Louise Wilson, British video artists, were given a grant to live in Germany and create *Stasi City*, which emerges as two opposing sets of video projections, sometimes replicating the area being videotaped from opposing points of views, at other times introducing new visual material into the mix. The piece takes roughly five minutes to perform, and then repeats, as the Wilsons' camera drifts through a series of deserted interrogation chambers, an abandoned television control center, and at the center of the facility, an abandoned operating room, with cabinets turned on their sides, a bleak operating table, and an ominous overhead light, apparently still functioning in this zone of hermetic decay and absence (see R. Smith, E37).

As the piece concludes, one of the Wilsons, dressed in the uniform of the East German Olympic gymnastic team during the 1970s, floats mysteriously through the debris suspended in midair, as an enigmatic silver cylinder floats in the air behind her. From another screen, another woman watches impassively, as the Wilsons' camera continues its effortless, dreamlike journey, drifting silently through this domain of torture and surveillance. The work ends abruptly: the metallic canister falls to the ground with a sharp, amplified noise, and both oppositional screens cut to black. Within moments, the loop will recycle itself, and the Wilsons will once again invite us into the domain of Stasi City, using only the natural sounds of the obsolescent machinery on the soundtrack, suggesting the horrific mechanisms of brutality which once operated inside these now-abandoned rooms.

Brief but brimming with menace and impact, the Wilsons' restrained video installation is both enigmatic and epigrammatic, but it also serves (ironically) to highlight the deficiency of narrative in conveying a sense of time and/or place remembered. Shackled with an eighty- to ninety-minute running time by arbitrary tradition and commercial considerations, conventional film and video production must rely upon narrative to hold the audience's attention. Indeed, as feature films become more expensive to make and produce, it seems that in addition to being driven by special effects and scenes of spectacular destruction, they are concomitantly informed by a need to formulate a cohesive narrative thread, linear and easily discernible, for their target audiences. Even motion picture coming attractions (or trailers) now feel obliged to lay out the entire narrativistic structure of the film they seek to herald; nothing is left for the viewer to discover. If one has seen the trailer, one has seen the movie. Yet the tyranny of the feature film format persists, driven by market economies and the audience's need to escape from the mundanities of everyday existence, linking commercial image production ineluctably to the demands of narrative closure, and thus sharply delineating the artistic realm of the conventional theatrical motion picture. It does not seem that this will change in the immediate future; indeed, it seems that the reliance on predictable, generic narrative stations of the cross has grown, rather than declined. This is precisely why video installations such as *Stasi City* are so important, and why they deserve a wider audience. Stripped of the demands for conventional narrative structure, as well as the need for a predetermined running time, works like *Stasi City* engage and challenge the viewer, demanding interpretation, resisting easy categorization, and evoking the banal yet real horrors of a defunct regime with understated yet sinuous effectiveness.

EL MEXTERMINATOR

Another performance/video installation of the late 1990s carries a good deal of cultural resonance in describing the politics of American racism with respect to Latino culture. Guillermo Gómez-Peña's *El Mexterminator*, presented at El Museo del Barrio in the summer of 1998, effectively critiques the dominant cultural bias of mainstream American/European culture through a variety of late twentieth-century invasive strategies. Co-created with Roberto Sifuentes and Sara Shelton Mann, *El Mexterminator* interrogates prevailing stereotypes of Latino/a culture as perpetuated by the mainstream media, as the polemicized manifesto for the presentation makes abundantly clear. Set in a post-apocalyptic America of 1999, *El Mexterminator* maps a cultural terrain in which Mexico and the United States have engaged in all-out, full-scale warfare, and in which Mexico has emerged the ultimate victor. The fictitious Minister of Aztlan Liberado announces to the citizens of the "ex-USA" that a new cultural, social, and political regime has thus emerged:

Dear Citizen:

As you well know, the nation-state collapsed in 1998 immediately after the Second U.S./Mexico War. The ex-USA has fragmented into a myriad [of] micro-republics loosely controlled by a Chicano prime minister. Spanglish is the official language, la lingua franca. Anglo militias are desperately trying to recapture the Old Order, which they paradoxically [seek] to overturn. The newly elected government sponsors interactive ethnographic exhibits to teach the perplexed population of the United States of Aztlan Liberado how things were before and during the Second U.S./Mexico War which Mexico won. What you are witnessing is an example of the new "official cultural hybrid." These five human specimens as well as unique archaeological artifacts are both residues of our dying Western civilization, and samples of an emerging Nova Cultura, a culture in which the margins have fully occupied the center. (Gómez-Peña n.p.)

The exhibit contains the video monitors, one with images of various Latino/a stereotypes and crossover hybridization prototypes as part of a videotape entitled *Border Stasis*, created by Gómez-Peña and his colleagues especially for this installation; the other monitor displays manipulated footage from old westerns, crime films, and footage of the gods on Mt. Olympus from *Jason and the Argonauts* (1964) slowed down to reveal the mechanics that inform the construction of the numerous fictive images Anglo culture has fabricated with regard to Latina/o society. Toys, face masks, magazines, garden implements, and other mundane artifacts of a society in collapse are showcased in a series of glass cabinets; a toilet, seated high above the rest of the exhibition, is displayed with a sign instructing potential participants to sit down, and role-play the part of "your favorite ethnic minority" for a maximum of ten minutes. The total effect is of a museum at the end of Anglo dominance after the complete and spectacular collapse of the inequitable infrastructure that has for so long kept it afloat. As the manifesto promises, the viewer will

meet El Mad Mex, Cyber Vato and La Cultural Transvestite. These undocumented "specimens" on display exhibit a variety of cultural characteristics: hybridity, hyper-sexuality, infectiousness, and unnecessarily violent behavior. They deal drugs and jalapeño peppers; speak Spanglish and gringoñol; practice experimental performance and witchcraft; and are highly politicized. Their political agenda includes invading El Norte and redefining the West. Their tableaux vivants, and arte-factos have been strictly designed by your fears and desires, with the help of thousands of anonymous internautas who have responded to Gómez-Peña and Sifuentes' "techno-confessional." (www.echonyc.com/`temple)

Part "Tex-Mex rave," "end-of-the-century freak-show extravaganza," and "Museum of the Apocalypse," *El Mexterminator* traces a new ethnographic and cultural map of Mexa York with performances in high fashion storefronts, impromptu public appearances, conceptual ads, posters and radio PSAs. These "information-superhighway banditos" and "media pirates" will cruise the media streams of the City with a live Internet chat and an interactive radio call-in show, encouraging individuals to participate as their "favorite cultural avatars," to discuss their fears and desires of the cultural "other" and reflect on the horror of a country perceived to be under siege by immigrants and people of color. El Museo del Barrio will host *El Mexterminator*'s "Techno-Museo de Etnografia Interactiva," featuring performances that are shaped uniquely by the audience's interactions with these ethno-cyborgs and new technologies, creating an embodiment of the visitors/turistas own psychological and cultural monsters. (Gómez-Peña n.p.)

As part of the performance schedule, in addition to the live Internet chat sessions and various unscheduled guerrilla "actions" citywide at unspecified times and locations, Gómez-Peña and his collaborations promised "two live Mexicans on display" for three days during the installation, and admonished the viewer to "look at these Mexicans on display at El Museo del Barrio. Watch for impromptu actions at other public locales including NYC hot spots, tourist attractions and other cultural destinations." Among these "actions" were a series of spontaneous performances through New York City, during which:

dressed in full regalia, El Mexterminator, Cyber Vato, and La Cultural Transvestite will go out on the town to provoke public response. Will elegant uptown restaurants let them in for lunch? Will Latinos on the street smile? Will tourists take a picture with them? *El Mexterminator*'s street interventions confront people and challenge them to admit and deal with their own ethnic issues of distance and preference as well as to enjoy the spectacle. (Gómez-Peña n.p.)

El Mexterminator is thus a combination video/theatrical/cultural artifact presentation that not only incorporates the "curios, paintings, and other artifacts referencing Chicano culture, [but also allows the artists to] create an installation which is the setting for these performances, shaped uniquely by the audience's interactions" (Gómez-Peña, *Manifesto*). *El Mexterminator* breaks beyond the boundaries of the museum space with its live performance "actions," but also retains the museum gallery as a "headquarters" for its cultural assault on the politics of racism and cultural/racial stereotyping. In addition to his work as a performance artist, Gómez-Peña is a MacArthur Fellowship recipient, a commentator for National Public Radio, and the author of several texts critiquing American cultural/social politics. As a whole, *El Mexterminator* seeks to expand the universe of the performance domain from the "sacred space" of privilege represented by the conventional museum and/or gallery, and also to fully incorporate, through a variety of means, audience input into their collaborative and provocative assemblage.

BEYOND THE FRINGE

A post-modern artist who has been working in film, video, theatre, and other mediums since the early 1960s is Jonathan Miller, who since his very earliest days as a performer, director, and writer has sought to expand the boundaries of the stage or cinema screen in search of a plastic, accessible, altogether kinetic approach to visual media. When his name is mentioned, most people think first of Miller's productions of Shakespeare's plays for the BBC, or his work staging operas in Salzburg, New York, Vienna and London, but in fact, Jonathan Miller is very much the renaissance personage. Having first trained as a medical doctor (he received degrees from St. John's College, Cambridge, and University College, London, in 1959), Miller has been, by turns, a satirist (in his work with the *Beyond the Fringe* review, where he co-starred with Dudley Moore, Peter Cook, and Alan Bennett), a critic, a writer, a stage director, an opera director, a producer, and a filmmaker. This last part of Miller's career is often obscured by his other accomplishments, but it forms a fascinating, and, I would argue, crucial portion of his overall accomplishment as an artist.

I first met Dr. Jonathan Miller during a lecture he gave at Rutgers University in the spring of 1968. He was there to present his feature film version of *Alice in Wonderland* (1966), shot in 35mm black and white as a BBC telefilm, and never released theatrically due to legal problems with actors' clearances (more's the pity). The huge ensemble cast included John Gielgud, Peter Sellers, Ralph Richardson, Malcolm Muggeridge, and Anne-Marie Mallik as Alice. To my mind, Miller's version is the very best adaptation of Carroll's oft-filmed classic, and its lack of public approbation is thus all the more unsettling. Miller also presented two shorter films, *Oh Whistle and I'm Come to You* (1968), a ghost story based on a short story by Henry James, and *The Drinking Party: Plato's Symposium* (1965), both also made for the BBC and running about an hour's length each. At a symposium after the screening, we began talking and became friends.

When I lived in London in the summer of 1968, I stayed at Jonathan's house. He was unfailingly kind, introducing me to the New Arts Lab in Drury Lane (then the hub of independent film production in the UK), and drawing me into debates in the basement kitchen of his Gloucester Street home (where he still lives today) on every imaginable topic under the sun, from pop music to politics. I was impressed then, as I still am now, with his candor, his concise and cutting use of language, and his unfailing honesty and good taste in all things, particularly film. Since Miller's filmic work has been so little distributed in the United States, and since so few people are aware of this aspect of his career, I decided that it would be a good idea to engage him in a dialogue on his film work. Late in the summer of 1997, we had an insightful conversation on Miller's life and work, some of which follows:

WHEELER WINSTON DIXON: In 1968, you had just finished *Alice in Wonderland* in 35mm black and white, and you were very much opposed to the use of color, and also to videotape, in your work at that time. Now, of course, you've done a lot of tape with your work in the Shakespeare plays, and also as a director/producer of opera for the BBC. How have your views changed since then?

JONATHAN MILLER: Well, I was really only opposed to the use of color in *Alice in Wonderland*, because I was trying to recreate a Victorian film, a film of the early cinema, with the effect of Victorian photography. I wasn't trying to re-create the Tenniel drawings, because there was no way you could do that on film, so I went for a much more naturalistic approach, but I wanted to get the effect of Victorian photographs, the sort of thing that Carroll himself would have taken. I'm still rather opposed to color under those circumstances. Making *Alice in Wonderland* was an absolutely delightful experience, because it wasn't a standard commercial production. I simply called up all my friends in the theatre and told each of them that the other was going to do it, and so in the end they all agreed, and the film was, I think, quite successful.

There are certain films that I think would always look better in black and white. *Alice in Wonderland* was one of them. If I was going to do a film about the 1940s, there are certain black and white photographs that look much better, and convey the spirit of the era with greater accuracy. But as my son, who is a photographer, keeps on saying: "It's a lie, because these events were, in fact, in color." For example, Steven Spielberg's *Schindler's List* (1993) was sort of a lie because of that. I also didn't like the way he threw in little splashes of color to direct your attention where he wanted it. But it was primarily a lie because, as Roman Polanski said, "I remember those events in color."

WWD: You were also quite opposed to videotape at that point in your career.

JM: That was only because in those days, videotape was an extremely crude optical device—it gave very undifferentiated results, the range of blacks and whites and greys was not nearly so full as it is now—and with increasing technological developments, and particularly with the introduction of digital videotape (DVT), I really now have very little against it. I've shot lots of things on tape subsequently, and been very pleased with them.

WWD: But don't you feel there's an essential difference between film and tape, the feel, the look, the essential characteristics of the two mediums?

JM: Yes, of course there are differences, and of course you can't satisfactorily project it on a big screen, although that day is coming. I think by and large that gradually the distinction between the two is getting less and less, and that, as my son just pointed out, you couldn't tell the difference between film and video in Peter Green-away's *Prospero's Books* (1991); the whole thing was, in fact, shot on digital videotape, and then transferred to film.

I think now that any objections one might have had to digital tape are very small, and from the point of view of convenience, and speed, and instant playback, video has the upper hand. When it comes to these big wide-screen productions, then obviously you would want to use massive, big format film for these projects, but I suspect that massive, big format digital tape will also become available for these productions in the future.

WWD: Are you suspicious of "these big wide screen productions," or to put it another way, are you suspicious of spectacle?

JM: No, I'm not suspicious of spectacle, I quite enjoy it, when it's there. But I don't think there are really many wonderful films which are ever great spectacles. Often times, these films are by definition "great spectacles" and that's it. There's nothing else to them. And in certain films, like John Ford's westerns, if you couldn't see Monument Valley in its entirety, it would detract considerably from the overall success of the work. That's the best kind of spectacle, because it's a marriage of thematic concerns with a sense of the broad sweep one needs in these kind of films. But if you're talking about films where the spectacle becomes the whole text of the narrative, then that's of no interest at all.

What I prefer are small, intimate films about real people. And often, for these projects, you could do them just as well on digital tape, and obtain some wonderful effects in the process. You can light productions now for videotape that are wonderful; you can do things with much greater subtlety than it was ever possible to do before. I've just got a new series coming out on the production of opera, which was shot in a very peculiarly moody warehouse, and it doesn't look that different from *Reservoir Dogs* (1992), and yet the entire project was conceived and shot on digital tape. I think the day is rapidly approaching, if it hasn't already arrived, when the distinction between film and video will disappear altogether.

WWD: Why did you abandon commercial filmmaking altogether after the production of *Take a Girl Like You* (1970), a feature film for Columbia which starred Sheila Hancock, Noel Harrison, Ronald Lacey, Hayley Mills, and Oliver Reed? I thought it was quite successful.

JM: Well, not from my point of view. As far as I was concerned, *Take a Girl Like You* was such a catastrophe, and I had such a bad experience doing it, working with stars and working with the conventional studio system, that I simply didn't feel inclined to go on in that direction. Nor did I want to go through the labor with studios of "packaging" projects, putting together this star with that story, getting "properties," going to meetings, and the like. I thought it much easier to go on directing plays and operas, and television documentaries. If the system had been more congenial, perhaps it would have turned out differently.

WWD: What can you tell me about your involvement as director in *What's Going on Now*, a film documentary that you did in conjunction with WNEW TV in New York in 1962–1963? Was that a series of telefilms?

JM: We only did one, which I directed, a full-length thing on the arts in New York at that time, and then we did some short shots on the Ed Sullivan show which he rapidly became impatient with because they were too subversive for *that* old Irish cop.

WWD: What led to production of your teleseries *The Body in Question*, which you wrote and appeared on, but didn't direct? That was shot on film, a thirteen-part series for the BBC in 1977. Wasn't this a rather gargantuan task to take on, an entire series about the concerns and conditions of the human organism?

JM: It was a very large and very difficult project, very long, arduous, and elaborate, but I had always wanted to do something on the history of medicine. But actually, as the production got under way, I found that I was not so much interested in the history of medicine as in the history of ideas, and that this was a very good framework for showing what became the history of the *mind*. The body became a sort of pretext for showing this interior landscape of the mind.

WWD: Then in 1979, you were appointed as head of another remarkably ambitious project, the complete Shakespeare series for the BBC. You served as executive producer for the entire series, as well as directing many of the plays yourself.

JM: Well, I only served on the project for three years, from 1979 to 1981. I took it on because it was an opportunity to do more Shakespeare, and that was the main attraction for me. It wasn't that I was interested in the mechanics of the entire production process at all, but I was deeply attracted to the opportunity to do as much of Shakespeare as possible, in versions that would appeal to contemporary audiences. So we used people like John Cleese of *Monty Python*, and Roger Daltrey, who had been the lead singer with the pop group the Who. Altogether, I did seven of my own productions of Shakespeare. I wasn't really attracted to the administrative end of the business, I can assure you!

This wasn't my first time directing Shakespeare for television; I'd done a version of *King Lear* on tape in 1975 for the BBC's Play of the Month series. But the experience with doing so many of these Shakespeare productions peaked for me with my direction of *Othello*, in 1981, which I was able to shoot on tape in a way which is almost indistinguishable from film. We used multiple cameras, and did live "vision-mixing" [known as "live-switching" in the United States] for *Othello*, but I was able to light it in such a way that it had real depth and intensity, and I feel it was every bit as good as film, and again, I feel that's becoming an increasingly artificial distinction.

WWD: How do you go about doing the blocking of the actors for film or tape? Do you do a lot of storyboarding? Is there a difference in your mind when you consciously set about to do something for the stage, as a theatrical experience, versus something for film or tape?

JM: Well, for a film or video production, I rough it out visually, not with storyboards, but during the rehearsals with the actors. I start very early on with the head cameraman, saying "look, we'll take this part of the speech up to here on that shot, and then we'll cut round to the other one of that." So it's very much a process of discovery, and by the time we've got round to the last rehearsals, and we're ready to go into the studio, we've got a shooting script.

WWD: In footage I've seen of you directing actors, you seem very much concerned with what I might call "externals," mannerisms, gestures, and facial expressions which might reveal the interior state of the performer's consciousness, and the use of her/his body as a performer.

JM: Well, you're quite right. I'm very interested in the minute details of human behavior. Most of the time, I find that as a director I'm reminding people of things they've known, but forgotten. I'm just not given to these sort of massive introspections when I'm dealing with actors; you hope that these people will come with sort of an idea as to what these internal emotions are, and then things will spring out of them quite naturally as they start playing the part. To merely utter the lines usually puts them in the frame of mind that will be appropriate for them; they discover themselves in the part through the language in the text.

We talk about people's states of mind, but most of the time, we know nothing about people's states of mind except through what they do. And so the best thing to do as an director is to keep on reminding the actors of this fact, and then they'll deliver the sort of performance that one wants. I always find it's best to go from outside in; to start with the exterior gestures and mannerisms, and they take them inside to find out why they seem appropriate to the actor.

Working with each individual actor is unique. Each person has a particular way of working, and it's mad to try to impose a way of working on them from the outset. Nevertheless, they come to recognize that I have a way of working as a director, in which I put tremendous emphasis upon subliminal human details that actually are part and parcel of the daily actions of the body.

WWD: In both your films and your video productions, it seems to me that you feel comfortable acknowledging the essential theatricality of your presentations, and you don't try to artificially break through the "fourth wall" in your films or videotapes. You seem to set it up as a given, the act of performance, and take it from that point. At the same time, your setting of costumes and props is very pared down to the essentials of the piece, and you keep concentrating the audience's attention back on the visuals and the performer's bodies and speech as the essential elements of the work.

JM: Yes, I like great simplicity in all my work. I don't like lots and lots of florid detail, and I want my film and video works to be recognized by the audience as theatrical presentations, or constructs, whether one is doing a project for the cinema or for television. It's much better to simplify, always, rather than elaborate.

WWD: What are your feelings about the current crop of period productions that are very popular now of Henry James's and Jane Austen's novels, films such as *Sense and Sensibility* (1996), *Emma* (1997), and *Portrait of a Lady* (1997)?

JM: Well, I hate them all. I hate them because they're utterly false. First of all, I have a basic objection to very elaborate settings, but secondly, when it comes to James's and Austen's work, these works have their primary existence as novels, and it is in their prior existence as novels that they have their plenary existence. To put in what the author doesn't mention is actually to abuse the work. As for Jane Campion's *Portrait of a Lady*, I think it's terrible. I'm not against updating, but if you're going to take that particular novel, everything that the novel is concerned with is contained in the prose that expresses those ideas. A person is not in the novel in the way that a person might be said to be *in* Birmingham, Alabama. A person is *in* the novel because they're *made out of the text*. And the text is in fact irreplaceable. And if you wrench the people out of the text which describes them, you've actually done away with *them*. That's the basic mistake these films make.

WWD: I couldn't agree more. What are your feelings about more commercial contemporary British filmmaking, things like *Four Weddings and a Funeral* (1994)? When the film was such an enormous success, there was a huge critical backlash against it in the British press. Yet it seemed to me that it was really nothing more or less than a very minor, modern Ealing Comedy, and didn't pretend to be anything else.

JM: Well, I didn't love it or hate it. I thought it was just a perfectly funny little sort of television comedy. It was just the teleseries *Friends*, English style. I wouldn't even say it was an Ealing Comedy, even a very slight one. It was *Friends*. It was a feature-length sitcom. As for the critical backlash, one might really call it more or less a category mistake. I mean, you might as well attack *Frazier*.

WWD: Most recently, you've moved most of your attention to live opera, which was prefigured by such projects as your 1985 version of *Cosi Fan Tutte* for the BBC, which you directed specifically for television. What led to this shift in direction from staged theatrical presentations, along with film and video, to live opera?

JM: Well, it wasn't a conscious plan. I just got more and more opportunities to direct opera, and as I fell more and more out of fashion in the English theatre, I tended to move the sphere of my operations abroad, and the only thing one could work in outside of one's own language is something where language doesn't take priority, and that's opera. So now I work almost exclusively in Europe, and occasionally in the United States, and it so happens that if you work outside your own country, opera's the best thing to work in.

WWD: What are your feelings about this whole "falling out of fashion" process you just alluded to? You started your career in the 1960s, when your contemporaries were people like John Osborne, Harold Pinter, and Tony Richardson.

JM: Well, we've all grown out of fashion. I don't deconstruct, and I don't like the French salon philosophers of the moment, such as Derrida or Baudrillard. I like Daniel Sperber's work a good deal, but the others seem to me to be rather fashionable without much real depth. That said, I think probably that my productions are as modern as anyone else's at the current moment. But there are certain adherences that I have still to the classical tradition, which make me in the eyes of some people slightly out-of-date. I occasionally update, but on the whole I have a certain sort of classical austerity which is not regarded as fashionable now. And, as always, the press is very interested in the latest thing. And when you're sixty-three, you're not the latest thing.

This happened to Noel Coward and Terence Rattigan, and then subsequently their works were rediscovered, and they had a sort of critical renaissance. But they were writers, and I'm a director, and as a director, one's work is more evanescent. One can't reconstruct my live productions, because once they're completed, there's no record of them. Directors don't undergo revivals. I mean, I'm as busy as I ever was, and in some senses, busier, but not busy in the theatre. I did a rather good production in London last year of *Midsummer Night's Dream*, a very updated version set in the 1930s, which was extremely beautiful, but much disliked by the critics. They said I'd "lost my magic" or something, whatever *that* means.

But one thing I must say: my work is very much my own. I don't pay very much attention to what's going on in the theatre; I do it, but I'm not involved in that world as a spectator. Because of my classical adherences, I'm busier than ever. I've just done two operas, one in Florence and one in Salzburg, and this coming Sunday, I fly to New York to supervise the lighting on a new production at the Metropolitan Opera of *The Rake's Progress.*

WWD: In the 1960s, it seemed that there was a great atmosphere of communal enterprise, and class and social barriers seemed to be crumbling. Then under the Thatcher government, it seems that all of this was built back up again, and this has had a very deleterious effect on the arts in Britain. Would you agree with this?

JM: Yes, I would. I think we went through a very bad eighteen years; it didn't rebuild class structures, but it built up new elitist structures based on economic inequality and racism.

WWD: How did this affect your work during this period?

JM: Well, I didn't work very much in England, that's all. There were more adventurous projects being done elsewhere, and so that's where I went.

WWD: Are you a supporter of Tony Blair's New Labour government?

JM: Not a very enthusiastic supporter. I mean, it's better than the other lot of crooks we've just gotten rid of. But what we now have is a lot of rather boneless conservatives. Blair had a party last night with Noel Gallagher, and all these famous people from the theatre, and I think he's like Bill Clinton: he just wants to be popular. He's sort of spuriously liberal, as well.

WWD: What's your favorite film of late?

JM: Well, the film that I've *hated* more than any I've ever seen, I think, is Anthony Minghella's *The English Patient* (1996). Just awful. It struck me as a combination of Biggles, which is a series of 1930s boys' stories about a daring English pilot, and Barbara Cartland, who writes all those romance novels which are so dreadfully popular. It's just piffle, like a Ralph Lauren commercial. My favorite film of late is Doug Liman's *Swingers* (1996). It's a bleak, quite funny sort of little movie. It's completely unpretentious; sort of like a series of Second City sketches. And it was made for nothing, because Liman was not only the director, but he was also the director of photography. You see, that's the sort of stuff that movies ought to do more often. On the whole, I like small, personal films, and documentary films like Steve James's *Hoop Dreams* (1994), or the films of Maysles Brothers, like *Grey Gardens* (1975), or Frederick Wiseman's *The Store* (1983), and things like that. Documentaries are really my favorite films; they seem to have the greatest accessibility and the least amount of pretension. For narrative films, I prefer low-key, low-budget movies about real life with a certain sort of satiric edge. I'm fond of the work of Hanif Kureishi, although I don't like Stephen Frears's work, which strikes me as trendy rather than genuinely interesting. Movies shouldn't be limited to spectacle; they do the simple things so much better. They should try to present real life in the simplest way possible, and be as unpretentious as possible. When they do that, they're successful. Films don't need to cost a fortune to be entertaining. They *do* need an interior sensibility and intelligence, which is really the most important thing that a film can have.

CHAPTER TWO

✠

Visions of the Gothic and Grotesque

A different sort of filmmaker altogether is the late Lucio Fulci, whose work is currently undergoing a decided renaissance. In 1998 Fulci's 1981 film *The Beyond* was re-released by Rolling Thunder Films, who used previously excised sequences, and restored a number of cuts made either at the behest of various censorship authorities and/or international distributors. Best known as a maker of "splatter" films, Lucio Fulci's best work partakes of a phantasmagorical, surreal atmosphere that transcends the requirements of the horror genre, and makes such films as *The Beyond*, *The Gates of Hell* (1980), and *The Black Cat* (1981) memorably original works of art. Fulci's ultraviolent, often deeply disturbing vision is the logical extension of work by his countryman and predecessor, Mario Bava, whose highly influential horror films (particularly *La Maschera del Demonio* [aka *Black Sunday*, 1961] and *Sei Donne per l'Assassino* [aka *Blood and Black Lace*, 1964]) set a new standard for stylishly graphic violence on the screen in the 1960s, and whom Fulci personally knew and admired. Bava, a director of photography before he became a director, created a series of sensuously sinister films in a career lasting from 1961 to 1979, before his death in 1980. Fulci, in a career that began in 1959 with the Italian low-budget features *The Thieves* (1959) and *The Jukebox Kids* (1958), went on to consolidate an international reputation as Bava's legitimate heir, even though, during his lifetime, Fulci's work was often ignored or denigrated by mainstream critics and theoreticians.

In this, Fulci is aligned with the work of the American filmmaker Stuart Gordon, whose films *Re-Animator* (1985), *From Beyond* (1986), and *The Pit and the Pendulum* (1991) push graphic violence to their fullest possible limits, with predictably controversial audience and critical response. *Re-Animator* and *From Beyond* are, as I'll shortly detail, ostensibly based on works by the twentieth-century gothic writer Howard Phillips Lovecraft, and *The Pit and the Pendulum*, with a stunning performance by Lance Henrikson as Torquemada, the Grand Inquisitor of Spain in the fifteenth century, is very loosely based on the short story by Edgar Allan Poe. Lovecraft, it seems to me, offers us a vision of what cinematic horror will be like in the twenty-first century, if only because the creatures he suggests in his short stories are so supremely ghastly that it takes a full complement of prosthetic effects and computer generated imagery to bring them to life. But there is more to Lovecraft's appeal than this, and a brief discussion of Lovecraft's gothic vision as a fictionalist, in tandem with a survey of some of the films based on his works, is of interest when considering the future of horror in the cinema.

Critically, Lovecraft's work has inspired a good deal of commentary, both favorable and dismissive. Kenneth W. Faig, Jr., and S. T. Joshi note in their essay, "H. P. Lovecraft: His Life and Work":

> The criticism of the . . . work of Howard Phillips Lovecraft (1890–1937) represents a singular chapter in the history of literature. . . . [H]e was a "ghastly writer" (Brian W. Aldiss), a "bad writer" (C. Wilson), "not a good writer" (Edmund Wilson) and an "atrocious writer" (C. Wilson); yet on the other hand he was "the supreme master of the tale of horror" (Drake Douglas), "one of the most sensitive and powerful writers of (his) generation" (J. O. Bailey), and "the greatest American author of horror tales since Poe" (John A. Taylor); his tales are "nearly always perfect in structure" (P. Penzoldt) and are "superbly written" (Drake Douglas), his style has been called both "distinguished" (August Derleth) and "undistinguished" (Edmund Wilson). It is difficult to find an author in this century whose writings were so unrecognized in his lifetime, yet so widely known after his death. We must look to Poe and LeFanu to find writers whose lives have accumulated such bizarre [legends]; to Conan Doyle to find one whose work has inspired such blatant imitation; and to Nathanael West to find one whose work has suffered such vicissitudes in critical acceptance. The reasons for all these occurrences are many, and to explain them requires an exploration not only of Lovecraft's life, work, and character, but many aspects of literature itself. (2)

Perhaps it would be best if I begin my analysis of Lovecraft's critical reception with some quotations from Edmund Wilson's well-known essay, "Tales of the Marvelous and the Ridiculous," which originally appeared in *The New Yorker* on November 24, 1945. It was during this period that an initial bid for respectability was being made by Lovecraft's literary executors, August Derleth, Donald Wandrei, and R. H. Barlow. Wilson read Lovecraft's work in the original Arkham House reprints of 1939 (*The Outsider and Others*) and 1944 (*Marginalia*), and wrote of it:

> The only real horror in most of these fictions is the horror of bad taste and bad art. Lovecraft was not a good writer. The fact that his verbose and undistinguished style has been compared to Poe's is only one of the many sad signs that almost nobody any more pays real attention to writing. I have never yet found in Lovecraft a single sentence that Poe could have written, though there are some—not at all the same thing—that have evidently been influenced by Poe. (It is to me more terrifying than anything in Lovecraft that Professor T. O. Mabbott of Hunter College, who has been promising a definitive edition of Poe, should contribute to the Lovecraft Marginalia a tribute in which he asserts that "Lovecraft is one of the few authors of whom I can honestly say that I have enjoyed every word of his stories," and goes on to make a solemn comparison of Lovecraft's work with Poe's.) (46)

Wilson grudgingly admits some respect for Lovecraft's work, however, when he notes:

> Now, when the horror to the shuddering revelation of which a long and prolix story has been building up turns out to be something like this (i.e., one of Lovecraft's "old ones"), you may laugh or you may be disgusted, but you are not likely to be terrified—though I confess, as a tribute to such power as H. P. Lovecraft possesses, that he at least . . . induced me to suspend disbelief. (46)

But his overwhelming feelings are clearly negative. Wilson also condemns Lovecraft's work because of its initial appearance in *Weird Tales*, a pulp horror and science fiction genre magazine of the twenties, thirties, and forties. Wilson writes: ". . . the truth is that these stories were hack-work contributed to such publications as Weird Tales and Amazing Stories, where, in my opinion, they ought to have been left" (46).

If I may dispose of this last objection first, Lovecraft's work appeared in pulp magazines, it is true, and he *was*, in the strictest sense of the word, a "hack writer." He wrote or revised stories for others to supplement his meager income from magazine sales. But certainly Poe was the meanest of hack writers, always living in penury, publishing his works in whatever magazines would take them, at ruinous rates. When his collected tales were finally published in hard cover, Poe's sole payment for all rights was a small number of volumes of the anthology for his own use. Poe also submitted his works to many publications simultaneously, and even let them be simultaneously printed in a number of competing journals. In general, Poe would seek any outlet for his work, and publish it at whatever rates he could get, just as Lovecraft did. To denigrate Lovecraft's work because it appeared in a popular, rather than scholarly or literary magazine, then, is simple snobbery.

But, unlike nearly all the rest of the *Weird Tales* authors, Lovecraft was not primarily writing for monetary gain. It is generally well known that Lovecraft wrote slowly, with great difficulty, and that he had an abysmally low opinion of his worth as a writer. Although he was recognized by the readers and editors of *Weird Tales* almost immediately as a horror fictionalist of excellent quality, and his submissions were usually readily accepted, Lovecraft remained skeptical of his abilities to the end of his life. On February 12, 1936, Lovecraft wrote to E. Hoffman Price that "I simply lack whatever it is that enables a real artist to convey his mood," and continued with the comment that "I'm farther from doing what I want to do than I was twenty years ago" (Lovecraft, *Selected Letters* 224). This nihilistic attitude towards his own work virtually assured Lovecraft's commercial obscurity. In fact, when a publisher wrote Lovecraft asking him if he had a novel for publication, Lovecraft did not even bother to reply, although he had his excellent novel *The Case of Charles Dexter Ward* ready and waiting for a publisher. One would have to look hard to find a more self-deprecating author, and these doubts certainly colored Lovecraft's chances of critical approval.

As to Wilson's objection that T. O. Mabbott makes "a solemn comparison of Lovecraft's work with Poe's," I will let Mabbott speak for himself:

> From time to time he [Lovecraft] is compared to Poe. There is little basis and no necessity for comparison. . . . The chief difference is

hard to explain although it is easy to feel; Poe was more interested in method of thought. Lovecraft more in a record of ideas; yet Lovecraft tried to make his tales consistent with each other, while Poe could allow the devil to read human minds in one tale and not in another with insouciance. It is also notable that Poe, like most writers, was only occasionally interested in the weird, while Lovecraft confined himself to a single *genre*.

But Lovecraft is not to be thought of an imitator of Poe. Almost every writer of weird stories since 1850 has either admired and borrowed some things from Poe or attempted to avoid being like him. Lovecraft was among the admirers. (Mabbott 44)

This seems to be something altogether different from what Wilson gets from a reading of Mabbott.

There is also an additional factor that works against Lovecraft's literary reputation, and that is August Derleth's intensive and often intrusive revision of Lovecraft's tales after the author's death. S. T. Joshi points out:

Derleth's unwillingness or inability to understand the Lovecraft works caused him to conceive and disseminate a highly distorted impression of Lovecraft; and, due to the fact that Derleth, being Lovecraft's publisher and champion, was considered the "authority" on his subject, his views, oftentimes fallacious, were adopted by the majority of critics and scholars. Perhaps Derleth's most serious fault was in writing his "posthumous collaborations" with Lovecraft, which are not only intrinsically poor but which present a perversion of Lovecraft's cosmic myth-cycle. It can be said that Derleth, though perhaps unintentionally and certainly with no malicious intent, has delayed the advancement of objective Lovecraft criticism for nearly thirty years. (24)

These are the very texts that Wilson was in fact examining, so his judgment here becomes further clouded by Derleth's emendations.

Wilson's initial doubting of Lovecraft has become, however, the dominant note in Lovecraft criticism to the present day. There are a number of reasons, over and above the obvious fact of Wilson's considerable reputation. First, critical reception of supernatural fiction has always been guarded and grudging. Each new advance in the genre is usually denounced by critics and self-appointed moral guardians as a new debasement of the human condition. Winfield Townley Scott wrote in an essay generally favorable to Lovecraft, that "the purpose of shocking—of frightening or horrifying—is in literature a meretricious one" (57). Yet this is exactly what Lovecraft set out to do. Horror fiction must intrinsically deal with precisely that subject matter which is often considered unwholesome or morbid. Concomitantly, each succeeding generation requires greater explicitness, and so horror fictionalists are driven by the demands of both their audience and the marketplace to graphic descriptions often intentionally bordering on the lurid and sensational.

How can a literary genre so dependent on the decadent, the macabre, as well as an appetite for violence and destruction, rise above these commercially compromised surroundings to create something of lasting worth and literary quality? There is only one answer possible: through the sincerity of the writing. Even Edmund Wilson, for all of his carping on Lovecraft's supposedly "prolix" style, admits that Lovecraft, through his writing, "induced me to suspend disbelief" (46) for the length of "The Shadow Out of Time." Yet, why is it that of all the literary genres one can name, only the western and the pulp romance novel can provoke the same the disdain with which most supernatural fiction is viewed by the literary establishment?

It seems to me that the answer is a simple one. Supernatural and horror fiction operate at the cutting edge of audience expectations; they must adhere to the conventions of the genre, but they must also shock and surprise the reader. Thus, the degree of graphicness in contemporary horror fiction removes it from serious literary consideration on grounds of subject matter and treatment alone. More than with most writing, a degree of historical perspective is necessary to accurately assess the quality of a work of horror fiction as writing. The shock factor must wear off first, to allow a clear view of a work's merits and/or defects.

Then, too, there is also the fact that in addition to Derleth's meddling, Lovecraft wrote a surprisingly large quantity of fiction, not all of it of the highest quality. But, like Poe, he was forced to write a great deal of material simply to survive. His ghost writing of stories which have since been reprinted under his name alone also gives his detractors much inferior work to buttress their unfavorable assessments. Yet despite all of these factors, and Lovecraft's admittedly narrow range of interests, in addition to the fact that Lovecraft's best work includes only a handful of short stories and one brief novel, I would nominate him as, thus far, the most *sin-*

cere supernatural writer of the twentieth century, and the best weird fictionalist since Poe. The true test of Lovecraft's worth lies in his creation of a believable "other," a world which, while blessedly lacking the artificial cohesiveness imposed upon it by Derleth (who arbitrarily schematized a supposed "Cthulhu mythos" and superimposed it on Lovecraft's works after Lovecraft's death), is nevertheless a real and tangible place. Lovecraft follows the Jamesian dictum of *sincerity* faithfully in all his work; what other possible reason could such a resolutely non-commercial author have for writing? Of course, sincerity is no guarantee of quality, but at its base, it separates the informing instinct of the quota writer from that of an amateur, or lover, of fiction, which is what Lovecraft always insisted he was. The degree of excellence in Lovecraft's writing, is, in any case, a highly subjective matter, as are all questions of aesthetic judgment.

I propose that if one is attracted to Lovecraft's vision, then one will probably find that he is successful as a prose stylist. Charles Brockden Brown, Bram Stoker, Hawthorne, Poe, Long, Machen, Mary Shelley, and other gothic horror fictionalists each possessed distinctive, and largely intuitive, self-taught voices that lent credence and dignity to their supernatural writing. Lovecraft's fiction combined Brockden Brown's reclusive scholar figure from *Weiland*; Stoker's sense of decay and mounting dread in *Dracula*; Hawthorne's interest in New England, Puritan ethics, and the fallen state of man from *Young Goodman Brown* and *The Twice-Told Tales*; Poe's fascination with madness, self-conscious archaism, and personal eccentricity, as displayed in nearly all his writing; Machen's quiet sense of impending disaster as shown in his short stories; Mary Shelley's theoretical argumentativeness in *Frankenstein*. Yet Lovecraft managed to make the resultant whole considerably greater than just the sum of these parts. Lovecraft's peculiar vision is his alone, influenced though he is by practically every major figure in the short history of American and British gothic literature. The rhetorical question is not really, Was Lovecraft a major writer?, which he was not; but rather, Was he successful on his own terms and turf as a writer of supernatural short stories and novels? To this refined question I would answer resoundingly, Yes. In spite of all the caveats, Lovecraft's clearest, purest work, as distilled in *The Case of Charles Dexter Ward*, "The Dunwich Horror," "The Colour Out of Space," "The Shadow Out of Time," and even his grisly serialized novella *Herbert West: Reanimator*, is a remarkable blend of all of its influences and yet is still an original contribution to supernatural literature. Lovecraft is a minor writer, but a major talent in his narrowly defined area. This does not diminish his considerable talents, but placed in context with his contemporaries—Hemingway, Fitzgerald, Stein, or even Sinclair Lewis—Lovecraft is clearly the smaller voice. Yet that voice is original and unique.

A certain cult aspect also swirls about Lovecraft and his work, which is unfortunate. Authors as diverse as Colin Wilson, Dean Koontz, Stephen King, Frank Belknap Long, Fritz Leiber, Robert Bloch, and others to attempt to copy his style, with little success. In view of all these dilutions of Lovecraft's actual oeuvre, it would seem that the first task awaiting Lovecraft scholars would be a definitive textual edition of his works, in chronological order, omitting all ghosted stories and "collaborations." With this corrected tool in hand, serious consideration of Lovecraft's work might begin anew. Until then, Lovecraft's work will remain mired in all the difficulties and shortcomings described here. But for those with the interest to seek him out, Lovecraft remains a vigorous original, possessed, in a very literal sense, of a sensibility all his own.

CINEMATIC VERSIONS OF THE WORKS OF H. P. LOVECRAFT

Although there have been a number of adaptations of Lovecraft's works for the screen, the essence of the Lovecraftian ethos to date remains outside the bounds of translation, seemingly beyond the craft of all those who have attempted to bring Lovecraft to life on the screen. Although a number of directors and scenarists have tried their hand at bringing Lovecraft to the screen, none have fully succeeded in this task. There are a number of reasons for this: one of the major problems is that Lovecraft has never had the benefit of a full-scale production, with the necessary values such a production would bring to the source material. Edgar Allan Poe has fared only slightly better in this regard. While many regard the 1960s Poe "adaptations" by director Roger Corman with affection, the films do not date gracefully, and seem hampered by Vincent Price's near-parodic association with the series. Of all the Poe-Corman adaptations, perhaps the most successful is *The Pit and the Pendulum* (1961), but even this film had very little to do with Poe, being more the result of an admittedly fruitful collaboration between Corman, set designer Daniel Haller, composer Les Baxter, scenarist Richard Matheson, and cinematographer Floyd Crosby. Perhaps American International's James H. Nicholson, who co-produced with Samuel Arkoff the early Poe/AIP films, put it best:

"Poe writes the first reel or the last reel; Roger does the rest" (in Pirie 47). Other adaptations of Poe have a decidedly more naturalistic feel than the studio-bound Corman films of the 1960s. Larry Brand's 1989 adaptation of *Masque of the Red Death*, produced, not incidentally, for Corman's new production company, Concorde/New Horizons, seems more adept and less visually stylized than its predecessor, and suggests that a new cycle of Poe adaptations may well outstrip the originals in quality.

Oddly enough, Corman's former key set designer, Daniel Haller, has the distinction of directing one of the better Lovecraft adaptations, *Die, Monster, Die*, based on Lovecraft's "The Colour Out of Space." This was Haller's first film as a director. The film was originally titled *The House at the End of the World* (released as *Monster of Terror* in the United Kingdom), and starred Boris Karloff, Nick Adams, Freda Jackson, and Suzan Farmer. Capable support was supplied by dependable character actors Terrence De Marney and Patrick Magee, but the film suffered from a lack of narrative pacing. Karloff's work in the film was mediated by the use of, in his own words, "a fleet of doubles;" Nick Adams, an actor of limited range, did very little with a conventional leading role, and Suzan Farmer was little more than a typical ingénue lead, in a part that allowed her little room for depth. Haller certainly was, and is, an excellent set designer—his work in the Poe films, as remarked, is excellent—but as a director he seems quite out of his depth.

Haller also directed the 1970 adaptation of *The Dunwich Horror*, with an excellent cast that included Dean Stockwell, Ed Begley, Sr., Sam Jaffe, Talia Coppola, and Barboura Morris. But this film, too, suffered from a fatal casting flaw (Sandra Dee in the leading female role), and, as with *Die, Monster, Die*, deviated so severely from the text that the end result bore very little relation to Lovecraft. Both films seemed sort of sub-par Poe films from AIP, as if the already cost-conscious company had set up a second, sub-"B" unit to grind out these two films with a minimum of financial risk or artistic adventurousness.

If *Die, Monster, Die* seems static and tedious in its exposition, and spends far too much time on an insipid love story between Adams and Farmer, *The Dunwich Horror* goes to great lengths to be flashy and superficially innovative, including one sequence photographed from the point of view of a dying man, whose vision changes from normal color to negative color to filtered color effects and even to pseudo-solarization as he dies. But the effect seems tacked on and arbitrary, a bow to the stylistic excess that marked late 1960s/early 1970s exploitation filmmaking (which had, in turn, been influenced by experimental and "underground" films of the period, such as Scott Bartlett's catalogue of video effects, *Off/On* [1967]). Taken as a whole, the film becomes a collection of sequences rather than a coherent work.

Haller migrated to direction for television, where he continues to work to this day. It is significant that he never went on to feature film work of any great accomplishment; certainly he deserved the chance to try his hand at a feature after his great success as an interior decorator for Corman. But, as with Mitchell Leisen, who did his best work as a set designer for Cecil B. DeMille and later directed a series of indifferent films, Haller simply wasn't up to the requirements of the assignment. If Corman's signature is more evident in his Poe films than that of the late author, Haller's signature in these two films seems that of a second-generation Corman, of one incapable of generating his own convincing approach to the material at hand.

This leads us to *The Haunted Palace* (1963), directed by Corman from Lovecraft's novel *The Case of Charles Dexter Ward*. It was advertised by American International as yet another film in the Poe cycle, which it manifestly is not. Starring Vincent Price, Lon Chaney, Jr. (who replaced an ailing Boris Karloff, originally slated to appear in the film), Elisha Cook, Jr., Leo Gordon, and Debra Paget, the film is an atmospheric yet stagebound work that looks and unreels as a minor effort in the overall Corman/Poe/AIP cycle.

The Case of Charles Dexter Ward is perhaps the most cinematic of all Lovecraft's works, and at near novel length, the only one of sufficient depth in itself to be brought to the screen pretty much intact, without the necessity of adding disparate material. Yet Charles Beaumont's screenplay displays no great fidelity to the original work, and Price and Chaney walk through their roles as the routine genre assignments they are. American International felt that Lovecraft's name would not guarantee sufficient audience recognition at the box office; thus, a few lines of Poe's poem were tacked on to the film purely for mercantile reasons. Certainly *The Case of Charles Dexter Ward* deserves to be filmed again, and no doubt it will be, but this version is not worthy of extended consideration.

The Shuttered Room, released in 1967 and based on a story that is almost entirely by August Derleth, was directed by David Greene (his first theatrical feature film as a director, after a long career as an actor in England and a director of teleplays for Canadian television, as well as a prolific stage director in New York and London), shot in Britain, and produced by Philip Hezelton. The cast included Gig Young, Carol Lynley, Oliver Reed, and Dame Flora Robson. Once again, an excellent cast had been assembled to bring a quasi-Lovecraft story to the screen, and once again, the results were much less than satisfactory. Poorly written dialogue, unadventurous direction, and a decided lack of involvement on the part of all the participants unite to make the film nearly interminable, and of all the Lovecraft adaptations discussed so far, this film is perhaps the least satisfactory. Greene's other work includes a number of TV movies; he also directed *Godspell* in 1973. In this respect, Greene is much like Daniel Haller: a stylist without vision.

The Crimson Cult, made in 1970, wastes the considerable talents of Christopher Lee, Boris Karloff, Barbara Steele, Michael Gough, and particularly director Vernon Sewell, who had done some excellent work in the past (particularly *The Medium* [1934], *Ghosts of Berkeley Square* [1947], *Ghost Ship* [1952], and many others), much of it in the realm of the supernatural. But Sewell, whose best work was clearly behind him, was unable to rise to the challenge of the material, and Karloff, confined to a wheelchair, struggles vainly with Lee to bring the material to life. *The Crimson Cult* is a film made by a director and a star who are both past their prime, but who still retain a great deal of affection for the genre they work in. This was one of Karloff's last films, except for a quartet of Mexican/American co-productions made just before the actor's death.

During this period, Rod Serling's television anthology program *Night Gallery* also did brief adaptations of Lovecraft's stories "Cool Air" and "Pickman's Model." Once again, although the source material in both cases is excellent, the end result leaves much to be desired. The real problem with the *Night Gallery* series is that Rod Serling, who served as the nominal host and figurehead for the program, had very little to do with the creation of the individual episodes, in direct contrast to his work on *The Twilight Zone*, one of the pioneer television fantasy programs. Episodes of *Night Gallery* were shot quickly and cheaply, using talent then under contract to Universal Studios for the going minimum wage. Work made under such inherently compromised circumstances has several strikes against it from the start; unhappily, these two adaptations seem hastily contrived, and lack any genuine suspense or artistry in their execution.

This leaves us with the two most interesting of the Lovecraft adaptations: two films by Stuart Gordon, *Re-Animator* and *From Beyond*. Because of their intense violence and graphic special effects content, both films have been hailed or reviled. Pauline Kael, the hard-to-please former film critic for *The New Yorker*, surprised many when she came out unreservedly in favor of *Re-Animator*, precisely because of its over-the-top Grand Guignol violence. Boasting a decent production budget for the first time for a Lovecraft adaptation, the film was based on the grisly "Herbert West—Reanimator," which is not generally considered one of the author's more accomplished efforts.

Despite the fact that the screenplay veered considerably from Lovecraft's original version, the film, of all the adaptations discussed here, has the most genuine Lovecraftian feel of the entire group. Set at the Medical College of Miskatonic University, the film is dominated by the performance of Jeffrey Combs as Herbert West, a brash young medical student who is obsessed with the notion of returning the dead to life. This isn't exactly new territory, but Gordon's fascination with the flesh and bone mechanics of the process raises the film above the level of a *Frankenstein* retread into an area distinctly its own.

When *Re-Animator* was first released, it seemed that Lovecraft had finally met an interpreter worthy of his talents, even though, in his predilection for scenes of excessive violence, Gordon takes Lovecraft's vision into areas the author would undoubtedly have felt in poor taste. Unlike all the other films cited here, however, what results is a genuine collaboration of styles, in which Lovecraft is not sacrificed on the altar of falsely commercial instinct, but rather melded with the ideas of a director and co-scenarist who has his own unique, if peculiar, vision. *Re-Animator*, no matter what else one might say about it, is a film that stands entirely alone: there is nothing quite like it, which perhaps accounts for a good deal of the film's success. In essence, the film represents a genre hot wiring feat of considerable proportions: it is part horror film, part gore film, part black comedy, and part love story. All these elements are pushed past the boundaries of parody into a zone of hyper-realism (aided by the unsparing graphic visuals) that sweeps the viewer along with the narrative into a unique and disturbing world that is Gordon's and Lovecraft's alone.

Although the score for the film is obviously reminiscent (if not absolutely derived from) Bernard Herrmann's score for *Psycho*, the film is remarkably lavish in its execution, with vivid color, a good deal of gallows humor, and special effects that, for once, do not disappoint. Indeed, it is only through the contemporary advances in special effects by such artists as Tom Savini and Ed French that a film like *Re-Animator* becomes at all possible: the special effects crew of Anthony Doublin and John Naulin deserve special credit in this area. One of the more memorable scenes in the film involves West's attempts to subdue one of a number of unruly, revived corpses; when one of his colleagues' efforts comes to no avail, West dryly pushes his cohort out of the way with a mild "excuse me," and plunges a whirring surgical saw into the entrails of the corpse, cutting a neat hole directly through the body's midsection. Combs's detached performance as West is directly complemented by the more theatrical work of Barbara Crampton as Megan Halsey and Robert Sampson as Dean Halsey, whom West reanimates from the dead with disastrous results.

Ultimately, what sets *Re-Animator* apart from the seemingly endless flow of tepid slasher films that dominate the cinema, particularly during the summer months, is the reflexive humor and intense self-examination that seem to have gone into the construction of every plot element, every frame of the final film. *Re-Animator* is a genre film that is fully cognizant of its ancestry; it takes the conventions and rules of the horror genre and breaks them into wildly configured shards of thematic material, pushing the normal audience tolerance for gore, and for outrageous plot exposition, past the boundaries that still, even in 1985, were rigidly enforced by audience expectations.

As many critics have remarked, the final reels of the film contain a graphic sequence of explicitly sexual material that seems designated to alienate all but the most jaded or passive viewers, and yet there is a good humor, a panache in the creation of the film that makes the entire enterprise seem the result of hard work, good humor, and a great deal of skill and knowledge. Gordon's own background before the film was as the director and co-founder of an experimental theatrical group that specialized in genre-bending exercises not unlike *Re-Animator*; Gordon and his company of actors were fortunate to find a sympathetic producer in Charles Band.

Then, too, the carefully thought-out art direction of Robert A. Burns gets the most from a tightly controlled budget, evoking the feeling of Miskatonic University's dark, forbidding halls and sleepy, ivy-covered buildings. The cinematographer, Mac Ahlberg, who has a number of productions to his credit as producer and/or cinematographer, is also a definite plus to the project. *Re-Animator* is certainly not pure Lovecraft, by any stretch of the imagination, but it is, on its own terms and turf, compellingly original, and true to its own sets of precepts. At the time it seemed that, along with Clive Barker (whose groundbreaking directorial debut was *Hellraiser*, which Barker also scripted), Gordon would emerge as the first new Gothic director of consequence in the late 1980s, after the late 1970s wave of Carpenter, Cronenberg, Dante, and others. The undeniable energy and nerve that went into *Re-Animator* (and into *Hellraiser*, for that matter) seemed to signal a new era in horror filmmaking. Yet sadly, this promise was to be short-lived.

Producer Charles Band announced plans for the production of more Lovecraft/Gordon "collaborations," the first of which would be *From Beyond*, which was released in 1986. Yet although production values remained high, and many of the original team members returned to the project, the film emerges as both schematic and joyless, as if everyone is simply going through the motions this time around, without much enthusiasm or desire. Perhaps this is because *Re-Animator* so successfully demolished what remaining audience boundaries there were in the area of shock filmmaking; perhaps it is because the film had a higher budget, and with more money comes more supervision, which does not always help the finished product. Then, too, Gordon and his compatriots were laboring under the enormous shadow of their first film, a film that had so successfully crossed over from the domain usually reserved for the exploitation film into the realm of serious filmmaking; how could they top themselves this time out? Mac Ahlberg's photography is suitably sumptuous; Combs is even more reserved as Dr. Crawford Tillinghast; and Ted Sorel's Dr. Pretorius is even more malevolent than Robert Sampson's Dean Halsey in *Re-Animator*. The film is also certainly not above a series of cheerfully morbid in-jokes, not the least of which is the casting of Gordon's wife, Carolyn Purdy-Gordon, as Dr. Roberta Bloch, an obvious reference to the author of *Psycho*.

The special effects in *From Beyond* are remarkable: the original two-man crew from the earlier film are joined by two additional members, John Buechler and John Shostrom, and their work throughout the film is never less than disturbingly realistic (assuming that, given the visions they are called upon to conjure up, such a thing as realism is even possible). Yet the film seems sadistic and ill-humored, something that the earlier film never gave the impression of being. Indeed, the violence in this film is presented with unflinching relish, as if Gordon has stepped over the edge of parody and found himself on the other side of the sadomasochistic chasm, and is, to our chagrin, enjoying the new position. *From Beyond* seems to me a dead-end thematically as well as in dramatic construction. It is no accident that the film did not receive the nearly universal acclaim of *Re-Animator*, did but a fraction of the earlier film's business, and, for all its self-knowledge, fails to hold the viewer's attention other than through the mechanism of some brutally misogynistic prosthetic effects.

Although the final reels of *Re-Animator* contain some rather problematic material dealing with the objectification of the feminine corpus (the notorious "cunnilingus" sequence being the most obvious example), there was something—a rather indefinite, yet certainly palpable diffidence and self-reflexivity—in the handling and playing of the material that made it seem as if Gordon and company were after higher stakes; making a claim on our psychic hidden ground with conscious deliberation, rather than simply seeking to revolt us with an unrelenting, inexorable catalogue of violent imagery. *From Beyond* seems to be interested *only* in this; for all the "in" humor, it is a film which, at base, is both deadly serious and uncomfortably linked to the image-making process of pornographic films, and their exploitation and representational processes.

There are two final additions to the Lovecraft filmography. They may be seen as footnotes, and as challenge to a new direction. On the one hand, now that Lovecraft's name has become marketable, a plethora of second-rate material, much of it produced directly for videocassette, is flooding the rental shelves, particularly such straight-to-video releases as *The Unnamable* and *The Curse*, both of which are pedestrian and boring films, having little to do with Lovecraft's work.

But the other intriguing footnote to the Lovecraft filmic legacy is the work of the previously mentioned Italian horror director Lucio Fulci who died in 1996. Fulci's works were initially distributed in the United States (when they were shown at all) under a variety of directorial pseudonyms, the most common of which was Louis Fuller. Fulci's films were designed for American distribution, either in theaters or on videocassette, and the American release versions are invariably subjected to horrendous dubbing and post-synchronization procedures, which seriously weaken (as a matter of course) the quality of the films. Nevertheless, Fulci is a director of some interest.

Beginning in earnest in the early 1970s, Fulci produced a group of cost-conscious but compelling features, including: *The House by the Cemetery* (*Quella Villa Accanto al Cimitero* [1981]); *Zombie* (1979); *A Lizard in a Woman's Skin* (*Un Lucertola con la Pella di Donna* [1971]); *The Psychic* (*Sette Note in Nero* [1977]); *The Black Cat* (1981); *The Gates of Hell* (1980); and *The Beyond* (1981). All of Fulci's films progress as if the protagonists are trapped in some awful, illogical dream, from which there is no escape. The circular entrapment of the characters in *The Beyond*, as well as the ominously pervasive atmosphere of nightmare that seeps into even the most pedestrian scenes in all Fulci's films, mark the director as an artist who possessed a genuine affinity for the Gothic, although he was forced to work under circumstances of crushing economy. Much of *The Beyond* takes place in Louisiana, where a young woman has inherited a hotel haunted by the spirits of those who have violently perished there. But his slight framing narrative is merely the excuse for Fulci to stage a series of macabre, distressing set pieces. A young blind woman's guide dog turns on her without warning, ripping out her throat; a succession of reanimated corpses stalk the living in somnambulant slow motion; events and actions follow one another without reason or seeming consequence, until the two protagonists of *The Beyond* find themselves penultimately trapped within a painting seen earlier in the film, sightless zombies without a destiny or a future.

Fulci's *The Gates of Hell* contains a nominal plot: a priest hangs himself, thus opening the gates of hell in both the town of Dunwich (one of Lovecraft's favorite fictive locations, as used in the author's *The Dunwich Horror*) and in New York City. Fulci shoots all his New York sequences on one blocked-off street of midtown Manhattan, in which star Christopher George walks through his role with a notable absence of conviction. Once the gates have been opened, the film becomes simply a series of grisly murders, photographed in clinical detail. The sets are modest, the photography is often blurry, and the dubbing is often out of sync. Yet none of this detracts from the overall mood and atmosphere of the film, and this, as with Mario Bava, is Lucio Fulci's strongest suit. Of the remainder of Fulci's films, the best known are *Zombie* and *The Black Cat*, yet another film "inspired" by Poe's short story. *The Black Cat* is notable as one of the last performances of Patrick Magee; visibly aging in his few linking sequences in the film, Magee nevertheless brings to his role an aura of genuine menace and authority, and serves as a suitable counterbalance to the rest of the film, which, in typical Fulci style, eschews narrative structure for a series of violent deaths.

It is perhaps odd that this consideration of the films and fiction of H. P. Lovecraft should end with the work of two directors noted for their extreme explicitness, yet Lovecraft must bow to changing standards of cinematic representationalism, as must all authors of supernatural and horror fiction. As image or as text, a good deal of the impact of horror depends upon the creation of a believable atmosphere of dread; once that atmosphere has been established, the narrative must be crowned with an image of dread that will both enthrall and repel the viewer. The horror films of the 1930s, '40s, and '50s now seem to us as if they were designed as "fairy tales for adults" (to quote the British Gothic director Terence Fisher, as cited in *Charm of Evil,* Dixon, iii); contemporary audiences demand a new degree of explicit gratification in their viewing experience. The future filmic adaptations of the works of H. P. Lovecraft will have to be cognizant of this axiom, and, in view of this proscription, it remains to be seen whether or not Lovecraft's Gothic vision will ever be faithfully transferred to the screen.

CINEMA OF THE DISENFRANCHISED

If the challenge of producing a quality adaptation of Lovecraft is taken up, it will inevitably occur at the margins of cinema, in what used to be called "B" films, but are now referred to as "low-budget independent productions." Such low-cost, low-risk enterprises are always in the vanguard of cinema/video production, if only because they must offer an alternative vision to the Dominant Cinema if they hope to appeal to the public. If one looks at the history of "B" production in the United States in the 1930s and '40s, for example, one sees a pattern in which the majors follow the independents in exploiting thematic trends at the box office, which is precisely the same phenomenon that drives Miramax, Rialto, Fine Line, and other niche distributors today. Although the major studios may eventually get around to tackling the major social problems of American society, it seems that, at least in the case of taboo subject matter, "B" films inevitably get there first. The "A" studios, such as Warner Brothers, Universal, Columbia, 20th Century Fox and MGM, are all essentially conservative operations: they want to make a return on their investment, which is often considerable. Consequently, these "A" studios tend toward safe, tried and true formula entertainment, and seldom stray into the area of social commentary, although the "B" unit of an "A" studio may tackle something more adventurous.

For example, during World War II, RKO's "B" unit, under the direction of producer Val Lewton, attempted one of the very first examinations of the rising problem of teenage gangs and juvenile delinquency, *Youth Runs Wild* (1944, directed by Mark Robson). The film was produced despite a good deal of interference from the front office, particularly from executive producer Jack J. Gross, who felt that no one would want to see a film so decidedly downbeat. But Lewton ultimately per-suaded Gross that since the budget was so low, RKO couldn't lose any money, and the film went on to gather excellent contemporary reviews. If RKO had been spending $1,000,000 rather than slightly under $100,000, the picture probably never would have been made. Slightly more than a decade later, Warner Brothers produced their own study of juvenile delinquency, Nicholas Ray's *Rebel Without a Cause* (1955), which had an "A" budget, glossy Technicolor and CinemaScope photography, and the undeniable impact of James Dean in the leading role. *Youth Runs Wild* had no stars, a small budget, and a shooting schedule of less than three weeks. However, the films are strikingly similar, and one cannot help but think that the production of the first film made the second fea-ture possible, if only by leading the way.

Since "B" films cost so little, and could be made in the 1930s and 1940s with a very small degree of front-office interference, directors such as Edgar G. Ulmer and William Castle were allowed to say what they wished, and deal with any subject they wished, so long as they got the film in on time and on budget. In a very real sense, "B" films were forced to be trailblazers, simply because they inherently could not compete in the area of spectacle: they had too little money for anything beyond the bare physical necessities of production. Monogram, Producers Releasing Cor-poration, Republic, and the other smaller "B" units could not afford to outspend the majors, so they had only one other avenue open: to deal with subject matter that the majors would not touch. It is true that a film such as Edgar Ulmer's *Girls in Chains* (PRC, 1943) was sold with an extremely sensationalistic advertising campaign; but once the patrons got into the theatre, they got a sensitive and serious examination of the hor-rendous conditions in women's prisons prevalent during the 1940s, and not the cheap and tawdry spectacle they had been implicitly promised in the ads. This "bait-and-switch" tactic was simply something that went with the territory of "B" film distribution: one could do anything with the actual content of the film at all, just so long as the title was highly exploitational. Because of this, we have a whole string of films from dif-ferent directors that are now considered social groundbreakers in their respective areas of interest. At the time of their initial release, however, because of the sensationalistic campaign necessary to make sure the pic-tures made money, the films were dismissed out-of-hand as trash. Only the more prescient critics even bothered to review them. But if the phys-ical realities of "B" films ensured cheap sets, uneven acting, and less than optimal production values, they also set their directors and scenarists free. However, a public unable to see beyond the enforced cheapness of the production would miss the value of the best "B" films altogether.

San Newfield's *I Accuse My Parents* (PRC, 1944) was one of ten feature films the director ground out during that year, and although the film offers for the first time the thesis that a juvenile's actions may be the result of indifferent or hostile parents, Newfield's execution of the theme is so hurried (two and one-half days for shooting, only three days to script the film before that) that the end result is so visually monolithic as to be almost unwatchable. Nevertheless, uncredited remakes of this film surfaced in such later films as *Knock on Any Door* (1949), another film by Nicholas Ray, in which Humphrey Bogart blames the parents of a teenage hoodlum for leading him into a life of crime.

In another area, King Vidor's 1934 *Our Daily Bread* (a "B" picture made on the slimmest of budgets, and only reluctantly released by United Artists), marks the first serious screen treatment of the problems and rewards of group farming, and serves as an effective and inspirational blueprint for farm groups to set up their own communal farming communities. By 1940, John Ford's *The Grapes of Wrath* was simply documenting the plight of migrant farmers in the dust-bowl of the late 1930s; the only solution the film offered was a government run relief camp, hardly the sort of practical self-help King Vidor's film endorsed. But any community run enterprise smacked too much of communism in the top circles of Hollywood filmmaking (and still does, today, despite a brief flirtation with radical politics in the mid-to-late 1960s), and so Vidor's vision remains one of the few practical "organize to survive" films ever made for the farming community: a "B" film that created practical social alternatives to government handouts, or starvation.

Black filmmaking started entirely as a "B" enterprise. The low-budget "B" films of Black filmmaker Oscar Micheaux are by now fairly well known, but other Black directors such as Spencer Williams produced innovative fantasies like *The Blood of Jesus* (1941), which Williams wrote, produced, and directed. In this film, and other Black-made films like Williams's *Go Down Death* (1944), and his *Dirty Gertie from Harlem, USA* (1946), the director forged a vision of a future society where Blacks would have an equal place with Whites. This is something major filmmakers would not touch even as late as 1971, when the later "B" picture, Melvin Van Peeble's *Sweet Sweetback's Baadasssss Song* (1971), was picked up only by an extremely marginal distribution company, Jerry Gross's

Cinemation (since defunct). White directors such as Edgar G. Ulmer, who later went to PRC precisely to obtain cultural freedom, pioneered the Black musical with such films as *Moon Over Harlem* (1939), an independent film so cheaply produced that Ulmer stated no one in the cast made more than fifty cents a day for their efforts. Within a few years, 20th Century Fox would make the expensive all-Black musical *Stormy Weather* (1943), which even at a meager running time of seventy-seven minutes was still the first Technicolor Black musical with a respectably "A"-level budget—but once again, the "B" picture had made the first move.

All these films were made by people who believed in what they had to say, and were content to put up with technical facilities bordering on nonexistence; again, no major studio would ever have touched any of these projects at the time; and finally, these films gave the public something they wanted, something that was not being supplied by the majors. At the same time, these visions of Black equality could not help but seep into the mainstream of filmmaking, even if only over a long period of time, and the very existence of a group of films, no matter how cheaply made, where Blacks did not have to portray bootblacks or porters, made the first dent in a long march to racial equality that still has not been achieved.

This book does not have the time nor space to list all the various areas in which a "B" film has paved the way for further explorations by an "A" film, but one can try to list a few more examples. There is the "B" work of Phil Karlson, whose *Phenix City Story* (AA, 1955) actually brought about the clean-up of a hopelessly corrupt real-life American town, Phenix City, Alabama, which had, until the release of the film, been completely ruled by vice, gambling, prostitution, and an utterly criminal local government. *Phenix City Story* paved the way for whole series of "A" films in *The Walking Tall* series (the first in 1973, also directed by Karlson), which pretty much recycled the plot of the first film, and showed that it was possible for one man to fight back against an indifferent and unresponsive local political machine. There are also the films of Roger Corman, who has managed to tackle a number of themes before his "A" brethren got hold of them, including the inequities of the sorority system on college campuses (*Sorority Girl*, 1957); the "psychologically motivated killer," in *Machine Gun Kelly* (1958), featuring a very early performance by Charles Bronson; *The Trip* (1967), which was, despite its advertising campaign, an extremely effective polemic against drugs; *The Wild Angels* (1966), the first modern motorcycle youth-gang film; not to mention a series of early films with exceptionally strong female protagonists, including *Oklahoma Woman, Swamp Woman,* and *The Gunslinger* (all 1956). As for women directors, who had been largely been prevented from working in Hollywood until the early 1970s, "B" films provided a forum. Such early feminist filmmakers as Dorothy Arzner, Ida Lupino, and more recently, Barbara Loden, Lisa Cholodenko, Kathryn Bigelow, Daisy V. S. Mayer and others used "B" films to tackle themes to which the majors could not commit an "A" budget.

There is one last comment that must be made about the "B" film: its inherent topicality. One of the things that ensures the "B" prescience is the fact that it must cater to fads, must deliver what an audience wants to see *right now,* in order to take advantage of the public's interest. This alone makes the "B" or exploitation picture perpetually ride the crest of the wave of public taste. But where this desire for "cashing in" meets with serious artistic intent, one can often detect in many of these modest pictures the seeds of themes that will be more slickly, and perhaps less honestly, tackled in later, major productions.

AN INTERVIEW WITH ROGER CORMAN

One filmmaker whose life and works have continually embraced the margins of moving image discourse is Roger Corman, the legendary producer, director, and entrepreneur. Corman began making low-budget, independent films in the mid-1950s, eventually forging an alliance with the distributor American International Pictures, and during the 1960s Corman created some of his most influential films (*The Masque of the Red Death* [1964], *The Wild Angels* [1966], *The Trip* [1967] and many others). It was also during this phase of his career that Corman began an informal sort of "film school" as part of his production process, and such mainstream luminaries as Jack Nicholson, Francis Ford Coppola, Paul Bartel, Monte Hellman, Peter Bogdanovich, Martin Scorsese, Joe Dante, Ron Howard, Jonathan Demme, William Shatner, Bruce Dern, composer James Horner (who later wrote the music for James Cameron's Titanic [1998]) started their careers with Corman, either at American International or Filmgroup in the 1950s and '60s, or later at Corman's own production/distribution company New World in the 1970s, and Concorde/New Horizons in the 1980s to the present. Corman has also appeared as an actor in a number of films, including Wim Wenders's *The State of Things* (1982) and Jonathan Demme's *Philadelphia* (1993).

However, with the inception of the videocassette, the films produced by Concorde/New Horizons now, for the most part, are straight to video release, with perhaps a desultory theatrical opening as a token gesture. The days when a modestly budgeted theatrical feature film ($100,000 or slightly more) could command national distribution are long gone. Corman himself traces this phenomenon from the date when *Star Wars* (1977) was released. Audiences began to demand spectacle above all other considerations in the Dominant Cinema, and spectacular physical production has traditionally been beyond the scope of the independent production companies. Now active more as an executive producer than a director, Corman directed his last film to date, *Frankenstein Unbound*, in 1990, but production at Concorde/New Horizons continues unabated in the late 1990s, with a continual flow of genre films, often lavishly produced, which are popular rented properties at Blockbuster and other major videotape and pay-per-view outlets. Corman has also continued a policy he started in the 1970s of securing distribution in the United States for foreign filmmakers whom the majors astonishingly won't assist, such as Ingmar Bergman (for *Cries and Whispers* [1972]), Federico Fellini (for *Amarcord* [1974]) and François Truffaut (*Small Change* [1976]). This in itself bespeaks a real interest in the cinema as an art form, not just a commercial medium, and despite his legendary respect for the production dollar, Corman has always been an artist who happens to be an astute businessman, rather than simply a commercial filmmaker.

In the late 1980s, I invited Corman to lecture at the University of Nebraska on his career in the cinema, in conjunction with a screening of *Cries and Whispers*, which Corman not only distributed in the United States, but also helped to finance. Corman was direct and forthcoming in his responses not only to my questions, but also to questions posed by members of the audience. In addition to *Cries and Whispers*, we also screened 35mm prints of some of Corman's finest work as a director, including the legendary *Little Shop of Horrors* (1960), which Corman produced and directed with intense efficiency. Corman's view of cinema production, direction, and distribution is both practical and deeply wedded to the aesthetics of the moving image, as his comments on his own films, and the future of the industry, made abundantly clear. Here is an edited transcript of our conversation.

WHEELER WINSTON DIXON: One of the films that we're running, *Little Shop of Horrors*, was shot in two days and one night. You were shooting roughly forty-five pages of script a day. You used two cameras on that film?

ROGER CORMAN: Yes.

WWD: Is that unusual for you?

RC: Yes. It's the only time I ever did that during dialogue scenes. We simply *had* to; we had no time. It's customary to use several cameras during action scenes. If you're going to cover it. But on that film, if I had a dialogue scene, I'd have a camera over on the left photographing one actor and a camera over there on the right photographing the other actor, and I might even—this is before the use of zoom lenses—be on a dolly. Now I'd probably use a zoom. I might start on an over shoulder shot, going into a close-up, and then an over shoulder shot on the reverse angle, dollying into a close-up, so I would have effectively four different angles to cut on the scene. It saves time.

WWD: How much rehearsal did you actually have with the actors?

RC: I had a fair amount of rehearsal, because what I did—this was a standing set at the studio—I made an arrangement to use it for shooting for two days. I got the head of the studio to give me the set, use of the stage, not to shoot on for three days, but to rehearse. You have to know the union rules. Screen Actors Guild charges more if you hire an actor for a day: if you do that, it costs more than one-fifth of a week—for obvious reasons. So I hired the actors for a two-day shoot on a five-day week. I hired them for five days, rehearsed for three, and shot for two.

WWD: Were the films pre-sold to the theaters with deficit financing? How did American International Pictures generate the cash to make these films?

RC: It was a complicated matter, different for every film. Sometimes they were pre-sold to the theaters, that is, to the theater circuits. Sometimes they were financed out of cash flow. AIP, although a small company, was rather successful. Their budgets were limited because of the money available, but they always did seem to have *some* money available.

WWD: Did AIP put out two black and white films on one double bill so they would control the entire double bill, so they wouldn't have to give away the top or bottom half to another film?

RC: Sometimes they did that. That wasn't the regular practice, but in a period of time, it became normal procedure.

WWD: What led into the production of the color films, such as the later Edgar Allan Poe cycle?

RC: The first Poe film, *House of Usher* (1960), had about a $250,000 budget. I was making black and white films generally on an eight-, nine-, or ten-day schedule for about 70, 80, 90, sometimes $100,000, and they would put them together as a kind of "theme" double bill, two horror films, two science fiction films, something like that. And it was rather successful. Then AIP came to me and wanted two more black and white horror films, and I was simply growing a little bit tired of this. And also I felt that we were beginning to repeat ourselves, and that other people were beginning to copy the concept. So I suggested that instead of doing two black and white films on a ten-day schedule that I do just one film on a fifteen-day schedule in color, and I suggested *The House of Usher* as the property. After some period of discussion, they agreed, and it was something of a breakthrough for them because they had never spent $250,000 for a film, and I never had a fifteen-day schedule. I felt I was to a certain extent in the "big time" with that. The film was something of a critical success and was commercially the most successful film they ever had. So it was a move forward for both AIP and for me.

WWD: And it was also the first film that AIP made that didn't have a monster, per se, in the film. You had a difficult time trying to convince Sam Arkoff, the head of AIP, that the house of Usher was the monster.

RC: Sam said, "What's a horror film without a monster?" And I said, "Sam, the *house* is the monster." And when we were shooting there's one line where Vincent Price says "the house *lives*." He didn't know what this was all about. I explained this to him, and he immediately understood—it really made the film.

WWD: The *Pit and the Pendulum* (1961) was the next film?

RC: Yes. And it was very successful, both critically and commercially.

WWD: And then you shot *The Raven* (1963). *The Raven* gave birth to a very peculiar sort of "side bar" film, as it were. I understand that you finished *The Raven* two days early and then went home and whipped up a script for a film that became known as *The Terror* (1963), which was shot on the existing sets of *The Raven* in two days, with the services of Boris Karloff.

RC: *The Raven* had the normal fifteen-day schedule, and after the first two weeks we had one more week to go. I was going to play tennis on a Sunday afternoon, and it rained. And I was sitting around the house, and I thought, "You know, these sets are pretty good." In fact, they were *very* good. I thought I could do another film on them, so I started fooling around, and I wrote a story outline that afternoon. The next day on the set we had Vincent Price, Boris Karloff and Peter Lorre, and I suggested to Vincent that I might come back and do another one. But Vincent, who is something of an art critic, was going on a lecture tour and was unavailable. So I spoke to Boris, and Boris said fine, he'd do it. So I made a deal with Boris to shoot two days. The two days seemed to be my standard. I figured you can't do anything in less than two days. And I got this guy who was a friend of mine, Leo Gordon, and we worked from the outline I'd written. We wrote only those scenes that Boris was in for two days. I got my good friend Jack Nicholson to come along, and Jack came for the two days. I told Jack, "Boris will work the two days with you, and I'll write the rest of the picture, and you'll be the star of the picture." Jack thought that was great. And that's exactly what we did.

WWD: Jack Nicholson, at the time, was not a very well-known actor.

RC: No. He got a little less than he gets today. And we did indeed shoot all that in two days. Then I shut down, and wrote the rest of the picture. I calculated that I was financing this by myself, and didn't have enough money to finish doing it because I was tied to the Directors Guild and a number of other things. The only way to finish the film was to go non-union. I couldn't do this as a member of the Directors Guild, so I got my ace assistant, Francis Coppola, to come along. I told Francis to go out and shoot the rest of this thing, and he said fine. He went up to Big Sur and shot a portion of it with Jack, and then he came back and he was offered a contract at Warner's to direct a film called *You're a Big Boy Now* (1966). He came to me and said, "Look, I got a great deal here at Warner's. This is the start of my career." I said, "Okay," and then I had Monte Hellman for a little bit. There were four or five directors, and finally Jack came to me and we had one more day of shooting and Jack said, with some justification, "Every idiot in town has directed part of this film. Let me direct the final day." I said, "Fine, Jack, you do it." So Jack directed the final day.

We then cut all this together and the film did not make a great deal of sense. It also wasn't particularly interesting, but by that time I was working on another Poe film. I had some sets again, so I asked Jack and Dick Miller to help me finish it. I told them, "When I finish shooting one day, I'm going to hold the crew over, and you guys come to the set around 7:00 at night, and we're going to shoot a couple of new scenes fast, and tie all this together." So we shot the sequence in which Dick played Boris Karloff's assistant or manservant or something, and Jack was the young officer who had taken refuge in the castle. So Jack grabs Dick, throws him against the wall and says, "I've been lied to ever since I've come to the castle. Tell me what's going on." And Dick told Jack the entire plot, tying all of this stuff together. The picture didn't have much of a twist at the end. Boris, according to the original story, had played Baron von Leppe. In order to get a little bit of a twist in my final rewrite, I decided that Boris was an impostor who had killed the Baron von Leppe and taken his place. That became the story Dick told Jack against the wall of the set. Weirdly enough, this film was fairly successful.

WWD: In the middle of all of these films for American International, you went off on your own and with your own money, on location, you made a film called *The Intruder* (1961).

RC: It was a film I wanted to do. At that time, things were going very well, and I had never had a failure. I think I directed seventeen or eighteen films, and they were all successful. So at that point independent distributors would back me on any idea I came up with. We never missed. So I bought this novel having to do with integration of schools in the South. This is around 1960. And I prepared the script with Chuck Beaumont, the writer of the novel. And to my great surprise—I was a little more naive than I am now—all the companies that had agreed to back me on any kind of idea I came up with turned me down on this one. So I decided to back it myself, and it's one of those things that sounds as if it's very logical, but it wasn't logical. I only worked with a couple of professional actors. Almost all of the people in the film were local townspeople, and I wanted to shoot in the mid-South which was where most of the integration problems were taking place. But I didn't want to be in a Southern state. I wanted to have, in my own mind, the protection of a Midwestern state, and the laws there.

Looking at a map of the United States, I found what's called the boot heel of Missouri, which runs along the Mississippi River in a little kind of wedge south of Missouri proper, between Arkansas and Tennessee or Kentucky, something like that. There I was able to get a Southern look and Southern accents for the townspeople. All of that worked right. But I was thrown out of two towns with flat-out threats, from the sheriff in one county and the chief of police in another. Being in Missouri really didn't make any difference. The sheriff actually told me, "If you're in town when the sun sets you're in jail. And don't ever come back." The final sequence of the film took place in a school yard, and we had shot in East Prairie, Missouri. The first day or two days of this final sequence went okay, and then the sheriff told me to get out of town. We couldn't go back, so I shot some swings in a part in Charleston for half of the next day, and the chief of police kicked me out of Charleston, and we ended up shooting at a country school yard. It was summer, and we were out in the country, where there were no police or anybody to see that we were there, and we finished the sequence. Nobody has ever noticed, but the size of the swings varies slightly from shot to shot because they were in three different areas. Luckily people were more interested in the scene itself.

WWD: There is a superb sequence in that film where William Shatner, as Adam Kramer, a fervent racist, delivers an impassioned pro-segregation speech that really stirs up the townspeople. You told me that many of the people who were at that rally were really pro-segregation, and they thought Shatner was the hero of the film.

RC: Oh, they loved him! They *believed* him. I recruited these guys out of the public park. They had great faces, and I said, "This is the man who is coming to town, and I want you to be part of this group." When Shatner said, "This country shall be free and White!" they cheered, and they believed him all the way. Some of them were heart-broken at the end of the film when they realized that Kramer was the bad guy. It was a great shock to them.

WWD: You continued working for American International as the Poe cycle ended. AIP wanted you to make additional Poe films, but you decided to opt out, feeling that the series had run its course. Then you made *The Wild Angels* (1966), which was one of the first Hell's Angels motorcycle pictures, then *The Trip* (1967), which was one of the very first drug pictures. And then after *Gassss*, which you made in 1969, was totally recut by AIP, you left the company. You had lots of interference on that, I understand. AIP eliminated the main character called God. *Gassss* has never really been released in this country, if I'm correct.

RC: It had some limited release, but not a major release. I was very unhappy with what AIP did to it.

WWD: Then you went over to 20th Century Fox and did *The St. Valentine's Day Massacre* (1967).

RC: Yes.

WWD: How was it working for a major studio after you had worked for AIP?

RC: I really didn't have any problems. At that time Dick Zanuck was running Fox, and I got along fairly well with Dick. There were a couple of differences. One, the ease of production was much greater. There was more money, and I had a very good crew. On the other hand, the crews worked slower. I became a little bit impatient at the slowness of the pace, but it wasn't a major factor. There was a little bit more interference in the casting. I did not get the cast I wanted.

WWD: Is it true that you wanted Orson Welles to play Al Capone?

RC: I *had* him! I wanted to do a gangster film with a very distinguished cast, so I wanted Orson Wells to play Al Capone and Jason Robards to play Bugsy Moran. Essentially I had them, and Dick Zanuck, rightly or wrongly, said, "Nobody can work with Welles. You just *can't*. He'll scream and yell and try to take over. He's driven every director he's ever worked with crazy. The only time he works is when he directs himself. If he isn't the director, he's *going* to be the director by the second day." So we switched and moved Jason to Al Capone and Ralph Meeker played Bugsy Moran. They were quite good, but Jason really was better fitted for Bugsy Moran, and Welles, I had made a deal with him through his agent without meeting him. I met him later on, and he said he was very disappointed he had not played this part.

WWD: After a brief period then at 20th Century Fox, you decided to set up your own company, New World, which was the most successful new studio and distribution outfit launched in the 1970s in the United States. A lot of people at that time were saying that you were never going to get it off the ground. Could you briefly describe why you decided to go into this, with such an enormous amount of risk involved, building up a studio, and a distribution network as well?

RC: I was really just tired of directing. I had directed so many films. I directed something like fifty or sixty films in thirteen or fourteen years, something like that. The last film I did was for United Artists, a picture called *Von Richtofen and Brown* (1971) in Ireland. We were shooting in an airport outside of Dublin, and I was living in an apartment in that city. And each day I would drive out to the airport, and the road would fork. One road would go to the airport, and the other would go, I think, to Dingo Bay on the west of Ireland, and every day I was tempted to go the other way and just drive through the rest of Ireland. I barely made it through the film. I was exhausted. So I just felt that I would stop directing for a year. I would quit and take a sabbatical, save a little bit of money, and start my own distribution company. I would work on it for a year and then turn it over to somebody else and go back to directing. I started the company and the first film, *Student Nurses*, was very successful. And the second film was a success. We did three pictures in six months, and they were all successful. And we just kept going and I never got back to directing. I couldn't really find anybody to run New World in what I thought was an efficient manner, so I just stayed with the company.

WWD: As New World moved along, you began to develop an enormous amount of new talent. That's something you've done throughout your career. At AIP, you discovered Francis Ford Coppola. You gave him his first chance to direct with *Dementia 13* (1963), an ax murder movie shot in Ireland on a twenty thousand–dollar budget.

RC: It grew to be a little bit over twenty, but Francis was pretty close to the budget.

WWD: And when you started New World, you picked up people like Joe Dante, who went on to direct *Gremlins* (1984), and numerous other people. How did you continue to find or develop these people? Would you watch student films, or go to local playhouses? How did you manage to keep on top of this?

RC: I watched some student films, and some people applied to the company. Others were recommended by certain people, people whose opinion I trust. Having been a writer and a director myself, I might be a little more qualified to judge on writers and directors. We had a kind of training program that not everybody went through, but Joe Dante is a good example. Joe started as an assistant editor, went on to be a trailer editor, then a feature editor, then a second director, and finally a director. So by the time he was a director, he had learned our style of work.

AUDIENCE MEMBER (AM): Do you think it would be as easy today to start a new independent film distribution company as it was in the early 1970s, when things were a little bit tougher for the major studios?

RC: It's a somewhat complicated answer. Overall, it's easier. For theatrical distribution it's a little bit tougher, however, because as I say, the lower-budget pictures aren't doing as well. However, with the rise of videocassettes it's easier, because you can get most of your money back from video alone today. So it's a *somewhat* safer investment and an easier operation.

AM: Is one of the reasons low-budget films aren't doing so well the demise of the drive-in theaters?

RC: It's partially that. It's a number of other things. It's very difficult to get somebody to spend five or six dollars a ticket to see a hundred thousand–dollar or even a million-dollar film, when they can wait and see it on television for nothing, or for the same five dollars they can see a twenty million–dollar film, or for one or two dollars a night they can rent a videocassette. The economics are working against low-budget films, and the demise of the drive-in is part of that. But these other factors are as important, or more important. That doesn't mean that there won't be any successful low-budget films. There will always be, at least for the near future, somebody who either is out of luck or skill or both who will break through with a low-budget film. But as a regular program of successful films, I think it's extremely difficult today.

AM: Does it concern you as a producer that the cost of film stock and getting everything done has risen so much in film? Do you think students are better off shooting in 16 mm, or is video the way to go?

RC: Video might very well be a way to go if you're not aiming directly for theaters. If you feel your film is going to television or to videocassette, I would recommend that you go video. It's clearly cheaper and faster. You've got it right there. It doesn't have to go to a lab. You can do your opticals, your effects, very quickly.

AM: What do you think of the reliance on special effects in today's movies? And with the TV network audience shrinking, don't you think it would be more profitable to work for a cable network, rather than one of the traditional networks?

RC: In regard to the first part of the question, special effects are getting better, and they're also becoming more expensive. But the audience expects them now. I think really the turning point was *Star Wars* (1977). I've done science fiction films all my working life. We had a certain level of technical expertise which was acceptable at the time. But *Star Wars* really moved everything onto a different level, and since *Star Wars*, the audience will not accept the simpler type of special effects. So we're forced, really, into more expensive films. This touches on an earlier thing I mentioned—to spend more money and get better special effects to get an audience into the theatre. I have my own special effects facility, and I find that works very well.

Regarding the second part of the question, it is indeed true that the percentage of the viewing audience held by the networks is diminishing. But it's diminishing at a very slow rate. It's losing one percent a year, or maybe two percent a year. So for the near future, the big money in television will continue to be with the networks. Public television is a possibility, and pay cable services such as Showtime and HBO are possibilities, but they're shrinking more than the networks. The most important medium in the last couple of years is home video. And the segment that's been hurt most by home video has been pay television. Motion pictures have been hurt a little bit, free television has been hurt a little bit, but pay television, pay cable, has been hurt dramatically. People can go and rent whatever they want: Why should they use a pay cable service?

AM: We just saw *Cries and Whispers*, which you distributed and co-produced, and it's a film that obviously you were attracted to for a number of reasons. I'm just wondering how you can make the shift from Bergman's *Cries and Whispers* to something like the *Wasp Woman*, which you directed. When you make a *Wasp Woman* (1959), do you think, "Oh, I'm just making another 'B' movie and throwing it out into the world," or do you care about what you're making, as a film, and perhaps as a work of art?

RC: That's a multi-part question, and I'll try to deal with it as well as I can. First, you find from experience that certain films and certain genres, as it were, work best at the box office. We referred earlier to *The Intruder*. When I made that, I had never made a film that lost money. With *The Intruder*, I did a film that I believe was very good, and it got wonderful reviews. One of the New York papers called the film a major credit to the entire American motion picture film industry. It won a number of film festival awards. But it was the first film that I ever made that lost money, which taught me something: The public simply didn't want to see that particular kind of film. So you learn fairly early on that unless you are as good as a Bergman or a Fellini, you can't do what you please. I think I was a pretty good director, but I had no illusions that I was working on that level. Unless you're that good, you have to stay fairly close to a commercial subject.

After *The Intruder*, I tried to do a film that would work on two levels. This is really the core of my filmmaking philosophy, without getting too grandiose about it. On the surface level would be an entertainment film, a genre film, an exciting film of a certain type, and on a deeper subtextual level would be a film that would have some meaning to me. It didn't always work out that way. Sometimes it has a meaning to me, but nobody else will find any meaning in there at all. But at least for me there was something there, and that type of filmmaking seemed to be a type of filmmaking that worked for me and was successful. So I got some satisfaction out of it, and the films themselves were a commercial success.

EXTREME ENTERTAINMENTS

Above all else, Roger Corman always gave the audience what they expected to see in terms of a genre picture. He created a film that fulfilled all of the audience's major expectations, and then hopefully moved beyond those requirements to create a film that was both artistically and commercially successful. In the late 1990s, genre expectations remain relatively stable—*Armageddon* (1998), *Madeline* (1998), and *One Fine Day* (1998) are all very much of a type in construction and execution (the action film, the children's film, the romantic comedy)—but television, in its need to compete with the surfeit of spectacle offered by the majors, has had to follow a different strategy. The chair-throwing confrontational antics of *The Jerry Springer Show* offer one low-cost solution to the problem of providing superficially engaging television programming. *Cops* is "reality television" at its least expensive, while E!'s *Talk Soup* simply recycles clips from other talk shows with a bit of added commentary delivered from a nearly nonexistent set. Foreign television takes these strategies to new extremes, particularly in Japan, offering what has become known as "extreme TV" to an audience that clamors for more sensation, and more violence, in their televisual offerings.

As Jon Herskovitz notes in an essay in *Variety*,

Extreme TV is a hit in Japan. The Nippon Television Network (NTV) show *Denpa Shonen* is bringing viewers a weekly feast of never-seen-on-air video segments. Although the program has a 10:30 P.M. timeslot Sundays, it has scored the top spot in weekly rankings with a 28% share. In terms of Japanese television, it stands alone. Where else on TV is it possible to see the exploits of a naked man who has to win his way out of a tiny apartment? The man is comedian Nasubi. About four months ago, the producers of *Denpa Shonen* contacted the struggling 22–year-old showbiz wannabe and said they had a gig for him. He was blindfolded, taken by car to an apartment, told to strip down to his socks and given his assignment. He had to win 1 million yen ($7,250) in free stuff from contests pitched in magazines in order to gain his freedom. A stationary video camera was set up in his apartment to record how Nasubi responded to slowly winning his freedom. The winnings kept piling up and the viewers keep tuning in. "The premise is so simple," says producer Toshio Tsuchiya. "All he has to do is eat, sleep and win prizes. It is the kind of life that people say they dream about, and we are showing it to them." (29)

As Hersokvitz comments, "NTV will not disclose the budget for the show or ad revenue figures. The talent on the show is all young and unproven, so their salaries are at the basement of the pay scale for talent in Japan" (29). Such manifestations of "reality based" programming, including *The Real World*, *Road Rules*, and *Fanatic* (in which a devoted fan gets to interview her/his rock and roll idols), all produced by MTV, as well as "clip" shows like *Talk Soup* and E!'s *True Life Hollywood Stories* (two-hour compilations of stock footage, stills, and interviews strung together with canned music and a sensationalistic voice-over), are at their core manifestations of the need to produce low-cost programming for television with great rapidity. Sitcoms and traditional hour-long shows now routinely cost between one and six million dollars an episode—more if the program is a substantial hit. Disposable, recyclable real-life or clip television programming uses casts of non-professionals obtained for minimal salary, or utilizes stock footage from such sources as the National Archives in Washington, D.C., where millions of feet of film in the public domain can be obtained for the cost of print duplication alone. *The Real World* and *Road Rules* regularly turn over their non-professional casts every few months to increase audience interest, and avoid excessive salary demands. Mastered on videotape, clip features using public domain stock footage and low-cost stills can be assembled in a matter of a few days, creating several hours of programming for minimal cost. "Extreme TV," now popular in Japan and elsewhere in the world, has yet to break through on a national, network scale in the United States, but it seems to be only a matter of time before this happens. NTV's *Denpa Shonen* is simply the logical, minimalist-extension of these low-cost strategies, cutting sets and cast down to a bare minimum: one man, one room, no script, no other performers, no performance royalties. As with old episodes of *The Real World, Cops,* and other reality based TV shows, completed segments can be broadcast again and again without SAG or AFTRA payments, since these shows do not use professional actors (to do so would, after all, violate the implied "reality" concept), and require no rights clearance.

There is a great deal of "extreme" television already available in the United States (for one example, *The Robin Byrd Show*, featuring explicit sexual encounters in a rapid-paced, half-hour format), if only in major metropolitan markets. But all of this image recycling is, in reality, nothing new, and is yet another example of the Dominant televisual culture catching up to, and appropriating, the avant-garde. Bruce Conner's collage films, such as *A Movie* (1958), paved the way for the found-footage assemblages that now crowd our airwaves; performance artists such as Raphael Montañez Ortiz, Otto Mühl, Hermann Nitsch, and other practitioners of "Deconstructionist Art" smashed pianos, draped themselves with butchered lamb entrails and blood, and directly confronted their audiences with a series of riveting and shocking images created at low cost and designed to compel the audience's attention while simultaneously critiquing the consumer culture that necessitated the need for such purgative performances.

Raphael Montañez Ortiz, in particular, is a marginalized figure from cinema history, even though his works were the subject of a 1988 retrospective at El Museo del Barrio. In addition to his *Piano Destruction Concert* performances, in which Ortiz would destroy an ancient yet still functioning piano before a typically astonished audience with an ax, Ortiz also created a series of collage films based on principles of total chance, including *Cowboy and "Indian" Film* and *Newsreel* (1958). Both of these films, much like today's compilation television programs, used found footage to create a compelling commentary on our existing view of the imagistic universe. Ortiz recalled that *Cowboy and "Indian" Film* came about after repeated viewings of American westerns; as a Latino who also traces his roots back to the Yaqui people of northern Mexico, Ortiz wondered why he should be cheering the cavalry in conventional westerns, when his own heritage so clearly forced him to identify with the colonized subjects in these racist, classist constructions (see MacDonald 324–346).

Using chopped up segments from Anthony Mann's *Winchester '73* (1950) to create *Cowboy and "Indian" Film*, and segments from an old Castle Films newsreel to complete *Newsreel*, Ortiz then relied on the principle of total chance operation to create the finished works. As he related to critic and theoretician Scott MacDonald, "I would chop the films up with the tomahawk and put them into a medicine bag. I would shake it and shake it, and for me the bag would become a rattle, and I would chant with it . . ." (325–326). When Ortiz felt that the images had thus been sufficiently "sorted," he would simply splice the bits together in random order, including bits of timing leader, scraps of head and tail leader, and other bits of cinematic detritus that emerged from his Deconstruction of the original work. What emerges is striking: *Winchester '73* re-edited in *Cowboy and "Indian" Film* becomes a meditation on the star power of James Stewart in the title role, and his positioning within the Manifest Destiny narrative as the nominal protagonist of the film. In *Newsreel*, Pope Pius XII seemingly blesses an atomic bomb explosion, a chance juxtaposition that nevertheless, according to Ortiz, was entirely in keeping with his thematic concerns in the work. Noted Ortiz, "I was interested in the fact that [the original Castle Films newsreel material] included footage of the Nuremberg trials, of the Pope, of war and death. It allowed me to have the Pope blessing the bomb, as a comment on the Catholic collaboration with the Nazis. For me, making the film was a way to purge all this, to release the good from the evil" (MacDonald 331).

In stark contrast to Bruce Conner's cheerfully macabre *A Movie*, which also uses a manipulated Castle "News Highlights of the Year" newsreel as a central source of its images, Raphael Montañez Ortiz's *Newsreel* presents the appropriated material in rapid-fire free-associational montage patterns that assault, rather than amuse, the viewer. Thus, Ortiz's vision is less directly accessible than the deliberate dance of death and destruction that Conner presents, but it is equally compelling, and arises out of an entirely different cultural context. As MacDonald notes, what Ortiz sets out to do in these two films is to attack the original film and tear it to metaphorical and actual shreds, in order to directly attack "the enterprise of conventional cinema and all that it represents" (326). Conner is one of the supreme ironists of the cinema; Ortiz, in both his piano destruction pieces, and his early collage films (as well as his later "digital/laser/video" works), seeks to destroy and deconstruct the mechanisms of western Eurocentric culture that have for so long oppressed Latino, Yaqui, and Native American peoples.

When Ortiz smashes a piano with an ax, his point is not simply to galvanize the audience, or to shock them for a moment. Ortiz seeks to call into question the entire process of valuation that Eurocentric culture attaches to its various totemic artifacts (newsreel images that seek to "capture" an event; the nascent colonizing influence of the piano), and to make us think about what is important to us as viewers, and *why* we attach significance to certain objects, faces, images of destruction, regeneration, and ultimately rebirth. Created on a virtual shoestring, Ortiz's early works are thus the comment of one artist directly confronting a society that effectively seeks to suppress him, and works that simultaneously turn the weapons of the Dominant Cinema back against their practitioners and adherents. In this, we can see in Ortiz's work, and the work of the Viennese Deconstructionists, a direct assault on the taboo of cultural destruction in our society. Bombing Nagasaki or Hiroshima is an acceptable act of warfare; smashing a piano to bits is cultural vandalism.

Interestingly, Ortiz's piano destruction performances gained wider notoriety when Ortiz was profiled in the *Village Voice*, and subsequently booked on Johnny Carson's *Tonight Show* (MacDonald 337). Though Carson obviously was interested in Ortiz's work for its novelty and/or shock value alone, this widespread dissemination of his work brought these acts of "cultural terrorism" to a receptive national audience. Indeed, Ortiz's work inspired a brief campus craze in the wake of his appearance on *The Tonight Show*, in which opposing teams would ritually smash pianos to smithereens with sledge hammers, and then pass the shards of the instrument through a hole six inches in diameter. The first team to complete the entire process would win the contest. Naturally, this appropriation of Ortiz's work entirely trivializes the political and social significance of his performances, but isn't that what mainstream culture always does? By reducing an act of cultural critique to a sophomoric team sport, Carson and the college students who imitated Ortiz's performance piece sought to undermine the impact of the artist's work through burlesque and mechanical replication.

The college craze, however, is forgotten; Ortiz's work, and the work of his colleagues, survives, creating a body of cultural activity that still reminds us of the symbolist value we inherently place on the artifacts of our appropriational social structure. Along with the performance works of Carolee Schneemann, Yoko Ono, and other activist artists in the 1960s, Raphael Montañez Ortiz sought to reconfigure the modern world through ritualistic destruction, and, in his films, reassemblage. The success of this shared enterprise is still evident today, serving as the springboard for populist entertainment, "extreme" televisual events in which societal boundaries and constraints collapse and implode. Locked in an apartment, the naked comedian Nasubi is a modern day performance artist, even if his "performance" is entirely designed by the same medium that seeks to exploit his self-inflicted plight for entertainment value. In this light, the producer of *Denpa Shonen*, Toshio Tsuchiya, may be the real orchestrator of Nasubi's epochal performance, and his comments show that he is not entirely oblivious to the ironic ramifications of the scenario he has constructed. When Tsuchiya comments that Nasubi's existence "is the kind of life that people say they dream about, and we are showing it to them" (Herskovitz 29), it seems to me that the hellish panopticonic zone of hypersurveillance Nasubi inhabits is more a zone of torture than the location of desire. And yet, audiences tune in with unrelenting zeal, eager to watch Nasubi's struggle to win his way to freedom. Like Peter Weir's *The Truman Show* (1998) in miniature, *Denpa Shonen* demonstrates that "extreme TV" can be produced cheaply and quickly, but it can also serve as a master (intentional or not) of cultural transgression. In this, low-cost "reality" programming echoes the stripped-down basics of 1960s performance art at its most confrontational, and questions the mechanics of consumer/audience culture, even as it operates within the zone of commerce itself.

CHAPTER THREE

❖

Images of Conquest
and the Colonialist Instinct

In the People's Republic of China, a different sort of hierarchy of images prevails. Under comparatively strict state control, China's cinema is continually called up to nakedly reinforce the rule of the central government. In the United States and Europe, of course, all cinema projects with a large funding base perform much the same function, but in the PRC, the intensity of this engagement with power is magnified. It remains to be seen which approach is more effective in keeping the general populace satiated, and China's annexation of Hong Kong brings an intensely capitalistic society for the first time within the realm of the mainland Chinese government. The by-now famous "Fifth Generation" of Chinese filmmakers began their work in 1982, after graduating from the Beijing Film Academy, and for a time created breakthrough films that were a radical departure from conventional Chinese cinema. But with a rising tide of international fame, such filmmakers as Chen Kaige and Zhang Yimou pursued widely variant directions as individual artists, and relationships forged in the early days of the Fifth Generation movement soon foundered. Chen Kaige used the talents of then-cinematographer Zhang Yimou, when the two worked together on *Huang tu di* (*Yellow Earth*, 1984), but when Zhang Yimou made his own directorial bow in 1987 with *Hong gao liang* (*Red Sorghum*), tensions between the two men erupted. Where *Yellow Earth* was seen as an earnest parable, *Red Sorghum* filled Chinese theaters to capacity, offering a diverting tale of period romance that caught the country's imagination. Subsequently, Zhang Yimou directed a series of box-office and critical successes, including *Daihou meizhoubao* (aka *Codename Cougar*, and/or *The Puma Action*, 1989), *Ju Dou* (1990), *Da hong deng long gao gao gua* (*Raise the Red Lantern*, 1991), *Qui ju da guan si* (*The Story of Qui Ju*, 1992), *Yao a yao yao dao waipo q iao* (*Shanghai Triad*, 1995), and *You nua hao hao shuo* (*Keep Cool*, 1997). In addition, Zhang Yimou directed one segment of the superb anthology film *Lumière et compagnie* (*Lumière and Company*, 1995), in which a number of directors from around the world (including John Boorman, Spike Lee, David Lynch, and others) were invited to direct one-minute short films using the Lumière Brothers' original camera.

In addition, Zhang Yimou got a lead role as an actor in Wu Tianming's *Lao jing* (*Old Well*, 1986), and won the Best Actor award at the Tokyo Film Festival for his work (Zha 80). Offscreen, he carried on a torrid relationship with Gong Li, who starred in Zhang Yimou's films, much to the consternation of Zhang's embittered wife. Zhang Yimou also co-scripted Shuqin Huang's 1993 film *Hua hun* (*Pan Yu Liang, A Woman Painter*) and received two Academy Award nominations for his work on *Ju dou* and *Raise the Red Lantern* (Zha 80). Chen Kaige, who had arguably reached his professional apex with *Ba wang bie ji* (*Farewell, My Concubine*) in 1993, when that film won the Palme D'or at the Cannes Film Festival, was not, despite his own success, pleased at the good fortune of his former collaborator. Once, when apprised that Zhang Yimou had won yet another award, Chen Kaige spat out to reporters "he's a fucking cameraman, *my* cameraman," leaving little doubt that was not sanguine about Zhang Yimou's continuing popular success (Zha 81). Where Zhang Yimou explored the terrain of "sex, lies and violence" (Zha 89) in his crowd-pleasing films, Chen Kaige's more sober and philosophical films such as *Hai zi wang* (*King of the Children*, 1987) and *Blan zou bian chang* (*Life on a String*, 1991) were seen as both commercial and critical failures. *Feng yue* (*Temptress Moon*, 1996) and *Gaing o chi chun* (*The Assassin*, 1998) have done little to improve matters, and while Zhang Yimou has become something of an international media darling, Chen Kaige's career seems in free fall, artistically and commercially. This is despite the fact that, ironically enough, both *The Assassin* and *Feng yue* starred Gong Li, and Chen Kaige apparently went out of his way to exoticize these later films as much as possible, adding enough sex and drug use to *Feng yue* to receive an "R" rating in the United States when the film was released through Miramax.

But what has really happened here is that an entire generation of Chinese filmmakers, working in the years following the Great Proletarian Cultural Revolution from 1966 to 1976, came up together at once, making films quickly and cheaply as a communal enterprise, driven by an intensity of shared vision, rather than a desire for box-office profits. Now, the star system (most notably in the figure of the charismatic Gong Li) had stepped in, together with Western-style hype and media exploitation that helped to sell the more controversial Fifth Generation films in the West. Chen Kaige acknowledged this implicitly in a 1993 interview in which he stated that

> there is of course an influence from the West. . . . [W]e were the first generation of directors to see so many foreign films. That must have influenced us, the style, the structure, the acting and so on. . . . [W]e did not like the Communist realism from Moscow. We were the first generation to discard it, to break away from this kind of filmmaking and the system based on it. . . . (Eder and Russell 91–92)

This Western influence helped to shape not only the vision and structure of Fifth Generation works, but also, I would argue, substituted the classical Hollywood model of commercial filmmaking for the traditional "ideological tract" filmmaking once in favor under Mao Tse-Tung, and Jiang Qing, Mao's wife, who controlled theatre, film, and the other arts in China from 1963 until 1976. When Mao died, and Jiang Qing was arrested as part of "the Gang of Four" and put on trial for her "cultural crimes," it signaled the end of a particularly arid period in Chinese cinema; however, in an intense period of artistic and cultural retrenchment and internal debate following the collapse of the Great Revolution, no clear new model for filmmaking activity emerged. The Fifth Generation finally embraced not only China's classical past, but also the technology and syntactical structures appropriated by the Dominant Western Cinema in an attempt to crack the international commercial and critical marketplace. And, as we have seen, this strategy was successful, generating new critical respect for the Chinese cinema worldwide, and turning films such as *Red Sorghum, The Story of Qui Ju, Farewell, My Concubine,* and *Shanghai Triad* into art house and video rental hits.

Ping He made an international name for himself with *Pao pa shuang deng* (*Red Firecracker, Green Firecracker,* 1994); Huang Jianxin did the same with his 1986 film *Hei pao shi jian* (*The Black Cannon*

Incident), which was his first feature film as a director. Huang Shuqin's most famous film is probably *Hua hun* (*Pan Yu Liang, A Woman Painter*), which was partially scripted by Zhang Yimou from the novel by Nan Shi. Huang Shuqin, one of the more noted feminist directors of the group, was born in 1940. Her mother was a prominent theater director. Huang Shuqin graduated form the Beijing Film Academy in 1964, and so she pre-dates many members of the Fifth Generation in her work. For a time, she assisted Xie Jin on his films, and made her directorial debut in 1981 with *Dangdai ren* (*Contemporary People*) (Eder and Russell 98).

Set in the early twentieth century, *Hua hun* tells the story of a young woman, Yu Liang, who starts her life in a brothel, but learns to paint despite numerous obstacles placed in her path. She is a student at the Shanghai Art Institute, but the institute is closed down for allowing the students to use nude models in their drawing classes. After further study in Paris, Yu Liang wins a prize for a self-portrait, painted in the nude, and returns to Nanking to teach art. But her academic career is cut short when the authorities discover that she started her life in a brothel, and Yu Liang is forced to leave for Paris. Finally, near the end of her life, Yu Liang is given a major one-person show of her work as a painter. The film is a Chinese/French/Taiwanese co-production, with financing from Canal +, Shanghai Film Studio and Golden Film Taiwan among other funding sources. It stars the ubiquitous Gong Li as Yu Liang, and in many respects, it is one of her finest performances. Unfortunately, perhaps because of its feminist theme, the film has not received distribution in the United States, although it was well received in France. Often compared to Bruno Nuytten's *Camille Claudel* (1988), the film is visually sumptuous, but also has considerable thematic resonance and conviction; it deserves a wider audience.

Li Shaohong is another woman making a mark in the Chinese cinema, and in many ways, surveying the work of the Fifth and Sixth Generation filmmakers in China, it becomes rapidly apparent that women with the new Chinese cinema are given many more chances to direct than their Western counterparts, though this has changed to some degree in Hollywood in the last few years. Born in 1955, Li Shaohong served in the military in 1976, and entered the Beijing Film Academy in 1978. Graduating in 1982, she directed her first feature film in 1988, a routine genre film. Her first personal feature is the 1990 *Xuese qing chen* (*Bloody Morning*), followed by *Sishi buhuo* (*Family Portrait*) in 1992, and *Hong fen*

(Blush) in 1994. *Hong fen* tells the tale of two women who form a deep friendship while working in a brothel, but who are parted when the Cultural Revolution disrupts their pattern of daily existence. Noting that "we make our films for the purpose of art," Li Shaohong told Klaus Eder that her journey to being a film director was not an easy or direct one. As she noted in Eder's interview with her,

> it was not my own choice . . . after the Cultural Revolution everyone had to face the fact of choosing a new life. . . . I was 23 at the time. I had to decide about a school which could accept me. So I chose this academy and entered the directing department. . . . [T]he graduates were accepted by the studios with difficulty. The studios did not accept our ideas—particularly the Beijing Film Studio . . . and then, the studio in Guangxi Province . . . first opened its doors for Zhang Yimou and Zhang Junzhao. The first film *Yi Ge he Ba Ge* (*One and the Eight*, 1983) was able to be made there. It was the first time that our generation could express itself. When the film was finished, it caused a sensation . . . it became the manifesto for our generation. (Eder and Russell 99–101)

Zhang Junzhao, the director of *One and the Eight*, has never had a major commercial success, but as Li Shaohung indicates, his film, on which Zhang Yimou served as cameraman, launched the Fifth Generation decisively on its path to international influence. Born in 1952 in Nanluo, Henan Province, Zhang Junzhao joined the army in 1969, and studied acting with the Modern Drama Troupe of Xinjiang Military Region. While still serving in the army, Zhang Junzhao learned the basics of direction while directing a number of military productions. In 1978, he entered the Beijing Film Academy's Directing Department, and graduated in 1982. Gravitating to the Guangxi Film Studio, he worked with Zhang Yimou to create *One and the Eight* (Eder and Russell 122). Li Shaohung describes the precise reasons that then-contemporary Chinese audiences, used to the staged dramatic pageants and "Revolutionary operas" favored by Jiang Qing, found the film so disturbing:

> An older generation did not accept the political point of view expressed in the film. *One and the Eight* described bandits, who fight against Japanese invaders. At that time people thought bandits cannot be good persons. In the film they are bandits, and at the same

time they are Chinese . . . but a lot of people could not accept the fact that "bandits" also had national and patriotic feelings. (Eder and Russell 101–102)

Zhang Junzhao's career did not flourish after this startling debut, and his influence is confined to his position as the first filmmaker within the Fifth Generation to actually undertake and complete a feature film. But others, including Tian Zhuangzhuang, pressed on to create films that were both controversial, and even more disruptive of the existing social order. Born in Beijing in 1952, Tian Zhuangzhuang's parents were actors. Forced to labor in the country during the Great Revolution, Tian joined the Beijing Film Academy in 1978, and, as was the case with many of his compatriots, graduated in 1982. Even before graduation, Tian directed a student film, *Womende jiaoluo* (*Our Corner*), with his fellow classmates, Xie Xiaojing and Cui Xiaogiu in 1980. Upon graduation, he went to work directing television, but soon gravitated to feature films, directing *Dao maze* (*Horse Thief*, 1986) and *Yaogun qingnian* (*Rock Kids*, aka *Rock and Roll Youth*, 1988). He steadily showed a taste for more controversial subjects in his choice of projects. This predilection came to a head with the production of *Lan fenq zheng* (*The Blue Kite*, 1993), a film so openly critical of the Chinese government that the authorities refused to allow it to be completed. The Hong Kong co-producer of the project, Longwick Film, prepared the final print in 1993 for presentation at the Cannes Film Festival (Eder and Russell 105). Seemingly seeking confrontation, Tian announced in one interview that if his films did not suit mass tastes, it was because, as Klaus Eder recounts, "he was making his films for an audience of the next century" (104). Such remarks understandably did not endear him to the authorities, and he was publicly attacked by Wu Yigong, head of the Shanghai Film Studio (104). *The Blue Kite* is openly critical of the Great Revolution, and depicts scenes of the Red Guards beating and imprisoning helpless members of the working classes without justice or compassion. The Communist Party is seen as an omnipresent, evil force, with huge pictures of Mao, blaring loudspeakers, and Red Guards on parade dominating the film's landscape. One of the film's protagonists dies in a prison camp; another starves to death. Only the hope that eventually the political situation will improve sustains the film's two main characters, the couple Chen Shujuan and Lin Shaolong. Tian paints in *The Blue Kite* a world of unremitting torment and hypersurveillance, in which the human spirit is crushed at every turn. It is easy to see why the film ran afoul of the censors. In an interview with Klaus Eder, Tian discussed the production of *The Blue Kite*, as well as other matters, but remained circumspect in his remarks, perhaps fearing further reprisals. In 1978, when he joined the Beijing Film Academy, Tian told Eder,

> There were no films. For twelve years, there were no films produced in China, with the exception of Peking Opera films. . . . From the UK for example, I saw only one film, *Hamlet* [1948] by Laurence Olivier. Later on, in the Film Academy, I saw quite a lot of films: the famous silent movies, the films of Eisenstein and Chaplin, Hollywood of the 1960s and 1970s, and of course also the best Russian films . . . Fellini, Antonioni . . . Ingmar Bergman, Fassbinder, Japanese films, the films of Satyajit Ray. . . . [T]he difference between us and the previous generation is, that this generation made films on China, on Chinese society, while we developed another understanding of the cinema . . . we went deeper, by researching the inner situation of society. . . . I think most spectators like very normal stories. I can understand it. . . . If you make a film dealing deeply with Chinese history and Chinese people, foreigners might not understand it. That's why [foreigners] prefer my first films, or films like Yellow Earth and Raise the Red Lantern. . . . But on the screen you do not see real Chinese people, you see only a symbol of China. (Eder and Russell 105–108)

THE SECOND WAVE OF HONG KONG CINEMA

With China's absorption of Hong Kong, a cultural cross-pollination that had been an uneasy alliance became an accomplished fact in cinema production. *The Blue Kite* was finished in Hong Kong before China absorbed the small nation; now, such a tactic would be impossible. But Hong Kong has been having its own production headaches of late. In the 1970s and 80s, Hong Kong action cinema under such early entrepreneurs as Run Run Shaw and Raymond Chow surged forward to international prominence with a variety of cheap martial arts movies. They finally cracked the market in the United States decisively with the films of Bruce Lee, who had abandoned a moribund career in the racist American cinema (as Kato in *The Green Hornet*, for example—always the sidekick but never the star, solely because of his Asian ancestry) for Hong Kong stardom. When he died suddenly and unexpectedly at the age of thirty-two in 1973, the Hong Kong film industry cast about for a solution to the loss of their major star, and decided that quantity—mass production and distribution—was the solution if Hong Kong films wished to keep their foothold in the West. Bruce Lee clones were introduced, such as Bruce Li, Bruce Lei, or Bruce Le, and production was speeded up to a terrific pace. Run Run Shaw and his brother, Run Me Shaw, created a huge cinema production factory where movies were ground out literally around the clock, shot silently, with dialogue added later, and edited without benefit of a work print. In these films, the editor would physically look through the negative of the film, and negative assembly would yield a complete final cut negative without ever making a work print; this final negative was then contact-printed in black and white, and sound effects, music, and dialogue were added in primitive dubbing studios. Most films were completed in less than a week, and the physical look of these early Hong Kong action films was often quite rough. With poor dialogue synchronization, minuscule negative scratches in every frame, smash zooms announcing major plot twists, and acting reduced to a series of cardboard stereotypes, the Hong Kong action film of the 1970s and '80s did well theatrically and on television throughout the world, but seemed to be playing to the law of diminishing returns in terms of quality and originality. The original formula had been over-exploited; something new needed to be added to the generic mix.

The second wave of Hong Kong action films began with the work of Jackie Chan, who rose to prominence in the 1970s Hong Kong cinema after years of training at the Chinese Opera Research Institute, where he began studying at the age of seven. An adept acrobat, Chan secured work initially as a child actor, then moved from stunt man and bit parts to star in such films as *Little Tiger from Canton* (1971), *New Fists of Fury* and *Shaolin Wooden Men* (both 1976), and *Dragon Fist* (1978). Though tapped to become the next Bruce Lee, Chan successfully resisted the tag, and invented a new genre of Hong Kong action film more indebted to such silent athletic comedians as Buster Keaton, Chaplin, Harry Langdon, and Harold Lloyd. Chan's films include outrageously dangerous stunts and precise choreography in the fight scenes, and have a light tone throughout which is missing from the deadly serious ambiance Bruce Lee brought to his films. Chan's amiable personality and his original approach to creating a new action persona made him an overnight star in Hong Kong, although his attempts to crack the market in the United States have been less successful. But even in the United States, Chan's frenzied dare-devil antics are a major box-office draw in an era of blue-screen process photography and stunts without genuine risk, and in his homeland, Chan is a superstar.

Yet with China's re-annexation of Hong Kong, another sea change was predictably felt in the Hong Kong cinema, the result of both the changing political climate and evolving technologies. Today, the VCD, or video compact disc, is the ruling medium of distribution and exhibition in Hong Kong; films are often pirated before they reach theatrical distri-bution, and released on VCD before a film opens its theatrical run. Pirate VCDs are cheap—about $2.50 in American dollars—and they are ubiq-uitous (Strauss, *Exit* 1). With this omnipresent video piracy permeating all aspects of the industry, box-office grosses for Hong Kong films have dropped drastically. But more ominous, perhaps, is the fact that rather than Hong Kong films influencing Hollywood products (as is the case with the exportation of Ringo Lam, John Woo, and other top Hong Kong action directors to Hollywood), Hollywood films are now beginning to dominate the Hong Kong box office.

In 1992, Hong Kong films took in an estimated $153,402,328 American dollars at the box office in Hong Kong, while Hollywood films accounted for only $33,210,605 U.S. in admissions, for a total of $186,612,933 in revenues, at an average ticket price of $4.27 per person. Just five years later, the results of an inexorable downward spiral in the demand for Hong Kong cinema were readily apparent. In 1997, Hong Kong films made only $71,782,891 U.S. in domestic box office admis-sions, down by more than fifty percent from 1992. Simultaneously, American films accounted for $76,572,457 U.S. in Hong Kong theatri-cal revenues, for a total of $148,355,348 at an average ticket price of $6.47 per person. This is a drop of more than $20,000,000 U.S. in five years in overall admissions, and a complete shift in the make-up of those films that draw audience dollars. In just five years, the Hong Kong cin-ema has experienced economic collapse, as cinemagoers flee the formulaic predictability of these once-fresh genre films for the lavish, yet even more formulaic films offered by Hollywood.

In 1993, *Jurassic Park* became the first American film to outgross domestic product in Hong Kong, and went to first place at the box office, something unheard of for an American film in Hong Kong at that time. Intrigued by the lavish digital special effects, audiences deserted home-made films for the super-spectacles churned out by the Hollywood majors, thus undermining the indigenous cinematic culture of the region. In addition, many of Hong Kong's most bankable stars and directors saw the writing on the wall, and left to pursue a career in Hollywood before the exoticism of the Hong Kong action film cooled off. The actors Chow Yun-Fat, Jet Li, and Maggie Cheung all went to Hollywood, and became involved in a variety of intensely commercial projects, from James Bond movies to the big-screen version of the 1970s teleseries *Charlie's Angels*. As of this writing, John Woo will direct Tom Cruise in *Mission Impossible 2*. And Hong Kong films are no longer being exported to the West in their original versions; like so many films from other countries desirous of theatrical bookings in the United States, such Hong Kong hits as Stephen Chiau and Lik-Chi Lee's *God of Cookery* (1998) are being remade in Hollywood versions, in this case starring Jim Carrey in the title role, with Stephen Chiau directing the remake (see Strauss, *Exit* 22 for more on this).

As if all this weren't enough, the Hong Kong gangs, or Triads, have invaded the Hong Kong motion picture production business, creating chaos at every turn in the motion picture production, distribution, and exhibition process. As Neil Strauss notes,

> Making matters worse was the incursion of real gangsters—organized crime, or the so-called triads—into the Hong Kong movies business. Film executives were murdered; stars were forced to accept roles in triad-backed productions. Then came the pirate-VCD market, which has robbed the Hong Kong industry of an estimated 40 percent of its business, forcing theater and video rental chains to close. As if things weren't bad enough, the Asian economic downturn hit, slashing movie budgets and destroying crucial ancillary markets and sources of investment in places like South Korea and Taiwan. (22)

In an atmosphere such as this, no creative community can flourish for long. Thus the wholesale defection of much of Hong Kong's talent to Hollywood seems arguably understandable, if regrettable. Many observers feel the Hong Kong cinema, in the space of less than half a decade, has simply collapsed, just as the British film industry collapsed in the early 1970s (though for different reasons) and became merely a series of postproduction and production facilities for the American product.

In the midst of this commercial and artistic disaster zone, there are a few bright spots. The director Wong Kar-Wai, creator of *Fallen Angels*

(1995) and the evocative, ultra low-budget gay-themed road movie *Happy Together* (1997) continues to create work of style, originality, and visual brilliance. Wai Ka-Fai, Fruit Chan, Eric Kot, and others are also making a series of audacious and complexly designed films that play well at home and abroad, where they are released in major cities to resounding critical praise. Neil Strauss's survey of Hong Kong offerings in his essay "Amid Decline, Some Standouts" singles out Wai Ka-Fai's *Too Many Ways to Be Number One* (1998), Ringo Lam's *Full Alert* (1998), Fruit Chan's *Made in Hong Kong* (1998), and Eric Kot's *First Love* (*Litter on the Breeze*) (1998), as being particularly successful. *Too Many Ways to Be Number One* is described by Strauss as being a "low budget gangster flick [turned] into a creative manifesto that has been interpreted, despite [the director's] protest, as a thinly veiled statement about Hong Kong's handover to China" (23). To give the film visual flair, Wai Ka-Fai shoots many of his scenes with deep focus, wide angle photography, and even stages "entire action scenes with a camera held upside-down" (23), to create a film that is both visually dazzling and thematically resonant.

Full Alert is another *policier* from the prolific veteran Ringo Lam, but Strauss feels that the film has particular energy and distinction; while Fruit Chan's *Made in Hong Kong*

> may be the most representative film of a new wave of directors who are making low-budget, more realistic youth-oriented movies. Starring the eminently cool, likable and scrawny Sam Lee, "Made in Hong Kong" is a tragic love rectangle chronicling the relationships between an aspiring gangster who would be better off in school, his mentally retarded sidekick, the dying 16–year-old girl he's in love with and a high-school girl he never met who has committed suicide. (23)

These films offer a compelling new vision to an industry that desperately needs a new direction, inasmuch as it cannot hope to compete with the financial clout of the major Hollywood studios, who can afford to release six thousand prints of Roland Emmerich's remake of *Godzilla* (1998) worldwide to saturate the international market at a cost of tens of millions of dollars, after spending nearly one hundred million dollars to produce the film in the first place. In contrast, the average cost of a Hong Kong film remains at around three million dollars U.S., with ten million dollars U.S. buying a super spectacle, such as the 1998 film *The Storm Riders*

(Strauss, *Exit* 22). For the rest of the industry outside the chained circle of big-budget filmmaking, the only answer is to shoot in 16mm, keep things cheap and simple, and hope that one can make it into theaters with the finished product before the video pirates hijack a print (or simply rephotograph the completed film off the cinema screen) and flood the home video market with thousands of pirated VCDs.

> "We have had bad situations in the past," says Hong Kong director Ann Hui (best known for her savage film *Boat People* [1983]), "but now we encounter problems on a daily basis. Funding for films is very difficult to come by." But Hui, too, feels that the answer is simply to turn out as many films as possible, even program pictures, to keep up Hong Kong's market share. "It's OK to have a lot of low-grade movies," Hui contends. "The important thing is to have a lot of movies." (Harris 34)

But as Neil Strauss reports, others are less optimistic:

> "Times are hard," says Richard To, the head of the Hong Kong Film Critics Society. "And the future is still very unclear. A lot depends on whether the mainland Chinese market will be more open than now to Hong Kong films. And a lot matters on whether pirate VCD's can be stopped. Otherwise, there's simply no hope."
> Perhaps the best evidence of this comes during an elevator conversation with the assistant of a Hong Kong director. Asked if he wants to become a director, he replies quickly, "No way." After a few seconds of silence, he shyly adds, "Are you interested in buying a digital camera while you're here? I can sell you one for very cheap." (*Exit* 22)

This is nearly the same situation that faces British filmmaking in the late 1990s, and has persisted in Great Britain since the late 1970s. The British film industry itself, while heavily subsidized by a variety of state grants, and production programs fostered by such agencies as Britain's channel 4, produces now for the most part either glossy romance films for export, or else highly personal local films that are not easily distributed abroad. Here, piracy is not the problem; it is simply that there is a shrinking international market for nationalist British cinema, while the parade of Merchant/Ivory films continues on unabated, creating a neo-colonialist fantasy zone for the foreign (American) viewer. Younger directors in Britain, such as Simon Beautoy, Eric Styles, Lynne Ramsay, Sandra Goldbacher, Corine Adler, Julian Henriques, Adam Tysoe, and many others, are making films with a strong personal bent on minimal budgets, but unlike Hong Kong cinema in the late 1980s, much of it does not do well in export to the United States, and winds up on the video shelves. While occasionally a film will break through to a mass audience, such as Peter Cattaneo's *The Full Monty* (1998), most contemporary realist British films seem destined for local consumption, and fail to find a larger international audience. This was not the case in the 1960s, when filmmaking in England was both cheap and had inherent international commercial appeal, whether for a frankly commercial enterprise, such as the British teleseries *The Avengers*, or in the more personal films of *auteurs* such as Tony Richardson, Karel Reisz, Richard Lester, and Bryan Forbes.

AN INTERVIEW WITH BRYAN FORBES

Bryan Forbes has had a long and varied career in the cinema, actively functioning as writer, producer, director, actor, and critic since the 1940s, but he has somehow never broken through in the public consciousness in the way that Richard Attenborough, Sir Carol Reed, Sir David Lean, or other of his contemporaries have been able to. And yet the range of Forbes's accomplishments is extraordinary, ranging from his appearances as an actor in such films as Henry Hathaway's *Of Human Bondage* (1964), Basil Dearden's *The League of Gentlemen* (1959), John Guillermin's *I Was Monty's Double* (1958), Guy Hamilton's *An Inspector Calls* (1954), Val Guest's *Quatermass II* (1957); his work as a director on *Whistle Down the Wind* (1961), *The L-Shaped Room* (1963), *King Rat* (1965), *The Wrong Box* (1966), *The Whisperers* (1966), *The Madwoman of Chaillot* (1969), and *The Stepford Wives* (1975), to name just a few of his many directorial credits; and his substantial career as a scenarist, from José Ferrer's *Cockleshell Heroes* (1956) and Guy Green's *The Angry Silence* (1960), to his own production of *The Naked Face* (1984) and Richard Attenborough's *Chaplin* (1992) (although this last assignment was not without problems, as Forbes details in the following interview).

In addition to all this activity, Forbes has also served as a chief of production at EMI Elstree from 1969 to 1971. Among the many, many actors he has worked with in any one of his numerous capacities are

Christopher Plummer, Michael Caine, Katharine Hepburn, Dame Edith Evans, John Mills, Ralph Richardson, Peter Cook, Dudley Moore, Peter Sellers, Albert Finney, George Segal, Leslie Caron, Paul Henreid, Donald Pleasance, Yul Brynner, Robert Morley, Richard Burton, and Honor Blackman. He is also the author of several novels and volumes of memoirs. Indeed, Forbes is one of the last survivors of the era of the great British studio system, but after some forty years in the industry, his energy and industry is unabated. I spoke with Bryan Forbes about his life and work, and his thoughts on the future of British Cinema, in July, 1997.

WHEELER WINSTON DIXON: In all the areas in which you've worked—as an actor, writer, producer, director, production executive—what's the area that gives you the most satisfaction?

BRYAN FORBES: Well, actually, I was a writer who became an actor who became a screenwriter who became a director, and I guess in the final analysis, because it's less ephemeral than most things, writing probably gives me the most satisfaction. But on the other hand, if you write a screenplay, and then you see it come to life, there's no greater pleasure. You have no idea how people react when they read your novels, because you're not there with them; but when you sit in an audience and say "My God, I've made them laugh, I've made them cry," that's a real satisfaction.

WWD: And yet there's nothing that's more "incomplete" than an unproduced screenplay.

BF: Yes, that's true. I've had better than average luck with my work, except for biographies. It's curious. I must have spent at least five years of my life writing major biographies, none of which have ever reached the screen. I wrote screenplays on the lives of Winston Churchill and Henry Ford. I wrote the first draft of the screenplay for Dickie Attenborough's *Gandhi* (1982), and then decided that I didn't like Gandhi as a person, and so I parted company with that production.

I did the first screenplay on *Chaplin*, which was abandoned, although I had a sort of credit on it. Actually, I don't think there's probably more than ten lines of my script in the finished film, but yet I received co-credit for the screenplay with William Boyd and William Goldman. But the Writer's Guild is very honest, and they figured that anybody who spends a year, and does most of the major research for the piece deserves the credit. At one time, I was going to take my name off it, because it was a very unhappy experience the way my script was not used by Universal. They walked away from it in a most arbitrary fashion; they wouldn't even agree to see me. This was all rather sad, because Richard Attenborough is my oldest mate, and we're still in partnership. But it did blight the friendship for about a year, and then I thought, "This is stupid, a screenplay is not worth a friendship," and so now we're back on again on keel. But yes, it did cause problems for about a year.

WWD: You were born July 22, 1926, and you're yet another graduate of the Royal Academy of Dramatic Arts (RADA).

BF: Yes, I won a Leverhulme Scholarship, but I didn't stay very long, because it was the middle of the war, and I knew I was going to be called up. Since there were only about eighteen young men in the academy at that time, and over two hundred rather nubile and pretty young girls, and about seven of the eighteen men were gay, the rest of us had quite a field day. But I just thought it was becoming rather a waste of time. When you knew you were going to be called up and possibly killed, it seemed more important to go out into the world. So I only stayed about a year of the three-year course, and then went directly into rep. There were a lot of reps, or repertory theaters, at that time in England, some two thousand or more weekly rep companies. I was on stage from the time I was seventeen, starting out in a rep company called the Intimate Palmer's Green, and then I went into Rugby Rep, and then various other reps, and then I finally got a West End job in a Terence Rattigan play, and of course, that's when I got called up, just as I was getting my first professional experience on the stage. I was called up in 1943, with British Army Intelligence, and served until 1947.

WWD: And this led to your screen acting debut in 1949, in Michael Powell and Emeric Pressburger's bomb-disposal thriller *The Small Back Room*, in which you played, pretty much, a corpse.

BF: Quite right. Mickey Powell was a bit of a little martinet, and he had a voice like General Montgomery, very high pitched, and he could be very cutting when he wanted to, saying things like, "Do you call that acting?," which gives one lots of confidence. But

I only had a one-day part, originally: the boy who picked up the bomb and was blown to pieces. I remember that I was paid twenty-five pounds for the day. So I lay there on the studio floor, amidst the rubble. I didn't have a stand-in or a double. In those days, filmmaking in Britain was very leisurely, and it wasn't until after eleven o'clock in the morning that Mickey actually looked through the camera at me. He didn't like what he saw, and so he asked the company at large, "What do people look like, who've been blown up by a bomb?" And a passing prop man answered, "Powdered gramophone records, guv'nor." So they got a bunch of old shellac gramophone records and smashed them up, covered my face in Vaseline and stuck all these bits of black all over my face. Mickey took another look through the camera and said, "I'll tell you exactly what that looks like. It looks like an actor with smashed up gramophone records all over his face." So then they decided they would bandage me to look like the Invisible Man, with only one eye. So now it's about half past three in the afternoon, and they hadn't taken a shot. Finally, they got the shot they wanted, but it took forever; no one seemed in very much of a hurry, I can tell you.

This was typical of British films of the period. There was a lot of waste. A lot of people seem to have the notion that British film-making during this period was carried on at an absolutely breakneck pace, but it's simply not so; perhaps on the quota quickies, but not "A" features, I can tell you. In fact, when I was directing, I always used to have a chess set with me on the stage, and I would play long games of chess with my soundman between shots. One of the major factors was that lighting took so long; they used enormous "brute" or arc lamps, which only lasted about twenty minutes and then all the arcs had to be switched off and trimmed and allowed to cool. So very often between shots, it wasn't unusual to be waiting twenty or forty minutes. Which gave one a good deal of time to pursue a quiet game of chess.

In 1950, for example, I had a job in a war drama called *The Wooden Horse* (directed by Jack Lee), for which I had an eight-week contract. Well, it stretched out to fourteen months! That was the insanity of the film units during this period. I mean, this was just after the war, and there must have been four hundred derelict prisoner of war camps all over Europe to use as sets. What did the producer do? He built a new one from scratch, clearing miles of forest and timber in the process. This was the madness of the film indus- try. Props were lost; they used extras who couldn't really act and so they had to reshoot a lot of it; but I didn't complain—I was getting paid. But it was sheer, extravagant waste, and the whole thing could have been made a good deal more efficiently with just a little bit of common sense.

WWD: In your early films as an actor, such as Derek Twist's *Green Grow the Rushes* (1951), Raoul Walsh's *The World in His Arms* (1952) and *Sea Devils* (1953), Ronald Neame's *The Million Pound Note* (1953, known in the United States as *Man With a Million*) and other of your films from the early 1950s, you're refining your craft as an actor, but you haven't started your career as writer yet. How did that come about?

BF: Well, I was out in Hollywood under contract to Universal as an actor in the 1950s when I made *The World in His Arms* for Raoul Walsh, and Cubby Broccoli, who was later to produce the James Bond films, was one of maybe seven hundred people in the world who read my first published book, a collection of short stories. As a result, he gave me a screenwriting assignment at seventy-five dollars a week, for a script that was never produced. But anyway, Cubby liked what I did, and so he sent for me when they ran out of pages on an Alan Ladd film called *The Black Knight* (1954, directed by Tay Garnett). And I sort of saved their bacon on that, because they had literally run out of pages; they had nothing to shoot. So I wrote that as fast as I could on a day-to-day basis, and somehow, we got through the film.

WWD: Where did you acquire your skills as a writer?

BF: Well, when I was at RADA I was already writing turgid, unpub- lishable novels. There was one that was published, but thankfully, it sank without a trace, and I don't even acknowledge it to this day. During the war, I didn't have time to write novels, but I did write quite a lot of short stories, and after the war, they were published under the title *Truth Lies Sleeping*. I also did a lot of journalism. I was fiction critic on the *Spectator*, I wrote for the *Evening Standard*, the *New Statesman*—anyone who would employ me. And it was very good training, because you had to meet deadlines, and of course you got paid. So I got the reputation as a fast man with a pen, and as a result of that, I got my first real screenplay assignment, for *Cockleshell Heroes* (1956).

WWD: That was directed by José Ferrer. Were you happy with the way it turned out?

BF: Not really, no. It was directed rather badly, and Ferrer brought in another writer to punch up the script, which I didn't appreciate. And in fact, with the associate producer, I was responsible for re-shooting a good deal of the film, without Ferrer's knowledge, because the producers weren't happy with the way it was going. So I sort of wrote new scenes for Trevor Howard, and although I wasn't really directing the scenes (the associate producer did that), I was on the floor all the time, and this was really valuable training that would serve me very well indeed later on. But it was not a happy picture at all. Ferrer was a megalomaniac behind the camera.

WWD: I'm struck by the fact that you seem to move from genre to genre very easily, as an actor, writer, and/or director. You've done everything from science fiction to comedy to war films, and yet you seem equally comfortable in each of your projects. To what do you attribute this?

BF: Well, I did a lot of films as an actor in the early to late '50s, even a film for the Danziger Brothers, Harry Lee and Edward J. Danziger, who built a rather cheap studio that they called New Elstree, which was mostly under water all the time. I acted in a film for them called *Satellite in the Sky* (1956, directed by Paul Dickson), but they were a very cheap outfit indeed. They'd come to films from the hotel business, from whence they should never have strayed. *An Inspector Calls* was quite a different affair; it was based, of course, on Priestley's stage play, and was a quality production all the way around. And I was in both of the first two Quatermass films in 1955 and 1957, both of which were made for Hammer, another outfit that was very small and made films very quickly. They were jobs, it was work; some were better than others, but I was always looking for the chance to direct and/or script my own films, and finally, in the early 1960s, I got the chance, with *Whistle Down the Wind* (1961).

WWD: What was that like?

BF: Well, Hayley Mills was a big star at the time, the number one juvenile star in both Britain and the United States. She'd been in J. Lee Thompson's film *Tiger Bay* (1958) and David Swift's film for Disney, *Pollyanna* (1960).

The whole thing came about because Dickie Attenborough and I were both working as actors on a picture I co-wrote called *The Baby and the Battleship* (1956), directed by Jay Lewis, which was filmed on location in Malta. We shared a room, and although I had known Dickie for a long time—we were friends—we had never really worked together before. We both decided that we'd come to a sort of crisis point in our careers; we weren't getting anywhere. We felt that we weren't less talented than some of the people we had to work for. So we decided to form a company called Beaver Films, and I wrote a script that never saw the light of day about a British army war cameraman . . . interesting script, but it never got filmed. And then I wrote a script called *The Angry Silence* (1960), and that was a kind of landmark movie. It was a labor drama; Dickie starred in it, along with Pier Angeli and Michael Craig; it really got a lot of people upset in its depiction of how labor unions can get out of hand. I think it's still very powerful today.

This was a great start for our company, as the film, which was directed by Guy Green, did extremely well. At the same time, Carl Foreman, the producer, asked me to write a thriller for him, and so I wrote *The League of Gentlemen* (1959). It was directed by Basil Dearden, and Dickie co-produced and acted in it. This led to the creation of another parallel production company, Allied Filmmakers, which consisted of Basil Dearden, Michael Relph, Dickie, myself, Jack Hawkins, and Guy Green. That company, Allied, went on to make six or seven more films, including Basil Dearden's *Victim* (1961, which was perhaps the first serious and sympathetic examination of homosexuality on the screen), *Seance on a Wet Afternoon* (1964, which I made), and the first one we made through Allied Filmmakers: *Whistle Down the Wind.*

I originally wasn't going to direct the film; Guy Green was going to do it. But about ten days before we were going to start filming, Guy came to Dickie and me and said, "Look, I've had this wonderful offer. You're paying me five thousand pounds, and MGM wants me to direct *Light in the Piazza* (1962), with Olivia de Havilland, and they're going to pay me fifty thousand pounds. So will you please release me?" And of course, we said yes, but then we had no director, and I took over. So I was lucky, because it was a great picture to start with. Hayley Mills was wonderful to work with.

WWD: You were still doing acting jobs at that time, and you've continued to do so. Tell me about your part in J. Lee Thompson's *The Guns of Navarone* (1961).

BF: Well, that was just two days' work, but Carl Foreman called me up, and so I did it as a favor to him, sort of a good luck gesture. It was just a brief scene, bringing tea to James Robertson Justice, or something like that. But you know something? If you start life as an actor, you never turn down work. People think I've had something of a charmed life, and ask me why I've done so many things. Well, one of the reasons is that I'm trying to earn some bread! So why turn down a part like that, when it means a nice check in a good film?

WWD: Tell me about the remake of *Of Human Bondage* (1964, directed by Henry Hathaway, Ken Hughes, and Bryan Forbes).

BF: (Laughs.) Well, as an actor, there are still sacred and profane remains of my performance in that film. I wrote the script, and I was also playing the second lead opposite Laurence Harvey and Kim Novak. And both Larry and I were so appalled by the way Henry Hathaway treated Kim Novak, that on two occasions, we actually walked off the set, and said we wouldn't come back unless he apologized. But things just got worse and worse, and finally Hathaway just walked out of the studio one day and got on a plane at Dublin airport and left, just like that. He'd been shooting the picture for three or four weeks, and suddenly, we had no director. Ray Stark, who was the producer, came to me and said, "Will you direct it?" and I said, "No, I won't. I really can't direct myself, I just can't be objective about my performance. It's impossible. But what I will do is direct for a fortnight to save your bacon, and in that time, you've got to find another director."

So Ray found Ken Hughes, and he took over the film and finished it. But we had a lovely cameraman on that, Oswald Morris, and so despite all these problems and interruptions, I think it turned out to be a pretty good film. John Box was the art director. And my wife Nanette Newman was in it. We've done about seven films or so together, and we enjoy working together very much. I was very sorry when Larry Harvey died so prematurely of cancer; he was a very witty, charming, generous man, and one who really made working on any project a great deal of fun.

WWD: Another of your key films of the 1960s was *The L-Shaped Room* (1963), which is one of the most beautiful films ever shot in black and white. Do you have any thoughts on the use of black and white vs. color when filming?

BF: Yes, I'm very fond of *The L-Shaped Room*. Leslie Caron did a superb job in it, and I've lately been receiving a lot of favorable press from the gay community here in England for my casting of Brock Peters as Caron's gay friend who lives upstairs, and for Cicely Court- neidge, who was wonderful as the lesbian character in that film. But the thing is that I wasn't conscious at the time of doing anything unusual in this casting; it just seemed that it made the film more realistic for the time and place it was set in. I feel it was really very much ahead of its time. And it could only have been made, in my opinion, in black and white.

I love black and white, but what can you do, commercially? I mean, right now, they're going to remake Sir Carol Reed's *The Third Man* (1949) just to make it in color, and as far as I'm concerned, that's obscene. It's such arrogance to say you can rewrite Graham Greene. Not to mention recreating the performances of Orson Welles, or the direction of Sir Carol Reed. But anyway, I love black and white. I made one of the last big black and white films in Hol- lywood, *King Rat*, which I scripted and directed in 1965. And sub- sequently I made *The Whisperers* (1966), with Dame Edith Evans, in black and white, and you see, you couldn't make that film in color. It simply wouldn't work. That was such a superb film, I thought, and Edith was so good in it. And during the making of that, I gave my editor on the film, Tony Harvey, a week off, and he shot his first feature film, *Dutchman*, based on Leroi Jones's play, in one week's time, starring Shirley Knight and Al Freeman, Jr. A really good first film for him. And then Tony went on to make, of course, *The Lion in Winter* (1968), with Katharine Hepburn and Peter O'Toole.

WWD: How do you set up your shots? Do you storyboard in advance?

BF: No, I never use a storyboard. I respond to the actors on the floor, and I work with the director of photography to get the shots and coverage I want. I start very gently with the blocking, planning all the entrances and exits, because it's very difficult to plunge straight in to what you think is going to be the style of the movie right away. I suspect that very few people do that. It comes upon you, as it were. You've got a general idea of where you're going, but how you'll get there is something you have to find out as part of the process. And what I normally say to the actors is, "I don't mind by which route you reach my destination, but you've got to reach my destination." Because actors don't hold the whole film in their heads. They memorize their "sides" and that's it. I remember when I got the chance to direct *Whistle Down the Wind*, I went to Sir Carol Reed for some advice; he was really my mentor, and a man I greatly respected as a director. So I said, "Carol, can you give me a couple of tips?" And he gave me two wonderful tips; you won't find them in textbooks, but I think they're really essential. He said, "Never humiliate an actor, and never cut before the actors have exited the frame." For editing and continuity, it really makes things much, much simpler.

WWD: What was it like working on a black comedy like *The Wrong Box* (1966), where you have a large cast of superb comic actors at your disposal, who are also at the same time a wildly competitive group of actors to contend with? It's a Victorian screwball comedy, in a way.

BF: I loved making it. It was a very happy movie. James Villiers, Ralph Richardson, Michael Caine, Peter Sellers, Peter Cook, and Dudley Moore in their glory years, Johnnie Mills, my wife Nanette Newman, Tony Hancock (and that was his last film), Thorley Walters, and so many others. It was a huge cast, and the logistics of getting it shot were formidable, but it came off very well, and I was very pleased with the result.

WWD: Let's talk about some of the cameramen you've worked with. You worked with Gerry Turpin on *The Wrong Box*. Who are some of your favorite cameramen from this period of British cinema? Unfortunately, there were no camerawomen at the time.

BF: Yes, that's right. Well I've been very lucky. I worked with some of the great cameramen. I worked with Burnet Guffey on two occasions; he shot *King Rat* for me, and did a wonderful job. He partially shot *The Madwoman of Chaillot* (1969) for me, as well. Guffey had started as a camera operator working on John Ford's *The Informer* in 1935, so he really knew his craft completely. I worked with Claude Renoir, who is one of the great, great artists of the cinema, and as far as English cameramen, I worked with Dougie Slocombe on *The L-Shaped Room*—he was a brilliant cameraman—Gerry Turpin, of course, and Tony Imi on *The Raging Moon* (1971), which was retitled *Long Ago Tomorrow* in the states (which I thought was a pathetic title). Gerry Fisher was a lovely man, but there were some strange ones, like Wilkie Cooper, who used to always cut down trees and wave them in front of an arc lamp to get an effect. "Burn 'Em Up" Basil Emmott, who used to move like lightning on the set, shot *I Was Monty's Double* (1958), which I scripted. And of course Chris Challis, but I only worked with him as an actor, and I never worked with Jack Cardiff, either, which I'm sorry about. He was always working with Mickey Powell. I know Jack, but I never worked with him.

WWD: How on earth did you wind up directing *The Stepford Wives* (1975)?

BF: Well, the producer of the film, Edgar Scherick, called me up and said, "Do you want to direct *The Stepford Wives?* I want an Englishman to do it, to get a new slant on it." So I went to Connecticut and directed *The Stepford Wives.* I enjoyed it, and it's become something of a cult movie. They made several sequels to it. I had a lot of fun doing it, and I never took it too seriously.

WWD: I wanted to ask you about *Deadfall* (1968), which you scripted and directed. A lot of people don't like it, but I think Michael Caine is excellent in it, and it has a convincingly bleak outlook that for some reason I find appealing.

BF: Well, I think it's my most stylish picture. Gerry Turpin shot that for me. We set out to make a really elegant film, and I think we succeeded. Eric Portman was marvelous in it, and Michael Caine, who had just been introduced to films with his first major hit in Sidney J. Furie's *The Ipcress File* (1965). I know a lot of people don't like

Deadfall, but I thought it was really rather effective for what we were trying to do: a psychological cat burglar film. I think the pacing was ultimately too slow, but I really admire the film in a number of ways.

WWD: You became involved with *The Madwoman of Chaillot* (1969) when John Huston left the picture. How was that experience?

BF: Making that picture was almost an unreal experience. When I used to look through my viewfinder, I used to think, "My God, there's Charles Boyer, there's Danny Kaye, there's Yul Brynner, there's Katharine Hepburn, there's Giulietta Masina, there's Maggie Leighton, there's Dame Edith Evans, there's Claude Dauphin, there's Paul Henreid, there's Oskar Homolka, there's Donald Pleasance." It was overwhelming, as a film buff. This was the history of the cinema I was looking at.

The only person who gave me any trouble on that film was Paul Henreid. He was just incredibly pompous. I took over that film on ten days' notice from John Huston, and inherited all sorts of things, including the main cast, and all of the cast members were tied to very tight contracts, and the whole film had to be shot on a very specific and tight schedule. Henreid was one of the first people to arrive on the film, and I had an enormous scene to film with him, with the French army and everything else, and he didn't know a word! He kept blowing take after take. I tried everything I could to placate him, I shot it from different angles, but finally we'd done something like thirty-seven takes, and nothing was usable in any of it. And this was the very first day! So I thought, "Jesus Christ, what have I gotten into here?"

So at the end of the day I went back to my rented house and said to Nanette, my wife, "My God, he must be sitting in the hotel alone cutting his wrists." So I rang him and said, "Hey, come on, let's all go out to dinner." So we drove back into Nice to take him out to dinner. And over drinks I said to him, "Listen Paul, don't worry, we all have days like that," and he said, "I'm not worried. Film is cheap." And in his own autobiography, he blamed me for all the problems he had on the film, and wrote, "I never had confidence in Bryan Forbes after that moment." Well, it's ridiculous. He was an extraordinary man, very ungracious. Nobody liked him; he was the only loner on the entire film. Katharine Hepburn was very gracious and the soul of professionalism; and other than Henreid, everything ran smoothly after that opening incident. But what a way to start the picture!

WWD: How did you become involved with *International Velvet* (1976)?

BF: Well, Dick Shepherd had been my original Hollywood agent, and he'd just taken over MGM, and he was looking to do all sorts of new projects, and so he called me up and said, "We've been looking through what we've got on the list; will you remake *National Velvet* (1944, directed by Clarence Brown)?" I said, "No. Reissue the old movie." But he didn't want to do that, so he said, "Will you write a sequel?" and after a lot of discussion, I agreed to do it. I never wanted to call it *International Velvet*; I wanted to call it *Winning*, but I never had a chance. They wanted to climb on the back of the old movie, which was a big mistake, but I loved working with Tatum O'Neal, who was completely professional and very pleasant to work with. Christopher Plummer, Tony Hopkins, and my wife were in it; it was a good cast. But when the film came out, it was as if I'd introduced a new strain of cancer to the United States; the notices were really, really bad in America, although in the rest of the world it did very, very well. In America, it wasn't the year for any film that was sentimental; they didn't like Tatum, for some reason, so it was sad. Nanette and I went over to do the promotional tour in the States, and every day, it was very unpleasant indeed. I'd never received notices like that before.

WWD: What about your most recent films: *Jessie* (1980, TVM), *Better Late Than Never* (1982), *The Naked Face* (1984), and *The Endless Game* (1990, TVM)?

BF: Well, *Jessie* is a beautiful film, a really sad period piece which was shown in the United States only on PBS, although it had a theatrical run over here; a really fine film I'm very proud of. *The Naked Face* was for Cannon Films. Roger Moore, who was in the film, was an old mate, and I always wanted to work with Rod Steiger, Art Carney, and Elliot Gould, so I took the job. It was based on Sidney Sheldon's first novel, actually; shot on location in Chicago. It was a difficult shoot, but in the end, I think it turned out pretty well. I was there for nearly a year, and I had a great time. *The Endless Game* was from my own novel. I had a really fine cast in that, including Albert Finney, George Segal, Ian Holm, Kristin Scott-Thomas, Michael Medwin, and Derek De Lint, who was in Philip Kaufman's *The Unbearable Lightness of Being* (1988); I spotted him in that, and cast him in this, and he was very good indeed.

THE MAN WHO CREATED *THE AVENGERS*

On the more commercial side of 1960s British cinema, as the person who created the format and wrote, designed, and supervised the day-to-day production of one of the most popular television series of all time, *The Avengers*, Brian Clemens holds a unique place in television history. Like just about everyone else who grew up in the 1960s, one of my favorite television programs was *The Avengers*. The program went through a variety of permutations and cast members before settling into its international success in the mid 1960s, starring Patrick Macnee as John Steed and Diana Rigg as Emma Peel. After breaking in with the legendary Danzigers production company at New Elstree studios, writing innumerable television shows and "B" features, Clemens drifted into work for the British television production company ITV, and was given merely the title (*The Avengers*) by Sydney Newman, head of ITV, and told to devise a series. This he did, brilliantly.

In addition to his work in the creation, storyboarding, and everyday writing of *The Avengers* (it was Clemens who designed the famous checkerboard opening for the series, and created many of the more bizarre sets and situations for the long-running hit program by storyboarding many of his scripts for the top-flight directors who worked on the show), Brian Clemens also created the highly successful British teleseries *The Professionals*, *The New Avengers*, and *Bugs* (a British hightech sci-fi espionage thriller which is just entering a new season on British television, with all new episodes). Clemens has also written episodes for such series as *The Champions, The Baron, Secret Agent* (starring Patrick McGoohan), *Randall and Hopkirk, Ivanhoe, Man in a Suitcase, H. G. Wells' The Invisible Man* and *Mark Saber*, as well as writing the screenplays and/or stories for the feature films *Operation Murder* (1957), *Station Six Sahara* (1963, starring Carroll Baker), *And Soon the Darkness* (1970), *See No Evil* (1971, with Mia Farrow), *Dr. Jekyll and Sister Hyde* (1972), *The Golden Voyage of Sin-*

bad (1974, a Ray Harryhausen special effects spectacular), *Captain Kronos: Vampire Hunter* (1974, which Clemens also directed for Britain's fabled production company Hammer Films), *The Watcher in the Woods* (1980, a Disney film starring Bette Davis in one of her last roles of substance), *Highlander II: The Quickening* (1991, with Sean Connery and Christopher Lambert), and several episodes of the American television series *Perry Mason* (three TV movies in 1991–1992), *The Father Dowling Mysteries*, and *Remington Steele*. He won a British Academy Award (a BAFTA) for the creation and production of his British comedy series *My Wife Next Door*. Brian Clemens has literally worked with nearly every important figure in British cinema and television, and his life story is a document that is fascinating and a compelling reminder that quality television can be both entertaining and well written at the same time. The following interview was conducted on May 22, 1997.

WHEELER WINSTON DIXON: Ken Taylor [the author of *The Jewel in the Crown*] gave me your number.

BRIAN CLEMENS: God, Ken and I started out together in the industry years and years ago, but I haven't heard from him in ages.

WWD: You both broke in working for the Danziger Brothers, two of the most legendarily cost-conscious producers in the business. They made features and TV series in Britain, often with American actors. And actually, I like the Danzigers' little crime thrillers, like the short features *Feet of Clay*, *High Jump*, and the *Mark Saber* crime television series.

BC: Well, the first feature film I wrote for them was called *Operation Murder* (1957), which was directed by Ernest Morris and starred the American actor Tom Conway, George Sanders's brother. Before I got to the Danzigers, I was working for J. Walter Thompson Advertising, and I had just had a play on BBC television, *Valid for Single Journey Only*, which I'd written. And then at a bridge party one evening, one of the guests mentioned that she was working for the Danzigers, and that they needed writers, and so I was tapped for that. Working for the Danzigers was wonderful, because I had the kind of grounding working for them that only the Hollywood hacks of years ago, like Ben Hecht, or the Epstein brothers, had. For a long time, the Danzigers didn't have any studios of their own, although they eventually built some studios at New Elstree, but before that, they used to work in Elstree, ABPC, MGM, and so on. They'd move in anywhere where there were still sets standing around from big movies. And then they'd come to me and say, "Look, we've got two weeks to shoot, so we want you to write something for these sets, a seventy-minute second feature, and it must have the Old Bailey, a submarine, and a mummy's tomb in it." So I'd write it to order. And no nobody believes that they made movies like this once, but it's absolutely true. And so nowadays when people say "rewrite this," or "lose seven sets," it doesn't phase me in the least, because I've had the best training in the world. The equivalent in the United States is, of course, Roger Corman.

WWD: What kind of schedules were these films shot on? Did you ever get a chance to get down to the set?

BC: Very rarely, because if I was on the set, they'd say to me, "Why aren't you home writing?" In all the years I worked for the Danzigers, I think I only went on the set eight times in four years. They made the *Mark Saber* and all the rest of the half-hour television series in about two and a half to three days. The budgets were minuscule. About seventeen thousand pounds for a feature, which would take eight to ten days to shoot. Jimmy Wilson was their key director of photography, and he worked very very fast indeed.

WWD: What happened next?

BC: Well, my big break came, I think, when I wrote the pilot for the series Ralph Smart created, *Danger Man*, known in the United States as *Secret Agent*, with Patrick McGoohan. I got involved because by that time I'd gotten an agent, and he was looking around for work for me, and he knew they needed some help. They were hour-long shows, shot in black and white, and they were shot in about five to eight days. That was one of the first series to crack the United States network market, on CBS. The pilot I wrote was called "View from the Villa," and it was set in Italy, but the production manager set the shoot on location in Port Marion, which looked like Italy, but which was much closer. And obviously the location stuck in Patrick McGoohan's mind, because that's where he shot his television series *The Prisoner* much later. There's an amazing story connected with this first episode of *Danger Man*: the second unit director on the show shot some location and background stuff and sent the dailies back to the editing room at Elstree. Ralph Smart looked at them, hated them, and called up the second unit director and said, "Look, these are terrible, you'll never be a film director," and then he fired him. The name of the second unit director? John Schlesinger [famous for *Midnight Cowboy* and many other films].

WWD: So were you working for *Danger Man* exclusively?

BC: No, I was kind of moonlighting from the Danzigers then. I was kind of locked in with them on a weekly payroll. They didn't pay me any more for a feature or a TV episode; they were just paying me a flat fee. It was something about sixty pounds a week, which was a fair amount of money back then. Then I was called to Madrid to rewrite a film called *Mission in Morocco* which starred Lex Barker and Fernando Rey, and was, amazingly enough, directed by Tony Squire. I was in Spain about three months. They had a terrible script, and they flew me out, and I rewrote it in the time-honored way of a couple of pages a day, which I would push under the door, and then they'd go out and shoot them.

And all along, I was still turning out stuff for the Danzigers, and British television shows like *Sir Francis Drake*, *Ivanhoe*, and *H. G. Wells' The Invisible Man*; at one time, all of British episodic television was written by about ten writers, and I was one of the them. I never worked on *Robin Hood* or *The Saint*, because by that time I was busy with *The Avengers*, but that's about it. I worked on nearly everything else.

Around this time, I started working on more features, and I co-wrote *Station Six Sahara* (1963) with my good friend Bryan Forbes (who later went on to be quite a director in his own right), which was directed by Seth Holt and starred Carroll Baker and Denholm Elliott. Then I did a feature for Arthur Brauner's CC films in Germany, called *The Peking Medallion* (1967), which was shot in Berlin. That starred Nancy Kwan, Robert Stack, and Elke Sommer and was co-directed by James Hill and Frank Winterstein. James Hill, of course, went on to direct a lot of episodes of *The Avengers*. And then in 1970 I produced and wrote a film called *And Soon the Darkness*, which was directed by Robert Fuest, who directed the very famous *Dr. Phibes* films with Vincent Price. He had a great sense of style and color in his direction. Ian Wilson was the director of photography. Then I wrote a script on spec, *See No Evil* (1971), and Columbia said, "Well, if Mia Farrow plays the lead, we'll buy it," and she read it and liked it, and so they bought it and we shot it. Richard Fleischer directed that; Gerry Fisher was the director of photography. After that, I produced and wrote *Dr. Jekyll and Sister Hyde* (1972), which Roy Ward Baker directed. It was a lot of fun to make. Then I wrote the screenplay for *The Golden Voyage of Sinbad* (1974) for Charlie Schneer. Gordon Hessler directed that; it was mostly a showcase for Ray Harryhausen's superb special effects.

And then I decided to direct something, after writing all these scripts for other people. I'd written so many, and storyboarded so many, that I figured if I couldn't do it by now, I never could. So I wrote and directed *Captain Kronos: Vampire Hunter* (1974) for Hammer Films, which was the first time I'd ever directed any-thing—not even a TV show before I stepped on the stage with that one. I could have directed *The Avengers* on many occasions, and I did direct a lot of second unit work for *The Avengers*. When we shot *And Soon the Darkness*, I storyboarded lots of that with Robert Fuest, and my partner on that, Albert Fennell, who's now dead, said "Well, I think it's about time that you directed something." So with *Captain Kronos*, I finally did.

WWD: What was it like working with the Hammer unit?

BC: It was fine; as long as you stayed on schedule, it was okay. I'm very much a first take or second take man. I'd learned a lot from the Danzigers and from Corman. Although I've never met Corman, I admired the fact that he got so much shot so fast, and it looked so good. That was the key: speed and quality. And of course so many people owe their careers to Corman.

WWD: How did you then make the jump to Walt Disney for the film *Watcher in the Woods* (1980) with Bette Davis?

BC: I wrote the screenplay from a book, but I thought the end was impractical, so I suggested an alternative ending. But they said, "Oh no, this is what we want." Disney's son-in-law Ron Miller was in charge at that point; he was a nice guy, but he really didn't know anything about making movies. So I said, "Look, this ending really isn't going to work," but they insisted on it. They shot it with John

Hough directing, and then they released it, and found out that it didn't work. So they pulled it, brought in another writer, and told him to tack on the ending that I'd suggested in the first place, and then they re-released it to fairly good business.

WWD: What about *Timestalkers* (1987)?

BC: That's a TV movie, really, directed by Jerry London; it was a time travel film, sort of a forerunner of *Timecop*. It was a good project. Klaus Kinski was the villain; it was Forrest Tucker's last movie, and William Devane was the lead. And more recently, I wrote three Perry Mason TV movies in 1991–1992, just before Raymond Burr died. They were really a stretch for me. And I did the story for *Highlander II: The Quickening* (1991).

WWD: Let's talk about *The Avengers*, because that's really what made yours an international name, and got you all this work doing movie scripts. It really was one of the biggest hit television series of all time. Actually, it should be pointed out that the series was originally suggested by the head of drama at Associated British Corporation (ABC) television, Sydney Newman.

BC: Yes, but in all fairness, the only thing he came up with was the title, *The Avengers*, and he said, "I don't know what the hell it means, but it's a good title, so now go up and write something to go with it." I wrote the pilot for the series, "Hot Snow," which featured Ian Hendry, who was left over from a show called *Police Surgeon* (which was a terrible series, but ABC liked him playing the role of a young doctor). So we started out with the title, and a young doctor, Dr. Keel, played by Ian Hendry, left over from the other series. Then Newman said, "We've got to have a CIA man, or a Scotland Yard man or something in it, and we'll call him Steed," and in truth, that's all Sydney Newman gave me when he said, "Go off and write the pilot for *The Avengers*." That was the brief, so to speak. The first shows were broadcast in December, 1960; they were done on videotape.

WWD: How did Patrick Macnee get involved?

BC: The reason Patrick got plucked in was because he was available and he was cheap. He'd been in a lot of films, like Brian Desmond Hurst's *A Christmas Carol* (1951), but he was very much looking for work. He was perfect for the role; the chemistry was stunning. But it was just luck, really. It went through a lot of changes early on; Honor Blackman was in the videotape episodes, and other characters were introduced, but it wasn't until Honor Blackman left the series in March 1964 to work on *Goldfinger* and other feature film work that the series really took off. That's when we cast Diana Rigg as Emma Peel in December of 1964; she came to us as a Shakespearean actor, and she was superb. That's also when I pretty much took over, along with Brian Fennell, creating the look and the scripts for the series—for example, the chessboard opening sequence was mine—right down to the storyboards. Julian Wintle produced, and Laurie Johnson wrote a new main title theme for the series, and it all just clicked overnight. From then on, all *The Avengers* were very much my pigeon.

WWD: Who was responsible for the "pop" stylization of the series visually?

BC: That was all mine. I storyboarded it like Hitch used to do. I was totally hands on with *The Avengers*. It sounds immodest, but the whole style of *The Avengers* was me. Diana Rigg was particularly fun to work with; she was a young, very young, inexperienced, unknown actress, who happened to have a lot of talent. She was very professional to work with. I have nothing but good things to say about her, and she never gave us a moment's problem all during the production of the series. She enjoyed herself immensely on the series; we all did. They were all shot on ten-day schedules, so we had to work very fast. But because we planned everything out to the nth degree, they all looked great.

Patrick Macnee was great to work with; Patrick's one of my best friends, actually. I always think that when he goes, it will be a bit like losing Trafalgar column. A consummate professional, and always grateful to *The Avengers*—he's not one of those actors who make their name in a series, and then spend the rest of their lives knocking it. The whole series was re-run on A&E in the United States to excellent ratings. There were something like 87 filmed episodes, one hour each, and with the video episodes added in I would guess that about 140 episodes survive; some went out live in the early days, or the videotapes were lost. Once we got onto film, we were able to save everything. Even in film, in black and white, our budgets were very, very low—under forty thousand pounds for an episode. Try to do that today! And we *begged* them, we begged them, for another three thousand pounds per week to put them in color, but they wouldn't do it. They had no idea what they had. We wanted to shoot in color from day one, the moment we got on 35mm film. And they said, "No, we're not gonna take that chance, that's another three thousand pounds per episode."

We cast so many guest stars that it became a weekly game. "What name star can we get in the series now." If we were shooting it now, we'd try very hard to get Steve Martin, for example. We'd see who we could get, and then we'd write the script around the guest star in lots of cases, depending on what they could do. In the end of the series, it was a bit like *Laugh-In*, because everybody wanted to be on the show; we were that big of a hit. As a guest star on *The Avengers*, you got money, you had fun, and you were in a very interesting and different series where you could do whatever you liked, really. We got John Cleese from *Monty Python's Flying Circus*; Peter Cushing worked on it, Donald Sutherland, Valentine Dyall, Clifford Evans, Nigel Green, Freddie Jones, Charlotte Rampling, Andrew Kier, Michael Gough, Patrick Magee, Dennis Price, Barbara Shelley. We got everyone we wanted, practically.

Wilkie Cooper, Gerry Turpin, Alan Hume, and Gilbert Taylor were rotating directors of photography; between them they shot most of the episodes. Alan Hume went on to shoot the Bond films; Gil Taylor went on to win an Academy Award for his work as a DP. You see, the difference in the look of *The Avengers* is that nowadays, if you shoot a TV show, you get a TV crew. But in those days, if you went on the studio floor, you got the very best theatrical motion picture crew you could imagine; these were all top, top professionals. Roy Ward Baker, Gordon Flemyng, Robert Fuest, Don Leaver, James Hill, and Charles Crichton were some of the directors, and they were all first rate. Roy Ward Baker had a long Hollywood career, and his films are really superb. So all of these people brought extra quality to the look and design of the series as a whole.

WWD: Who was the person who cast Linda Thorson to replace Diana Rigg in *The Avengers*?

BC: Well, that was a producer named John Bryce. Albert Fennell and myself had a falling out with ABC television UK, and we left the series for about five or six weeks, during which time they pursued us all over the place trying to get us to come back, and it was then that John Bryce cast Linda Thorson as Tara King. Linda's okay, but I wouldn't have cast her.

WWD: What can you tell me about the episode "The Forget-Me Knot," in which Tara King (Linda Thorson) and Emma Peel (Diana Rigg) exchange places? Wasn't Linda Thorson already a part of the show by this point?

BC: Well, there was that hiatus when we left the series, and when we came back, we said, "Well, we've got to have an episode to introduce Linda Thorson to the audience, and I *hate* killing off characters, so let's just figure out a way to have Emma Peel make a more graceful exit." I think it's an act of weakness when you kill off the lead; everybody hates that, and you've also closed the door to any possibility of doing anything with the character in the future, as well. I'm very proud of that show, because Steed loses the girl and gets the girl, so to speak, in virtually the same shot. It's something I'm very happy with.

WWD: How involved are you in *The Avengers* (1998) movie?

BC: Not at all. What happened was that EMI, who owned *The Avengers*—because I don't own it—they sold it to Cannon, who sold it to someone else, and eventually it wound up at Warner Brothers. Sean Connery is going to play the villain, and Ralph Fiennes will play Steed, Uma Thurman will play Emma Peel and Jeremiah Chechik will direct the film. [Note: Clemens made these remarks before the final film was completed. *The Avengers* movie was released in 1998 to nearly universal critical pans; the overblown epic failed utterly to capture the economy and style of the original series. This is sad for a number of reasons, but primarily because it prevents anyone else from doing another film based on the characters for the foreseeable future.]

WWD: What about other series you were involved in during this time?

BC: Well, *The Champions, The Baron, Randall and Hopkirk*, and all those other series were being made in the next office practically at Elstree by my good friend Dennis Spooner, who unfortunately is no longer with us, the guy who wrote *Pennies from Heaven*. Whenever he had an opening in one of his series, he'd say, "Come on over and write a *Champions* for me," and whenever I had an opening in *The Avengers*, I'd say, "Come over and write one for me." So we swapped back and forth, and I wrote a bunch of episodes for these series.

WWD: How did *The New Avengers* come about? Were you responsible for the series?

BC: Totally. I mean, I produced it, and wrote it, and so on. In retrospect, I think it came out very well. All the episodes that we shot in England came out very well, indeed. In fact, I think that one episode, "Dead Men Are Dangerous," is one of the best episodes of any of *The Avengers* series, along with perhaps "The House That Jack Built" from the first series. But then we ran into money problems from the French, who were co-producers of *The New Avengers*, and as a result they said, "You've got to make some in France, and you've got to make some in Canada," and it made an enormous difference in the quality of the episodes. As soon we moved into another country, we started to lose control.

WWD: What about *The Professionals*, the next series you created?

BC: Well, that was quite simple. We stopped making *The Avengers*, and the guys who showed it over here in the UK said, "We'd like you to make us a new series." And we said, "What kind of a show?" And they said, "A cop show." And so that's how *The Professionals* was born. "We'd like a buddy show," they said, "not like *Starsky and Hutch*, but something with a bit more bite." So I invented *The Professionals*, with Gordon Jackson, Lewis Collins, and Martin Shaw in it. Again, we had great writers on it: Dennis Spooner, Chris Wicking, and Tony Barwick were just a few. Charles Crichton directed a few of those shows, as well. A very dear man.

WWD: What about *The Protectors*?

BC: Well, that was a Gerry Anderson show, one of his first stabs at directing live actors instead of puppets, as on his old shows *Thunderbirds* and *Captain Scarlet*. Well, instead of directing bits of wood, he decided to get actors. Robert Vaughn and Nyree Dawn Porter were the stars; a lot of people took turns directing, including Don Chaffey, Charles Crichton, Michael Lindsay-Hogg, Roy Ward

Baker, Cyril Frankel, even Robert Vaughn himself directed an episode. I wrote some episodes, which were all thirty minutes; Dennis Spooner, John Goldsmith, and Sylvia Anderson wrote others. They produced a total of fifty-two shows; it even ran for a time in the United States.

WWD: Tell me about your latest series, *Bugs*.

BC: Well, that's a high tech series, and Carnival Films came to me here and said, "Nobody's doing escapist TV series anymore, they're all very nitty-gritty, and would you like to do something that's high-tech escapism along those lines, the kind of series you used to do?" And I said, "Sure," because I love those sort of pop, upbeat, escapist kinds of series, and I think the audience needs this sort of entertainment, particularly in difficult times. There's a place for brutal realism, like the British TV series *Prime Suspect*, but you need something to balance it, so that the audience has a choice.

WWD: Could you share a bit with us on your working methods? How fast do you wrote a script?

BC: Well, I do write them very quickly, it's true. Sometimes I write them very quickly indeed. *And Soon the Darkness* I wrote in a weekend. But I'd been blocking it in my mind for several months, so all I was really doing was putting it down on paper. Series episodes were also written very quickly: I had to write "The Forget-Me Knot" in a weekend, simply to keep up with the production schedule. What I had to do was block it in my mind, put it on paper, and then give them the design for the set so they could go ahead and build it so we could get it shot on time and on budget. So they built the sets before they'd seen the script.

I don't dictate scripts; I don't use a computer. I have a number of little old portable typewriters—one in Hollywood, one in Spain, and about five here in my house—and I just write my scripts on those. You see, when I was a little boy, about five years old, my father said to me, "What do you want to be?" I said, "A writer," and so very wisely he bought me a typewriter. And then when I went into the army for two years, I got a little bored, and I took a typing course to brush up. That really got me started on the craft of writing.

My normal procedure for writing is I block it out roughly in my head what's going to happen in what order, and then I write telegrams to myself, just one line for each scene. Then I expand upon that, and of course, as you write it, it changes, mostly for the better. My general principle is if I'm writing television, I aim for ten pages a day; for a feature, five pages a day. That's about my average pace. Writing screenplays is second nature to me now; there are a dozen things I want to write. Right now I'd like to do a *film noir*, something like John Dahl's *Red Rock West*, or a Raymond Chandler kind of thing. I think I'm going to start on it this weekend. My two favorite directors, by the way, are John Ford and Hitchcock—the old masters. I like the "little" films that nobody seems to notice but me; the little suspense films like *Time Lock* that really get the suspense going. Films like *Trainspotting* are okay. I wasn't entertained by it, but I had to see it, because it's part of our industry now. Another example is *Reservoir Dogs*. I thought *Reservoir Dogs* was a wonderful film, but I hated it. Every so often nowadays you get a really good film like *Speed*; that was a terrific film. But films lack style somehow these days. The other evening I watched *Pat and Mike*, the old Katharine Hepburn and Spencer Tracy film, and it had style and charm. It really worked as a piece of filmmaking.

WWD: Of all the projects you've worked on, what was the most satisfying for you?

BC: *The Avengers*, without a doubt. It was such a wonderful time, it was the '60s, they were the halcyon days, and I was living in a Golden Age. You never really know you're living in a Golden Age until it's over, you know? Golden Ages are always then, not now, aren't they? But I had so much, and I met so many wonderful people, like Charles Crichton, Roy Ward Baker, people like that. I was working with the best of the British film industry, and learning from them. And things were inexpensive; now everything costs a fortune. But with *The Avengers*, we really lucked on to something. Without a doubt, it was the most fulfilling time of my life.

A SOCIETY WITHOUT IMAGES

In direct contrast to the panoply of filmic representations of society and self created by the British government from the earliest years of cinema onward, the cinema in New Zealand has been marked mostly by the absence of film production, until a recent boom of production in the 1980s. As Helen Martin and Sam Edwards document in their superb survey of New Zealand cinema, *New Zealand Film 1912–1996*, indigenous feature film production in New Zealand as late as 1976 was distressingly sparse, and the country survived on a diet of films imported from the UK, the U.S., and other countries to keep the local audiences satisfied. Indeed, the first multiplex cinema didn't arrive in New Zealand until 1991, a six-theatre facility in Palmerston North dubbed the Downtown 6 (Katz 1009). While the New Zealand cinema in the late 1970s to the present has given us such diverse talents as Roger Donaldson (director of *Sleeping Dogs* [1977] and *Smash Palace* [1981]), Jane Campion (director of *Angel at my Table* [1990] and the international box-office hit *The Piano* [1993]), and Peter Jackson (whose film *Heavenly Creatures* [1994] also did well in theatrical screenings around the globe), as well as the actor Sam Neill, to name just a few artists currently dominating public attention, for the first seventy years of the twentieth century, practically no films were made in New Zealand at all.

This is doubly surprising because, at the turn of the twentieth century, New Zealand's amateur cinéastes were engaged in cinematographic experiments similar to those conducted by Augustin Le Prince, Thomas Edison, and The Lumière Brothers. In 1895, A. H. Whitehouse exhibited motion pictures for the first time in New Zealand using Edison's kinetoscope (Martin and Edwards 8), in which viewers had to use a "peep show" device to watch each short film individually. On October 13, 1896, the Opera House in Auckland, New Zealand, was the site of the first projection of motion pictures in that country, again using Edison's equipment, in this case the kinematograph (Martin and Edwards 8). By 1898, Whitehouse was filming brief, Lumière-like actualities (the opening of the Auckland Exhibition on December 1, 1898; a horse race at Ellerslie in Auckland on December 26, 1898), and it seemed as if New Zealand would soon join the international "boom" of film production (Martin and Edwards 9). But it was not until 1905 that the Bioram 9 Company began filming "actualities" throughout New Zealand, in which local people and places were filmed on the road, hastily developed, and then shown the next day to the participants, a process emulated in the Soviet Union by Dziga Vertov's Kino Eye Collective in the early twentieth century, and still used by ethnographers in the age of digital video today (Martin and Edwards 9). From this point on, progress was slow and painful, particularly in the realm of feature films.

The pioneer French filmmaker Gaston Méliès (brother of George Méliès) brought a crew with him to New Zealand to film *Loved by a Maori Chieftess* (1913), *Hinemoa* (1914), and *How Chief Te Ponga Won His Bride* (1913), but these were really foreign projects that used New Zealand legends and locations as the backdrop for the productions, and in any event, no known footage of any of these films survives today (Martin and Edwards 20–22). Local feature film production began in earnest with George Tarr's *Hinemoa* (1914), a version of the Maori legend of Hinemoa and Tutanekai, but again, this film, shot (naturally) on nitrate stock, has been completely lost to posterity (Martin and Edwards 23). The same fate befell Rawdon Blandford's *The Test* (1916), and Raymond Longford's *A Maori Maid's Love* (1916) and *The Mutiny of the Bounty* (1916) (Martin and Edwards 24–26). William Desmond Taylor's *Beyond* (1921) is another foreign production using New Zealand as a narrative location, in this case an American melodrama produced by Famous-Players Lasky (Martin and Edwards 27), but surprisingly, although the film was set in New Zealand, it was shot entirely in Hollywood. It is interesting to note that between 1916 and 1921 not one feature film was produced in New Zealand; rather, United States films such as the pedestrian *Beyond* were allowed to dominate the New Zealand box-office. As Sam Edwards notes,

> *Beyond* seems only peripherally associated with New Zealand, but it represents the first example of a feature utilizing exotic New Zealand as a setting while actually being shot in the United States. It is typical also of the melodramatic romances which appeared on screens around the world and which influenced filmmakers far beyond Hollywood's environs, despite their rapid production time and rather unremarkable production values. Furthermore it was typical of what audiences [in New Zealand] would see, as within the next five or six years the American studios would supply between two-thirds and three-quarters of all films registered by the New Zealand censor's office. (Martin and Edwards 27)

In 1921, Beaumont Smith directed a romance entitled *The Betrayer*, but this film also disintegrated with the passage of time (Martin and

Edwards 28). The epic film *The Birth of New Zealand* (1922), directed by Harrington Reynolds, followed this production, a 132-minute series of historical reenactments of which only fragments remain in the New Zealand Film Archive (Martin and Edwards 29). In 1922, Rudall Hayward wrote, produced, and directed *My Lady of the Cave*, a film which Hayward completed on a budget of £1000 at the remarkable age of twenty-two (Martin and Edwards 30). Still, it can hardly be said that the New Zealand film industry was developing at a rapid rate. By this time, in both America and Britain, an entire industry, complete with sophisticated studios and distribution systems, had been well-established, and because of the technical sophistication and availability of foreign product, it continued to dominate the New Zealand box-office, much to the detriment of local entrepreneurs. Nor did matters improve much in the ensuing years. George Tarr's 1922 *Ten Thousand Miles in the Southern Cross* is a documentary feature of a tour of the South Pacific, of which only sixteen minutes survive (Martin and Edwards 31). Henry J. Makepeace's *The Romance of Sleepy Hollow* (1923) has vanished altogether, leaving only a poster to advertise its phantasmal existence, and a record of censorship and required cuts in the film (from 5700 feet in November of 1923, to 4800 feet in December of that year) before the film was released to the public (Martin and Edwards 32). James R. Sullivan's *Venus of the South Seas* is a pearl-diving romance starring Annette Kellerman which has survived the ravages of time, a modest and engaging action melodrama which seems both fresh and authentic in its execution. At the brief feature running time of fifty minutes, the film is also economical and captures the attention of even the contemporary observer through its innocence and charm (Martin and Edwards 33).

As the silent era drew to a close, the New Zealand productions remained few, and surviving materials are scarce. Rudall Hayward's first filming of *Rewi's Last Stand* (1925), Beaumont Smith's *The Adventures of Algy* (1925), Arthur Messenger's government-sponsored documentary *Glorious New Zealand* (1925), Edwin Coubray's *Carbine's Heritage* (1927), Gustav Pauli's *The Romance of Hine-Moa* (1927), Pauli's *Under the Southern Cross* (1927), and Hayward's *The Te Kooti Trail* (1927) and *The Bush Cinderella* (1928) survive in varying states—on some titles, no footage is available; on others, a complete print can be viewed (Martin and Edwards 34–41). Gustav Pauli's *The Romance of Hine-Moa*, in particular, seems a beautifully composed film, although one's opinions must be based solely upon the single surviving reel of the production, which was "discovered in a garden shed outside London in 1981" (New Zealand Film Archive Database). The film, which was shot "in 1925 on various locations around Lake Rotorua and on White Island" (New Zealand Film Archive Database) was premiered in London on December 16, 1926, and released throughout New Zealand in 1927. In its unaffected naturalism and evocative use of color tints, the surviving fragments of *The Romance of Hine-Moa* offer a tantalizing glimpse of a lost vision of early New Zealand cinema.

But still it seemed that simplistic romances, travelogues, and historical pageants preoccupied New Zealand's filmmakers, while Hollywood seemed only too content to relegate New Zealand to the status of a "filmic colony"—a useful, if not particularly profitable place for the exportation of American feature films, and a location for the occasional "exotic" feature. One such film was Lew Collins's 1929 *Under the Southern Cross*, a sound/silent hybrid film initiated by Carl Laemmle of Universal Pictures, who originally financed one Alexander Markey to direct the film, under the working title *Taranga*. When Markey went over-schedule and over-budget, Laemmle ordered Collins, who had been serving as assistant director on the film, to take over the project, which was released in both sound and silent versions in Great Britain as *Under the Southern Cross*, and in the United States under the more sensationalistic title *The Devil's Pit* (Martin and Edwards 42). Despite the hand of a Hollywood studio, only fragments of the film's outtakes survive. Matters did not improve with Edward T. Brown's sound production *The Romance of Maoriland* (1930), which was to have been the first full-length "talking" picture produced and released in New Zealand. Another historical pageant, the film sought to illustrate New Zealand's history for then-contemporary audiences, and remind audiences (according to the film's prefatory intertitles) of the "romantic foundation upon which our far-flung Empire is built" (Martin and Edwards 43). Although the film was passed by the New Zealand censor on August 14, 1930, the film was never released, and exists today only in a thirty-minute fragment, as yet another evanescent project in the history of New Zealand cinema.

In 1934, the 35mm color and black and white sound documentary *Romantic New Zealand*, partially shot in Trucolor (or Trucolour, as it was spelled in New Zealand), was produced by the government as an inducement to tourism. Featuring the usual assortment of scenic splendors and fleeting historical reenactment, the film was shot by Bert Bridgman, Cyril Morton, and Charles Barton, and projects the image of New

Zealand as "a fully established outpost of the British empire," as the narrator intones (Martin and Edwards 44). *Down on the Farm* (1935) followed, directed by Steward Pitt; unfortunately, only disjointed fragments of this early sound film remain today (Martin and Edwards 45), with rather terrible picture and sound quality. Other early sound films, including *Hei Tiki* (1935), directed and produced by the colorful impresario Alexander Markey; *Phar Lap's Son* (1936), a racing drama directed by Dr. A. L. Lewis, of which no known footage still exists; J. J. W. Pollard's *The Wagon and the Star* (1936), of which only "one reel and some out-take footage" remains; and *On the Friendly Road* (1936), directed by Leonard P. Leary for the New Zealand Film Guild (see Martin and Edwards 46–49) are all rough-hewn films produced under considerable strain and budgetary economies. The budget for *On the Friendly Road*, for example, was a mere £800, and this for a full-length, 84-minute film! But even at this relatively late date in sound film production, the drought of product wasn't over. After Rudall Hayward's production on *Rewi's Last Stand* (1940), which documented a famous historical battle between Maori and colonial forces in the 1860s, feature film production in New Zealand effectively ceased for an entire decade. This is a pity, because both *On the Friendly Road* and *Rewi's Last Stand* are remarkably polished efforts. The figure of the Rev. Colin G. Scrimgeour as Uncle Scrim dominates the sunny optimism of *On the Friendly Road*, a film that was inspired by the Reverend's popular radio broadcasts presented under the same title. The film's tale of a man falsely accused and then absolved of guilt is both slight and fanciful, yet Rudall Hayward's cinematography is both deft and graceful, as is Hayward's editorial supervision of the project. Even more impressive is *Rewi's Last Stand*, which Rudall Hayward wrote, produced, and directed, centering on a decisive battle between Maori and colonial forces during New Zealand's pioneer era. Evenly portraying both sides, *Rewi's Last Stand* stands in stark contrast to John Ford's westerns of the same period, for example, and portrays Maori society as both noble and under continual attack from the colonial forces who, somewhat reluctantly, seek their destruction. *Rewi's Last Stand* depicts a battle that is still being waged in New Zealand society: a conflict that is both profound and unavoidable in any telling of the history of the formation of New Zealand as it is today.

As astounding as it might appear, between 1940 and the 1950 production of the glorified newsreel *British Empire Games 1950*, not a single feature film was completed within New Zealand. World War II came and went, the twentieth century entered the Atomic Age, and New Zealand's filmgoers were still obliged to subsist on images imported from Hollywood and Great Britain, with Hollywood films still comprising the bulk of the imports. No doubt, New Zealand audiences could take some marginal comfort in their "transgressional reinscription" reception of these imported visions of human existence, reinscribing their own culture across the narratives they were forced to consume. *Broken Barrier* (1952), directed and produced by Roger Mirams and John O'Shea, ended the long dry spell with a pioneering tale of interracial relationships which seemed quite daring for the period. In my interview with John O'Shea, he told me that the film came about when Mirams suggested that the two of them film a documentary about Maori life. "How boring!" responded O'Shea, and suggested that the pair tackle a fictional film, with what O'Shea described as the "simplest, oldest plot in the world; boy meets girl, boy loses girl, boy gets girl back. We stuck to this very simple scenario, and the film worked" (Dixon interview). This film, too, was shot on a shoestring and yet, with a voice-over sound track, rather than sync sound, an indication of the fact that the film was shot with "two [silent] 35mm 200 ft. load Arriflex cameras, one on loan from Movietone News and the other picked up from an allegedly dead German in the Western desert . . . [coupled with] a rickety dolly and some lights cobbled together from scrap metal," as O'Shea later recalled (Martin and Edwards 52). The film, though somewhat crude, was perceived by most critics and viewers as a deeply felt, personal, and authentic film, and at a running time of only sixty-nine minutes *Broken Barrier* is an almost mesmerizing neorealist document.

But matters did not improve with Ken Annakin's 1964 *The Seekers*, a British-based production starring Jack Hawkins, which used New Zealand merely as a colorful backdrop for yet another fable of colonialist domination (Martin and Edwards 52–53). In fact, from 1952, it was not until 1964—twelve years later—that John O'Shea would again try his hand at directing a feature film, with the bizarrely downbeat *Runaway* (1964), which originally ran one hundred and two minutes, but was retitled *Runaway Killers*, and slashed to eighty minutes, for British release (Martin and Edwards, 54). Essentially a "road picture," *Runaway* tells the story of David Manning, a young accountant who lives beyond his means and is forced to abandon his career and attempt a metaphorical escape back into his own childhood. Picked up by a wealthy young woman on the road, Manning becomes involved in a series of tangled relationships, ending in a scene vaguely reminiscent of Raoul Walsh's *High Sierra* (1941), in which Manning, finally alone, seeks to escape across a mountain pass with the police in pursuit (Martin and Edwards 54). Of all the surviving films of New Zealand's formative years, it is *Runaway* that impresses me most. I was fortunate to conduct an interview with John O'Shea on August 5, 1999, and he astounded me by telling me that *Runaway* was shot without sync-sound for a total budget of £28,000, with all the sound added later (Dixon interview). *Runaway*'s existential downbeat feeling echoes the 1960s films of Losey, Richardson, Anderson, and other British filmmakers, but O'Shea told me that Michelangelo Antonioni's *L'Avventura* (1960) was the major influence on the film, and that the cast and crew would screen sections of Antonioni's films each night "to keep in the proper spirit" during production (Dixon interview). Oddly enough, the middle section of the film (in which David, the young protagonist tries to drop out of New Zealand society) has eerie echoes of Edgar Ulmer's *Detour* (1945), although O'Shea claims never to have seen the film. Early on in the film, David hitches a ride with an obnoxious businessman who has a heart condition, and then steals the man's car and papers when the man unexpectedly dies of a heart attack. Manning continues on his journey despite this, picking up a young woman, Diana (Deidre McCarron) along the way, before hiking alone into the mountains to his death in a final attempt to escape the police. Not surprisingly, the character of David Manning became something of a counter-cultural hero among disaffected New Zealand youth, but O'Shea denies that this was his intent. O'Shea saw the central character as "a weakling who can't face up to the responsibilities of life" and a character who, as another member of the cast observes "likes things too much" (Dixon interview). With its moody black and white cinematography, picturesque dialogue and subdued cool jazz score, *Runaway* is a superb film that demands repeated viewing. Unfortunately, *Runaway* is not available on commercial videocassette, and my viewing of the film was confined to the New Zealand Film Archive. When I asked O'Shea how he felt about this, he suggested that perhaps the film wouldn't turn a profit on a commercial video release. Perhaps he's right, but that's hardly the question. *Runaway* is a masterpiece of international 1960s cinema, and should be seen by the widest possible audience.

This brooding, reflexive film was nevertheless not a particular hit at the box-office, and O'Shea followed it up two years later with a lightweight musical, *Don't Let It Get You*, in which a group of popular musicians essentially play themselves, with the narrative stripped down to near nonexistence, a job that O'Shea simply took on as a commission, and on which he actually fell asleep during the shooting of one sequence because he was both over-tired (from other projects, such as commercials and industrials) and bored with the film as a whole. *Don't Let It Get You* was a commercial hit, precisely because of the various pop acts it so effectively showcased, but it was hardly a great leap forward artistically. Nevertheless, despite the financial success of this rather unambitious film (reminiscent of Richard Lester's *It's Trad, Dad* [1962], *A Hard Day's Night* [1964]) and other musical revues of the period), it was not until 1972 that New Zealand produced another native feature film, *To Love a Maori*, a 16mm low-budget production that proved to be Rudall and Ramai Hayward's swan song as producers/directors (Martin and Edwards 56). Forced once again to compromise in terms of their budget and use the smaller 16mm format rather than 35mm, the Haywards were nevertheless the first New Zealanders to create a full-length color film shot entirely in New Zealand (Martin and Edwards 56), an astonishing situation when one considers the state of international film production by 1972.

This brief survey of the New Zealand feature film up to 1972 is frustrating primarily because, despite the fact that a number of talented men and women tried to bring the feature film into full flower, and even with government support (of a limited kind), in the end, very little was accomplished, and even less survives. In addition, low budgets and hurried production schedules conspired to isolate New Zealand cinema from the international marketplace. However, in an effort to see for myself what it would be like to live in a "society without images," I traveled to both the Amsterdam Filmmuseum, and the New Zealand Film Archive in the summer of 1999, to see not only the surviving segments of those New Zealand films that have managed to escape the ravages of time and neglect, but also to better understand precisely why it took so long for the New Zealand film industry to establish itself as a world force. Why, for so many years during the first part of the twentieth century, had New Zealand feature film production existed only as a personal, highly independent and marginalized affair, bereft of studio support, swamped by American and British imports, and unable to sustain growth and continued expansion as the commercial cinema was able to do in so many other countries throughout the world? The results that I brought back were both surprising and disturbing.

As Sarah Davy of the New Zealand Film Archive told me in an e-mail exchange prior to my visiting the archive, the problem with understanding the New Zealand Cinema is that it is not [a] straightforward [task] to arrange for a "representative selection" of NZ feature films. Ours is not a cinema of "canonical classics." Filmmaking in this country up to the 1970s was of a more local, personal and irregular nature. We have, for example, a series of 2-reeler "community comedies" ([such as] *Daughter of Dunedin, Frances of Fielding*) which were made by traveling filmmakers using the resources, locations and people of towns and cities in NZ in the 1920s. Many features made prior to 1940 only survive in fragmentary form ([such as] *The Romance of Hine-Moa, Birth of New Zealand, Down on the Farm*), and there were only 3 features made between 1940 and 1970 (*Runaway, Don't Let It Get You* and *Broken Barrier*). (e-mail to author, July 27, 1999)

But why, I continued to wonder, was there no major film studio established in New Zealand until the 1970s? Why has the industry flourished in the period from 1970 to the present, yet remained relatively moribund for the first seventy years of this century, when in nearly every other country one cares to mention the establishment of a film studio system was, by this time, an accomplished fact?

The answer lies partly in the fact the American and British films were so easy to export, and on the colonial stranglehold that the American star system had on the local populace, coupled with the continued influx of films from Great Britain. Another factor seems to have been active interference on the part of the New Zealand government; as director John O'Shea noted, his film *Runaway*, for example, was not warmly received in certain official quarters. According to O'Shea, a certain bureaucrat told him that "never again would [Pacific Film Productions Ltd., O'Shea's company] make another feature film, because 'films should be happy'" (Martin and Edwards 12). This may account for the fact that O'Shea's next film, *Don't Let It Get You*, is a relentlessly upbeat musical, one which would have no problem with censorship or government interference.

Censorship itself seems to have had a firm grip on the New Zealand film industry for quite some time, to deleterious effect. Violence was heavily censored in the early 1960s, particularly the output of Hammer Films in England, who were then involved in reigniting the heritage of the Gothic cinema at the world box-office (see Churchman 40–49). Sexual material was also heavily censored. When the relatively tame production by Joseph Strick of James Joyce's *Ulysses* was released in

1967, the film was shown in New Zealand in separate cinemas for men and women. When the film was shown at universities or in smaller towns, a rope was erected as a makeshift barrier in the middle of the projection area to prevent the sexes from mixing together during the screening (Watson and Shuker 48). It was not until 1976 that Vilgot Sjöman's relatively tame sex-themed film *I Am Curious–Yellow* (1967) was passed for screening to private film societies, and on the whole, the New Zealand government seemed more interested in the first three quarters of the twentieth century in producing bland documentaries to increase tourism rather than forging new ground in the cinema. It was, finally, economic considerations rather than artistic ones that sparked the first wave of aggressive feature film production in New Zealand in 1980, when a series of tax regulations and loopholes allowed producers to write off production costs on their films, creating a boom which led to the production of fourteen feature films in 1984, as compared to two in 1980 (Martin and Edwards 13).

But a deeper, more disturbing factor was suggested to me by John O'Shea during our August 5, 1999 interview. The lack of indigenous New Zealand cinema between 1900 and 1972 stems, according to O'Shea, not only from censorship problems and a lack of government support, but also from the fact that the New Zealand National Film Unit "was not interested in drama—it's a denying society [in New Zealand]. They [the Colonial government] stole the land from the Maoris, in a very proper way, and they didn't want to tell the truth about it" (Dixon interview). Continuing along these lines, O'Shea noted that he felt "we will soon have a Balkan situation here" in the ongoing conflict between the Maoris and the Pakehas (whites), a conflict which is omnipresent in every aspect of contemporary New Zealand society. Despite conciliatory gestures by both sides, O'Shea feels that "the rednecks" on both sides will keep pushing until the situation explodes, which presents a rather grim prospect for New Zealand's future. Nevertheless, O'Shea's bleak prognosis goes a long way toward explaining why mainstream fiction filmmaking was never actively taken up by government or industry. In O'Shea's view, it is only recently that New Zealanders have come to grips with their past. O'Shea also points to the continued Americanization of cinema as "an ominous thing—audiences are used to opulence and special effects. Hollywood degrades the world and seduces the innocents of the world—teenagers, children, the 5 to 35 set—with glamour and hype. Because of this confection, the world faces indigestion and early heart attacks [from Hollywood product]" (Dixon interview). Now, as then, the majority of films shown on New Zealand screen are Hollywood product, and the occasional contemporary New Zealand film, such as Robert Sarkie's *Scarfies* (1999), a mordant dark comedy about a group of potentially murderous college students, is a welcome exception to the general commercial rule.

But in the formative years of New Zealand cinema, there was a distinct segregation of Maori and colonial white culture, with Maori rites and customs being relegated to curiosity status in a variety of shorts and documentaries (as we have seen), and the use of "exoticized" women in "action" roles to cross the racial barrier in early commercial cinema. One such example is *Venus of the South Seas*, a 1924 romance/adventure film directed by James R. Sullivan, and starring Annette Kellerman as Shona Royal, a young woman who acts as a figure of transgressive reinscription across the racial divide that separated the culture. Kellerman, an accomplished diver and champion swimmer, first attracted public attention when she was arrested in Boston in 1907 for appearing in public in a one-piece bathing suit (New Zealand Film Archive Database). While the plot of *Venus of the South Seas* is slight, the film affords the contemporary viewer an excellent example of the ways in which simple melodrama could be used to subvert the Maori's claim to New Zealand soil. The exterior scenes of the film were shot in Nelson, while the film's interiors were completed in improvised studios in Christchurch. The public reception to this simple fable was guardedly favorable:

> The story concerns a lonely pearl-diver and his beautiful daughter, Shona. She is a child of nature, a goddess of the seas, and one [moonlit] night romance comes to her when she swims out to a strange boat and meets the hero. A rival pearl pirate, on the death of the old man, attempts villainy, but the young man pits himself against him, and, naturally, all ends well. Playing opposite Miss Kellerman is Mr. Norman French, who does excellent acting, and makes a manly hero all through. (*Evening Post* review, June 7, 1924, as collected in the New Zealand Film Archive Database)

Venus of the South Seas thus commingles the exotic and the prosaic within the compass of a predictable genre narrative, while simultaneously displacing Maori culture from the center of the film's fictive world.

Other early domestic comedies were less spectacular, and relied more upon location shooting, the use of well-known local personalities to enhance box-office appeal, and a slapstick framework to deliver a reassuring message of social order to the filmgoing public. *Frances of Fielding* (1928) is typical of this genre, a two-reel comedy directed by J. S. Vinsen. The plot is aptly outlined by the New Zealand Film Archive Database in a few terse sentences:

A community comedy set in Fielding using local people in the leading roles. The new school teacher is courted by Ken the journalist and part time fireman and Tom the grocery clerk, who play tricks to discredit each other. Kidnapping and a car chase follow. Scenes of Fielding include: stockyards, main street traffic, bowling green, primary school pupils at assembly and attending classes, exercises and games. (New Zealand Film Archive Database)

As critic Clive Sowry noted of these "community comedies,"

Community films used a stock script with a simple story that could be filmed quite cheaply against a background of familiar beauty spots with a cast of local players. By travelling from town to town in the silent days, producers could make the same film over and over again relying on local interest to make the venture profitable. The idea of making such community films originated in America and came to New Zealand via Australia early in 1928. The script called for a leading lady, a hero, a comedian villain, and as many local people as could be fitted into the crowd scenes. (Clive Sowry, April 1994, as collected in the New Zealand Film Archive Database)

Rudall Hayward cut his cinematic teeth on these cheerfully primitive two-reel farces, directing, among other projects, *A Daughter of Christchurch* (1929) and *A Daughter of Dunedin* (1928), both silent two-reel films. The plot of *A Daughter of Dunedin* is much the same as that of *Frances of Fielding*, as the following synopsis attests:

A community comedy set in Dunedin. The arrogant Freddy Fishface causes trouble trying to woo the pretty school teacher from Dogtown. His efforts are no match for the romantic "he-shiek" Bill Cowcocky.

A Daughter of Christchurch followed much the same mold.

> The arrogant Freddy Fishface is no match for the handsome Bill Cowcocky and his friends from the country. He wins the hand of the pretty school teacher in a battle of wit and goodness. (New Zealand Film Archive Database)

That these films were popular with the general public is beyond dispute, as the following review of *A Daughter of Dunedin* from the *Otago Daily Times* for Thursday, November 29, 1928, makes abundantly clear.

> The Dunedin public has shown a great deal of interest in the filming of "A Daughter of Dunedin" which is the first screen story to have been made in this city and which will make its first public appearance at Everybody's Theatre today, and it is confidently expected that the interest will not only be maintained, but greatly increased during the picture's season. Enterprise in the film industry has been sadly lacking in the Dominion in the past, and Mr. Rudall Hayward, the producer of this film, may rightly be called a pioneer in the business as far as the South Island is concerned at least. It is very probable that this initial effort will result in further pictures being made in Dunedin, and there is no doubt that they will be eagerly awaited. The principals in the picture, a private screening of which was witnessed last evening by a *Daily Times* reporter, are well known locally. They are Miss Dale Austin, Dunedin's own "movie" star, Mr. Norman Scurr and Mr. "Tiff" Bennett. Miss Austin holds the role of a school teacher from "Dogtown" with great credit to herself, while Mr. Scurr is seen as Freddie Fishface, a reporter. As Bill Cowcockeye [sic], a farmer, on a visit to town, Mr. Bennett makes an excellent hero. The first scene depicts Dunedin in the neighbourhood of the Stock Exchange with its street almost bare of people. There follows the arrival of the heroine and her reception by Freddie, who "does the honours" in his own inimitable fashion. Though the latter's depiction of the private life of a newspaper reporter is scarcely true to fact, it serves the required purpose admirably, for a better comic villain would be hard to find. Immediately after the meeting of the heroine and the potential villain there comes on the scene the hero—Bill, in leggings and other trappings which advertise his vocation—and from

that point a fierce rivalry comes into being. Both men stand for election to the committee of the school where the girl teaches, and Freddie, seeing defeat staring him in the face, causes the evening newspaper to print a fictitious report in which his rival is depicted as a thief.

His efforts are not successful, however, for Bill is elected by a large majority. So Freddie is forced to take more drastic action. Luring the heroine to a local garage, he steals a car and kidnaps her. Bill is told of this, and he and his friends who have come to town for the election "to see that the eggs used are fresh ones," set off in hot pursuit on horseback, and then follows a stirring chase on the Tomahawk road. Finally, of course, retribution falls heavily upon the villain, and Bill is restored to his adored one with his fair name happily cleared at the right moment. Despised and thoroughly disgusted with life, Freddie decides upon suicide, but even that is denied him, for there is insufficient water in the Leith for his fell purpose. There is not a great deal in the story, but at the same time, it is sufficient to hold the interest and provide genuine entertainment. Perhaps the most notable feature of the film, as far as Dunedin residents are concerned, is the variety of views of familiar places. In addition, not a few local residents will be gratified to find themselves appearing in a real picture. The remainder of the programme is extremely interesting, and a fine programme of music will be supplied. (New Zealand Film Archive Database)

Silent filmmaking was relatively easy and cheap. With the introduction of sound, all that changed. As John Reid notes in his study *Some Aspects of Film Production in New Zealand,*

The introduction of sound, thereby making large sums of capital investment necessary, took its toll on early New Zealand film producers. Production fell and Filmcraft, the only large production house, went into bank receivership.

What film production there was between this time and the second world war, was largely confined to the National Film and Advertising Studios at Miramar. Independent production was sporadic and small.

After the second world war, interest in local film production re-emerged and a number of small production houses tried to get off the ground. While some lacked the necessary skills[,] others managed to survive in a business and professional climate that was, if not indifferent, openly hostile. What was to become the largest independent production house, Pacific Films Ltd., was started by two young film makers in 1948. One of the founders, Alan Faulkner[,] left New Zealand within the year but his partner Roger Mirams carried on and was joined by the present head of that company[,] John O'Shea. Forming Pacific Film Productions Ltd., with the same two partners, the company produced the first New Zealand Feature for almost twenty years. *Broken Barrier*, a film about race relations in this country, was financed on a miniscule budget and its completion in 1951 [it was released in 1952] was secured not so much by large investment[,] but rather by the determination and skill of the personnel involved. If nothing else this production proved one point, that it was possible to make feature films in New Zealand that would stand up favourably with overseas productions. The requisite skills and the personal drive had already manifested themselves, and all that was lacking was the financial investment necessary to bring these skills into production.

Having survived what many commentators felt was the premature entry into feature film production, Pacific Films then concentrated on making sponsored documentary films of many kinds. After 1957, Pacific Films was led by John O'Shea as its head producer maintaining a production schedule of sponsored documentaries.

In 1964, Pacific Film Productions produced its second feature, *Runaway*, followed nearly two years later by a third feature *Don't Let It Get You*. While being received in a most patronising manner by many local film buffs, these two features further established the important precedent that feature film making was not only desirable in New Zealand but also possible.

In the mid '50s Rudall Hayward returned to New Zealand from London to continue production here. However high production costs have kept him confined to short films with the exception of *To Love a Maori* which he and his wife completed [in 1972]. Rudall Hayward and his wife have produced films in many countries throughout the world. To date their output has manifested a skill and dedication far in excess of the recognition they have received. (Reid, *Some Aspects* 29–30)

Thus, while John O'Shea and Rudall Hayward soldiered on practically alone, the New Zealand government was far more interested in the production of a seemingly endless series of newsreels, travelogues, and informational short subjects, such as *Monkey Tail*, a 1951 production by the National Film Unit, described in the New Zealand Film Archive Database as "a road safety film for school children starring a family of *chimpanzees* [original emphasis] (New Zealand Film Archive Database). *Monkey Tail*, which was written and directed by one of the first women to direct in New Zealand, Kathleen O'Brien, is nevertheless typical of the sort of jocular inanities inflicted on the New Zealand populace in the 1950s. John O'Shea's Pacific Film Productions Ltd. company produced its own "newsreel," *Pacific Magazine*, in the early 1950s, while also making commercials for such products as *Gregg's Coffee* (1970), which was, stunningly, "New Zealand's first multi-racial television commercial, directed by Tony Williams" (New Zealand Film Archive Database).

Political films also took up a large portion of the New Zealand production horizon, with such titles as *Regained Horizon* (1937), a "docudrama" on the state placement service, and its efforts to combat unemployment; *You Must Decide* (1949), a bizarre production of the National Party equating socialism with Communist dictatorship; *Indictment* (1950), a brutally frank look at the lack of care for the elderly, and surprisingly free of the sentimentality or, perhaps more accurately, superficiality that marred most of these synthetic productions. If, in John Reid's words, "at the end of the silent era, film production in New Zealand was quite well established" (*Some Aspects*, 28), by the 1940s and '50s it had become impoverished and monopolized by state interests keen solely on keeping the viewing public pacified with modest travelogues, and a plethora of imported feature films, mostly from Great Britain and Hollywood.

And it was equally clear that Hollywood and Britain didn't relish the idea of an additional competitor in the feature film arena, and preferred to use New Zealand as a backdrop for "tropical adventure" films and the like. As John Reid notes,

The American Bureau of Foreign and Domestic Commerce Report described the situation in 1929 in the following way. "To date there have been three feature films based on Maori or native Polynesian life or the life of the farmer in the back country." The report quoted the expenditure on these films as in the vicinity of $5,000 each with not more than $30,000 total capital tied up in local film production. In addition the report noted a local production featuring, in the star role, a girl who, as Miss New Zealand, had been given a screen trial in Hollywood. An American company were also engaged in making a travel film featuring "pictures of geysers and the native Maori life of New Zealand." The production cost for this venture was quoted as $60,000 and the film was intended for release throughout the United States.

The New Zealand Government Travelogues (at that time produced by Filmcraft Ltd.) were praised as works of art by the Bureau's Report, and mention was made of their successful distribution throughout the United Kingdom, Canada and the United States. The absence of suitable studios was the major reason given by the report, for the lack of a film industry as such. Until adequate studios were established, film production in this country would be very slow in getting under way. (Reid, *Some Aspects*, 28–29)

But as we have seen, this was not the sole factor mitigating against feature film production in New Zealand. As John O'Shea convincingly argued during our interview, no one—not in New Zealand, America, or Britain—really wanted those studios to be built, for a variety of economic, social, and political reasons. It was much safer, and more profitable, to simply keep churning out sanitized newsreels and "Orientalist" "documentaries." John O'Shea amplified these comments in an essay entitled *Some Notes on Film Production in New Zealand*, a report prepared for the Department of Industries and Commerce, and held in the New Zealand Film Archive. Commenting on the fact that in the twenty-six years between 1940 and 1966, only four feature films had been successfully completed in New Zealand (*Rewi's Last Stand* [1940 version], *Broken Barrier, Runaway*, and *Don't Let It Get You*), O'Shea noted somewhat acerbically that

This is a remarkably small number for even as small a country as New Zealand. Part of the reason lies in the fact that, whereas in other countries['] Governments, realising the "national image" value of feature films, make grants and subsidise feature film production, in New Zealand all Government finance for film making is directed towards its own National Film Unit. As part of a Government Department, the National Film Unit does not possess the freedom required to make feature films, some elements in which might bring

FIGURE 1. Ritual performativity in Heiner Carow's *Coming Out*, the first (and last) East German film to explore homosexuality within the confines of Communist society, directed by Heiner Carow. Courtesy DEFA Films.

FIGURE 2. The two lovers confront each other in *Coming Out*. Courtesy DEFA Films.

FIGURE 3. A scene from *Four Women of Egypt* by Tanahi Rasched. Photo by Jacques Leduc, courtesy The National Film Board of Canada.

FIGURE 4. Social discourse in the marketplace; a scene from *Four Women of Egypt* by Tanahi Rasched. Courtesy The National Film Board of Canada.

FIGURE 5. Jonathan Miller directing John Cleese. Courtesy Jonathan Miller.

FIGURE 6. The pre-digital Titanic. Roy Ward Baker's *A Night to Remember*. Courtesy Jerry Ohlinger Archives.

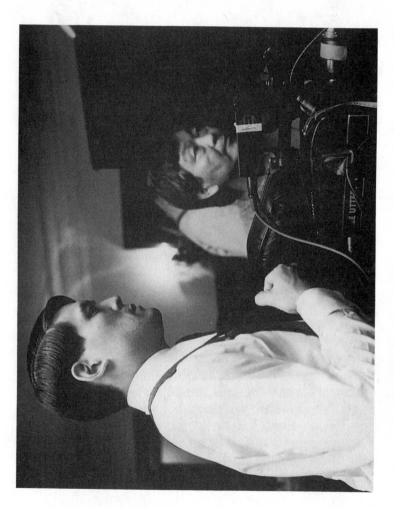

FIGURE 7. Chris Tashima and director of cinematography Hiro Narita on the set of *Visas and Virtue*. Photo by Gayanne Feitinghoff, courtesy Cedar Grove Productions.

FIGURE 8. Silvia Águila and Jorge Perugorría at gunpoint in Arturo Sotto's *Amor Vertical*. Courtesy Pandora Cinema.

FIGURE 9. Jorge Perugorría and Silvia Águila build a makeshift house to escape overcrowding in government apartments in Arturo Sotto's *Amor Vertical*. Courtesy Pandora Cinema.

FIGURE 10. Women of Vovchkivtsi grieve three victims of Stalinist terror in David Pultz's *Eternal Memory*. Courtesy David Pultz.

FIGURE 11. The huge ensemble cast of Bryan Forbes's *The Madwoman of Chaillot.* From left to right: Oskar Homolka, Nanette Newman, Donald Pleasance, Charles Boyer, Paul Henreid, John Gavin, Yul Brynner, Danny Kaye (reclining), Katharine Hepburn, Giulietta Masina, Margaret Leighton, Dame Edith Evans, Claude Dauphin, and Richard Chamberlain. Courtesy Jerry Ohlinger Archives.

FIGURE 12. Kim Stanley in Bryan Forbes's *Seance on a Wet Afternoon*. Courtesy Jerry Ohlinger Archives.

FIGURE 13. Patrick Macnee and Diana Rigg in the long-running teleseries *The Avengers.* Courtesy Jerry Ohlinger Archives.

FIGURE 14. A scene from Jane and Louise Wilson's video installation *Stasi City*. Courtesy 303 Gallery.

FIGURE 15. A still from James McDonald's 1923 "documentary" *Scenes of Maori Life On the East Coast*, a typical example of colonialist New Zealand cinema practice. Courtesy Nederlands Filmmuseum.

FIGURE 16. Staged "ethnography" in action: the film *Fiji battalion Comes Home*, produced by the New Zealand National Film Unit. In this scene, according to the original caption, we see "relatives awaiting return of a Fiji Battalion" on the beach. Courtesy Nederlands Filmmuseum.

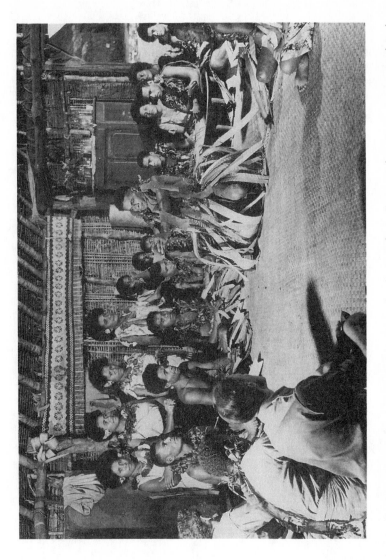

FIGURE 17. A "traditional Kava ceremony of welcome" from *Fiji Battalion Comes Home*, produced by the New Zealand National Film Unit. Courtesy Nederlands Filmmuseum.

FIGURE 18. The New Zealand Film Archive in Wellington, New Zealand. Photo by Gwendolyn Audrey Foster.

FIGURE 19. Annette Kellerman in *Venus of The South Seas* (1924), the "pakeha" in Maori guise. Courtesy Stills Collection, New Zealand Film Archive.

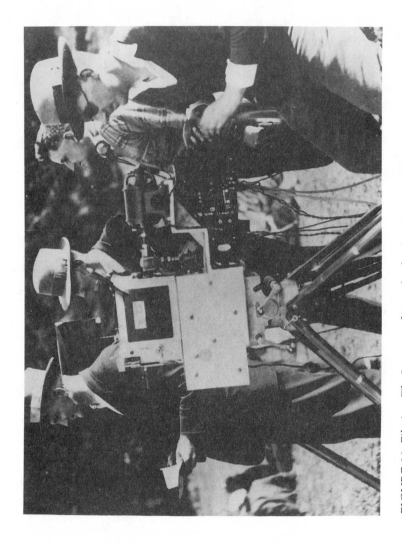

FIGURE 20. Filming *The Romance of Maoriland* with early sound equipment, in New Zealand, 1929. Courtesy Coubray Collection, New Zealand Film Archive.

FIGURE 21. The poster for John O'Shea and Roger Mirams' *Broken Barrier* (1952), the first fictional New Zealand film to deal with race relations in that country in a relatively straightforward manner. Courtesy Pacific Films Collection, New Zealand Film Archive.

FIGURE 22. The existential ending of *Runaway*, as David Manning (played by Colin Broadley) leaves his companion Diana (Deidre McCarron) on an isolated, snow-capped mountain, and continues on alone to his death. Courtesy Pacific Films Collection, New Zealand Film Archive.

FIGURE 23. John O'Shea (left, hand to head) directs the absolutely minimal crew of his final feature film, *Don't Let It Get You* (1966). An innovation created by the New Wave in the France in the 1950s, this "bare bones" crew is a fore-runner of the approach used by today's filmmakers in digital film and video pro-duction. Courtesy Pacific Films Collection, New Zealand Film Archive.

FIGURE 24. Filmmaker David Leigh examines the bizarre case of the Jersey Devil Murders in Lance Weiler and Stefan Avalos' *The Last Broadcast* (top photo); from left to right, Lance Weiler, Esther Robinson and Stefan Avalos, who created this digital feature for a mere $900. Photo by Rob Featherstone, courtesy Wavelength Releasing.

FIGURE 25. Peter Broderick, president of Next Wave Films, one of the major distributors of digital cinema. Courtesy Next Wave Films.

FIGURE 26. A scene from Christopher Nolan's *Following*, which was completed with funding from Next Wave Films. Courtesy Next Wave Films.

FIGURE 27. A computer "phone booth" in Amsterdam, where internet and web access are available on many street corners throughout the city. Photo by Wheeler Winston Dixon.

FIGURE 28. The exterior of "De Waag" in Amsterdam, home of the Society for Old and New Media, one of the most cutting-edge digital/computer production facilities in Amsterdam. The offices and production facilities are on the second floor; the bottom level is a public restaurant. Photo by Wheeler Winston Dixon.

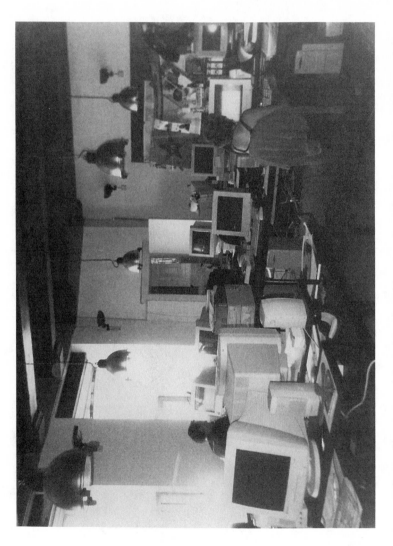

FIGURE 29. The interior of the Society for Old and New Media in Amsterdam, where commercial and non-profit digital productions are created on a daily basis. Photo by Wheeler Winston Dixon.

FIGURE 30. A scene from Sally Cruikshank's *Quasi at the Quackadero*. Courtesy Sally Cruikshank.

down on politicians criticism by the electorate. It is not surprising then that an independent company has been the only producer of feature films. (cited in Reid, *Some Aspects*, 33–34)

This line of reasoning was confirmed by Lindsay Shelton of the New Zealand Film Commission, who noted that, in addition to government interference, many New Zealanders simply felt that their story wasn't worth presenting to a cinema audience, although one could easily construe this reluctance to hold up to a mirror one's national past as avoidance of unpleasant truths rather than innate modesty. As noted by Simon Sigley in his paper, "The Cinema in New Zealand: A Short Survey,"

> . . . three features in thirty years hardly constitutes a film industry. One of the reasons for this lack of interest on the part of the government, and on the part of New Zealanders themselves, may be found in the fact that New Zealanders did not take cinematographic representations of themselves on the screen very seriously. They were not convinced that they were worth looking at: "We were very embarrassed by seeing ourselves," said Lindsay Shelton of the New Zealand Film Commission. "We were uncomfortable." (Sigley 5)

And so, because of a combined series of circumstances—lack of international marketing, censorship, government interference, fear of the past, and the convenience of maintaining the status quo—feature film production in New Zealand drifted along in an ineffectual haze, save for the efforts of a few individuals, until, as previously noted, tax laws in the 1980s made investing in feature films a potentially profitable enterprise, or at any rate, a solid tax write-off. As Sigley comments,

> Investment in the cinema in the later seventies and early eighties was considerable thanks to the short-lived benefits of a tax system which, by astute financial management, could be geared up to two or three times the actual investment in a film. This tax shelter had an important effect on private investors (doctors, dentists, lawyers . . .) in the cinema. A tax deduction of . . . $2 or $3 dollars for every $1 dollar [NZ] invested was the norm. The legislation which made this possible was adapted from other high-risk investment areas. (Sigley 6)

This general scheme opened the floodgates of cinema production in New Zealand at long last, solely on the basis of cost efficiency. Eventually, the tax shelter scheme was abandoned because of a number of abuses; quite a few films were being produced that lived up to no one's expectations of quality (see Churchman 62–66). Since that time, however, such films as Roger Donaldson's *Smash Palace* (1981), Vincent Ward's *The Navigator* (1988), Merata Mita's *Mauri* (1988), Peter Jackson's *Meet the Feebles* (1990) and *Heavenly Creatures* (1994), Jane Campion's *An Angel at My Table* (1990) and *The Piano* (1993), Alison Maclean's *Crush* (1992), Lee Tamahori's *Once Were Warriors* (1994), and numerous other films, to say nothing of the internationally popular teleseries *Hercules* and *Xena: Warrior Princess*, effectively demonstrate that, at last, the New Zealand film industry has come into its own. In addition, at presstime Peter Jackson was working on an ambitious three-part version of *The Lord of the Rings*, with an estimated budget of $315,000,000 NZ, for worldwide distribution. These films are shown internationally, win awards, and command respectable returns at the box office. Has the New Zealand cinema, then, at last been liberated from the forces that hindered it in the past?

Perhaps. Although more feature films are being made in New Zealand than ever before, *Hercules* and *Xena* are teleseries designed for export specifically, and there is, at this moment, only one homegrown teleseries regularly produced and broadcast in New Zealand, a night-time soap opera, shot on videotape, entitled *Shortland Street*. Set in a variety of locations, including a hospital and a series of middle-income homes and restaurants, *Shortland Street* is produced in a frankly assembly-line manner, using numerous writers to stitch each multi-plot episode together to meet the grueling production schedule. In each episode, "there's always a drama, a romance, a medical dilemma, and a comedy story to keep as many viewer tastes satisfied at once" (Christian 62). "The only New Zealand drama series currently screening in prime time" has an average nightly audience of 650,000 viewers (Christian 62), but in its direct appeal to melodrama and the commercial instinct, it can hardly be cited as a beacon of artistic triumph, even as it celebrates its seventh year on the air. *Shortland Street*'s producer John Bennett addressed both the appeal and the limitations of the program in a discussion with writer Dionne Christian. Said Bennett,

> Having worked in theatre and television for a long time, I believe we have the talent to make very good dramas in this country.

I think it's vital that our own culture is reflected. We need to tell stories so we have a sense of what it is to be a New Zealander. It's very easy to believe that we're living in the United States, and that does our country a disservice.

Dionne Christian continues,

> Television drama also creates jobs, and *Shortland Street* has certainly done that for a large number of New Zealanders. But our affection for the show doesn't necessarily transfer for the individual cast members, as many a former *Streeter* has found to his or her cost after leaving the show.
>
> The show makes good use of some established acting talents, but for those who enter the *Street* as their first real acting job, there are few other locally made shows to provide work once they leave. To survive they need to turn to the vagaries of live theatre work, roles in New Zealand's limited film industry or the ignominy of fronting a "real TV" show. Otherwise it's back to the day job. (Christian 62–63)

So at least in television, the horizons seem distinctly limited at present.

Yet, when I spoke with John O'Shea, he was enthused about New Zealand's first commercially successful digital feature film, Campbell Walker's *Uncomfortable Comfortable* (1999), which was produced on a modest budget, and has caused quite a stir in the country, much as *The Blair Witch Project*, *The Last Broadcast*, and *Cruise* have in the United States. In an interview with Simon Vita, O'Shea had this to say about *Uncomfortable Comfortable*, and the current condition of film in New Zealand:

> The malady [facing New Zealand's feature film industry] is institutionalised poverty. We have to find a way around that one. *Uncomfortable Comfortable* is really good. One's used to seeing amateur films sort of . . . amateur films aspiring to be professional films shot on digital cameras and that sort of thing and they made a really good job of it, I think. The Cocteau dictum states that when every means of visual communication is as easy as using a pencil and a paper, one can express one's self to one's full potential using anything. I see that [the film's director] Campbell [Walker] has really taken it to an extreme and his actors have done likewise.

From this year's film festival, O'Shea speaks very highly of Danish director Lars von Trier.

> He has come at it from knowing about films. He says he's not an artist anymore but of course he's an artist. He expresses things artistically. His film made under the auspices of [Dogma] 95 was *The Idiots*. It's absolutely hair-raising because it reveals absolutely everything about people's lives. Someone coming out of the film said to me, "My goodness John there are no families like that here," and I said, "Come on, you scrape away the surface gloss and NZ will conform very much to that." (Vita 13)

CHAPTER FOUR

※

The Commodofication of Desire, and the Disruptive Figure of Paul Robeson

The desire to memorialize the past that Brian Clemens speaks of, an attempt to recall the artifacts of a lost age of creative energy and synthesis, is also apparent in contemporary gallery offerings, in which the props, costumes, and other bits of cinematic detritus involved in the creation of a film become separate works of art, endowed with lives of their own. The show *Spectacular Optical*, presented at the Thread Waxing Space in the summer of 1998, brought together the artists Lutz Bacher, Jeremy Blake, John Brattin, Lygia Clark, Bonnie Collura, Gregory Crewdson, Bryan Crockett, Keith Edmier, Jason Fox, José Antonio Hernández-Diez, Luisa Lambri, Julian Laverdiere, Miranda Lichtenstein, Charles Long, Greg Lynn, Fabián Marcaccio, Mariko Mori, Tony Oursler, Laura Pames, Randall Peacock, Alexis Rockman, Alexander Ross, Jana Sterbak, Shellburne Thurber, and Jane and Louise Wilson in a show dedicated to the cinematic work of David Cronenberg, from his earliest 16mm films such as *Stereo* (1970) to his contemporary works. Collating fake advertisements, newspapers, bits of old costumes, and videos into a spatially and aesthetically component whole, *Spectacular Optical* offers the viewer an extension of the vision Cronenberg creates in his films, making that which is phantasmal concrete in the fetishistic display of these various artifacts.

Contemporaneous with this event, the Russian filmmaker Vadim Pevzner presented an evening of his films and videos at a New York screening space, the Void, showing the brief films *After World, Clutch,*

Pulp, Charlie Don't Rave and other works, all completed in either 35mm film, various video formats, Super 8mm, or 16mm film, and then transferred to VHS video for final presentation. The hour-long program of Pevzner's work was refreshing both for its anarchic flair and its recycling of previously used images, intertwined with new film and/or video material photographed directly by Pevzner. Of his life and work, Pevzner offers this brief account, on a flyer he distributed at the screening:

> Vadim Pevzner, a native of Russia, moved to the U.S. after living for several years in France. He received an M.F.A. in film making from the School of The Art Institute of Chicago. In his work, he experiments with the qualities inherent in formats from super-8 to 35-mm. to hi-8 to digital video, and mixes formats deliberately. He also incorporates found footage and optical-printing techniques. Whether through frame-by-frame montage or long, static takes, his editing tests the limits and endurance of visual and psychological perception. His works are meditative, voyeuristic, and direct, and many of them possess a sense of playfulness and black humor. The particular texture of his work is further intensified by striking sound designs. In terms of "subject matter," he continually tries to evoke *diffOrance.* Pevzner attempts to chip away at the surface of subjects and objects, looking for as many ways through the looking glass as possible. (Pevzner n.p.)

Pevzner is part of a new underground of cinema, creating works, as others did in the 1960s, using little or no money and whatever facilities he finds at his disposal. For these new artists, video projection is now the normal method of presentation, and 16mm projection is no longer routinely used. No matter what the source material of Pevzner's raw imagistic material, the end of the image chain is a videographic presentation. One should also note that none of Pevzner's films, which run between two and eleven minutes, expects to make any money in terms of exhibition fees—a purity of construction reminiscent of the underground cinema in the 1960s, when everyone involved knew instinctively that art would be its own (and only) reward.

Levi Asher, a New York webmaster and digital artist, produced an adaptation of Dostoyevsky's *Notes from Underground* and advertised it on his web site, offering 750 copies free to the first interested parties who logged on. As Austin Bunn reported of Asher's project in the *Village Voice,*

Notes from Underground is a project so resolutely noncommercial that you can't help but feel it's from a different age. . . . Local programmer Levi Asher, the one-man band behind the beat-literature altar Literary Kicks (litkicks.com), is releasing 750 *free* copies of the CD-ROM based movie *Notes from Underground* beginning August 4 at his site. Filmed on 8mm and starring his friends, Asher's 64–minute, updated Dostoyevsky looks more like a thoughtful, earnest film-school project than a professional venture—and he wants it that way. "Venture capitalists stay away, nothing about this project has anything to do with money," writes Asher in the liner notes. Come October, he'll be selling the disc for $12, but he's realistic about its potential. "This is a pretentious dream, but I like what Lawrence Ferlinghetti did—he never got lame or sold off to Bertelsmann to start producing Tom Clancy books," he says. With *Notes from Underground*, Asher, like the rest of them, has his eyes fixed on his ideal audience. "One of my secret hopes," he says, "is that it will catch the student audience of kids who don't want to read the book—like Cliffs Notes." (27)

Asher's work (and his ethos) is echoed in numerous web sites, particularly Scott Stark's Flicker Pages (located at<http://www.sirius.com/~sstark/>), with individual web pages attached for each artist that spotlight the most radical, not-for-profit cinema and video being produced today. In his liner notes for the CD-ROM of *Notes from Underground*, Asher details his "no budget" production process in egalitarian completeness.

The project began as a technology experiment; I wanted to see how good a movie I could make on a standard-issue home computer, not with a low budget but with no budget. I shot all the video with a Sony 8mm camcorder (the one I use to take videos of my kids) and did all the digitizing, editing and graphic design on the family Mac, a 7500 with 80 MB of memory and 6 GB of disk space. I mastered the PC version on a Gateway 486 with 32 MB of memory, and burned test CD's on a Phillips CDD2000.

I edited the video with Adobe Premier and created the interface with Macromedia Director. I also used Macromedia SoundEdit for audio, Adobe Photoshop for still images, Adobe Illustrator for package design, and Terran Interactive Media Cleaner Pro for video compression (Quicktime Cinepak at 180 KPS, 15 fps, IMA audio).

I was using many of these programs for the first time, and was blown away by their power, intelligence and elegant simplicity. (Liner notes, n.p.)

As Bunn notes, the project does feel as if it is "from a different age," but whether that age is the past, as evidenced in 1960s experimental film production, or the future, in which entire features can be produced for a fraction of the cost of even the cheapest 1960s experimental 16mm sound film (and with sync sound, to boot), *Notes from Underground* offers the viewer an early clue to a new direction in personal film production. For in *Notes from Underground*, Asher proves that one really can make a compelling film with minimal resources. His elegantly stark vision of urban alienation is both true to Dostoyevsky's original novel, and faithful to the best spirit of independent film production, as well.

Lynn Hershman Leeson's *Conceiving Ada* is an alternative example of a low-budget, digital "feature film" being constructed entirely in the domain of hyperspace, with slightly more sophisticated equipment, but still for the fraction of the cost of its Hollywood counterpart. Unlike *Notes from Underground*, which was shot on actual locations, *Conceiving Ada* uses what Leeson describes as "virtual sets." As William Kelly found out when he interviewed Leeson,

> To realize the idea for her first feature film, Leeson drew from the extensive digital experience she'd gained from working in various media since the seventies, and developed a process she calls, "Virtual Sets." Asked how these virtual sets differed from the traditional blue screen process with images matted in after shooting the actors, Leeson [noted that the difference is that] "the images are already there in real time while the scene is being shot, not added later. Actors stand in front of a blue screen but they can see themselves on a monitor composited with their environment. For example, they could see if they were near a fireplace or a window and react accordingly. . . . The actors loved it. . . . I took thousands of still photographic images of Victorian Bed and Breakfast Inns in the Bay area from all angles. Then they were digitized, altered in Photoshop to take out any reference to contemporary life, and colorized. On the set these images were altered through several computers where [mattes] were added and images were put into perspective or enlarged. They were then laid onto digital videotape while the actors were performing." (Kelly 32)

The film, which tells the highly complicated story of a late 1990s computer whiz travelling back through time to "jack in" to the brain of Ada Byron King, Lord Byron's daughter, featured Tilda Swinton and Timothy Leary in its central roles, and was edited and shot using Macintosh workstations to composite the actors within the synthetic sets (Kelly 32). Such an audacious project can only exist at the margins of cinema; yet this is where the future of the moving image undoubtedly resides.

Far more commercial is Indiewire.com, a sort of clearing house for semi-commercial independent cinema, films designed to hopefully play at the Angelika Film Forum, or the Quad Cinema. These "commercial" indies are produced for minimal amounts of cash, but such projects as Vincent Gallo's *Buffalo 66* (1998), Hal Hartley's *Henry Fool* (1997), Susan Skoog's *Whatever* (1998), Tommy O'Haver's *Billy's Hollywood Screen Kiss* (1998) and other semi-marginal films all expect, or hope, to at least return their production and exploitation investment. Those who work on the true margins of cinema expect nothing for their labors, other than the fulfillment of seeing their vision on the screen.

FILM DISTRIBUTION IN THE NEW MILLENNIUM

One of the few remaining truly independent theatrical feature film distribution companies left in existence as of this writing is Kino Films, whose president is Donald Krim. Krim, who at one time worked as an executive at United Artists, formed Kino in 1976 with the rights to distribute classic 16mm prints of films in the Janus collection, as well as films from the estate of Charlie Chaplin. The entire company is comprised of twelve individuals who do all the booking, publicity, and shipping of prints. As Krim explained in an interview with Dennis Lim,

> The field is particularly crowded right now, but at the same time, the bigger companies are leaving the smaller foreign films to the ten or so companies like us that are not attached to multinational corporations. We compete for the foreign films that aren't expected to gross a million dollars . . . we can be profitable even with a film that does $300,000 to $500,000 at the box office, partly because video makes up the difference. (128)

Kino's biggest hit to date has been Julie Dash's 1991 film *Daughters of the Dust*, which grossed nearly two million dollars. Kino has also distributed

Wong Kar Wai's *Happy Together* and *Fallen Angels* to good, if unspectacular, results (Lim 128). The critical commentary is another story: universal approbation. Yet distribution outfits such as Kino will have to continue to operate on the margins to eke out a profit, and obviously, a love of cinema is far more central to Kino's operation than any hope of a gigantic commercial success. With so many ancillary markets available—cable, pay TV, videocassettes, CVDs, and the like—theatrical presentation of these films is a decided luxury, and yet it is an essential act for critical reception in the late 1990s. Without the cachet of theatrical distribution, these films would be lost in the limbo of straight-to-tape releases, unnoticed by all but the most observant critics and viewers. Kino, and other small independent distribution outfits like them, give foreign and low-budget "art" films a potential foothold in the public's consciousness in a brutally overcrowded marketplace of images, and for this, we are indebted to them. Obviously the majors won't take the risk. And without Kino and its brethren, the contemporary foreign feature film—other than the mainstream costume drama—would surely cease to be commercially viable as an international release.

There are numerous examples of marginalized films that received exposure from smaller distribution companies, either independent or corporate owned. Manoel de Oliveira's *Viagem as Princípio do Mundo* (*Voyage to the Beginning of the World*, 1997) was the actor Marcello Mastroianni's last film, a gorgeous Portuguese/French co-production concerning a film director, Manoel (Mastrioanni), and his troupe of actors, who are on their way to a shoot. While Manoel indulges in desultory conversation with an assistant, Judite (Leonor Silveira), and stops to revisit the locations of his youth, one of the actors, Afonso (Jean-Yves Gautier) gradually appropriates the film's narrative, and steers the group to a meeting with his relatives, whom he has completely lost touch with. A detailed, mesmerizing and transcendental meditation on aging, mortality, memory, and loss, *Viagem as Princípio do Mundo* would never have received even a limited theatrical run were it not for the intervention of Strand Releasing, another small theatrical distribution company. Shari Springer Berman and Robert Pulcini's *Off the Menu: The Last Days of Chasen's*, recounting the final days of a legendary Hollywood restaurant, would also have escaped the public's attention were it not for a brief theatrical appearance at the Quad Cinema in Manhattan, an engagement which led to favorable critical reviews, and thus increases the chances that Berman and Pulcini will have the chance to create another project in the future.

Gone, sadly, are the days in which a foreign film such as Shiro Toyoda's *Gan* (*The Mistress*, 1953), a superb Japanese black and white film, could hope to have a general "art house" release in 35mm in the West; gone, indeed, are the days when such a film would even have a profitable engagement in its native land. Color is a nearly ineluctable requirement for theatrical distribution, and above all, spectacle sells to the masses, not an intimate drama that audiences could just as easily see on their television sets, without leaving the comfort of their homes. Benoît Jacquot, director of *La Désenchantée* (1990) and *La Fille Seule* (1995), known in America as *The Disenchanted* and *A Single Girl* respectively, makes small-scale dramas of everyday existences in contemporary French society that are commercial successes in France and even modestly in the United States. But Jacquot, a charter member of the post New Wave French cinema, who worked on various projects with the late Marguerite Duras, and is a contemporary of André Téchine, Chantal Akerman, and other post '60s *cinéastes*, realizes that cinema is an inherently compromised art form. While he has produced numerous works for French television, as well as a documentary on the life and work of the French psychoanalyst and philosopher Jacques Lacan, Jacquot, from the early 1990s on, decided to make a determined effort to become more accessible, and more commercial in his work. As he told Kent Jones,

> Really, I think that my career started over again with *The Disenchanted*. I like the earlier films but they're too . . . dry, hermetic, sealed off in a world of cinema, which is a trap. *The Disenchanted* is the first film where I made a real effort to connect with the public. You know, it's so easy to lose yourself in the cinema, and you must never forget that it's an impure art form. That's what keeps it alive. That's what I love about it. (106)

While *The Disenchanted*, a resolutely serious chamber film that nevertheless managed to strike a resounding chord with the viewing public, was a solid commercial hit (due in no small part to Caroline Champetier's superb photography, and Judith Godrèche's leading role), it was *A Single Girl* that finally put Jacquot on the cinematic map after years of work. *A Single Girl* is a real-time tour de force starring Virginie Ledoyen as Valerie, a young girl in her first day on the job in a large metropolitan Parisian hotel. One can see in *A Single Girl* not only the romantic influence of the first New Wave of French *auteurism* in the late 1950s, but also the rigorousness of Akerman and Jean Eustache in Jacquot's use of long handheld tracking shots to follow Valerie on her daily rounds, as she struggles to keep up with internal political machinations at her place of work; tries to steal a few minutes with her less than sympathetic boyfriend, Remi (Benoît Magimel); and delivers room service orders to unreasonable, demanding, and occasionally psychotic hotel guests. Valerie is the heroine and central focus of Jacquot's ninety-minute slice of life, and his camera is constantly on the prowl with her, tracking down hotel corridors or drab city streets as Valerie attempts to bring some order and dignity to her difficult life.

Despite the formal intensity of the film, *A Single Girl* offers enough visual pleasure to seduce its audience, and Virginie Ledoyen's performance as Valerie is stunning in its simplicity and directness. The humanity and pathos of Valerie's quest is so searingly conveyed that the audience is mesmerized by the film's singularity of purpose. Surprisingly, although *A Single Girl* embraces a near-Rouchian insistence on observation and the long take, Jacquot himself is resigned, even appreciative, of the current mainstream offerings filling the multiplexes. "Look," he told Kent Jones, "I liked *Titanic*. Of course it was an absolutely idiotic film, but then the older I get, the less I think intelligence is a valuable attribute in the cinema" (106). Whether this is merely fashionable cynicism or philosophical fatalism on Jacquot's part is open to debate, but for other contemporary filmmakers, this battle between the mercantile and the ideal in cinema is an ongoing struggle, the outcome of which is still being contested on a daily basis. With his film *Seventh Heaven* (1998), Jacquot continues his examination of bourgeois French life in present-day Paris, in a film that is both light and transcendent, and a refreshing reminder that small-scale commercial films are still economically feasible in contemporary French cinema.

COMMERCE AND CONTESTATION

Daisy Von Scherler Mayer, who signs her films "Daisy VS Mayer" for the sake of simplicity, came up through the ranks of the commercial feature cinema with *Party Girl* (1995) and *Woo* (1998) before she directed her first full-fledged mainstream film, *Madeline* (1998), based on the famous series of children's books by Ludwig Bemelmans. Directing a superb cast, including Frances McDormand as Miss Clavel, Nigel Hawthorne as Lord

Covington, and Stéphane Audran in a brief role as the dying Lady Covington, *Madeline* is a film for children that also speaks to adults on such issues as power, responsibility, friendship, and the need to do what one perceives as morally imperative. *Madeline* is a heroine for the late 1990s in much the same way that Valerie in *A Single Girl* is: she is tough, self-reliant, and unafraid to confront authority when she knows that she is in the right. While *Madeline* is a children's film, its exquisite production design (by Hugo Luczyc-Wyhowski), faithful to the illustrations in the original books, coupled with the judicious use of location shooting in France, give the film an air of fantasy and authenticity. *Madeline* becomes a moral fable more than anything else. *A Single Girl* and *Madeline* both offer us instructions for life, one in the form of a series of parables for youngsters, the other in a *cinema verité*–styled cautionary tale for young adults.

Woo and *Party Girl* are primarily genre entertainments, and yet even in these frankly commercial enterprises, Von Scherler Mayer scores solid points in her feminist vision of self-determination in an often hostile world. *Woo* (played by Jada Pinkett Smith) charges through her world with confidence and self-determination, creating the world that she wants rather than subjugating her will to the desires of others. Venus (Nicole Bobbitt) in *Party Girl*, assisted by a supporting cast that includes the always reliable Parker Posey (as Mary), strides through the club scene with similar aplomb, unwilling to be exploited even as she seeks to exploit those around her. *Madeline* strongly suggests that Von Scherler Mayer will soon be graduating to projects of even greater consequence; clearly, she is an artist who understands the requirements of genre filmmaking, but who nevertheless injects all of her projects with a positive, self-actualizing vision that is both refreshing and underplayed.

Betty Thomas is another contemporary genre director who has scored a considerable commercial success. Her version of *Doctor Dolittle* (1998) is an Eddie Murphy vehicle which is *very* loosely based on the children's books by Hugh Lofting. Before that, Thomas worked as an actor in a variety of films and television series, including the long-running series *Hill Street Blues* (where she played the character of Lucy Bates) and Robert Zemeckis's early film *Used Cars* (1980, still one of his most effective works). Turning to direction in 1990, she helmed several episodes of the series *Dream On* before her first major commercial success with *The Brady Bunch Movie* (1995), followed by *Private Parts* (1997) and then *Doctor Dolittle*. Thomas's work is certainly more assembly line than Von Scherler Mayer's oeuvre, but she offers to her public a compellingly direct form of address in her work as director and, as *The Brady Bunch Movie* readily confirms, she is adept at satirizing the cookie-cutter mentality of television series production with both affection and accuracy. Even as her vision is resolutely mercantile, it never condescends.

The same cannot be said for Adrian Lyne, whose projects (*Foxes* [1980], *Flashdance* [1983], *Nine and 1/2 Weeks* [1986], *Fatal Attraction* [1987], *Jacob's Ladder* [1990], *Indecent Proposal* [1993] and his remake of *Lolita* [1997]) constitute a litany of commercial calculation and cynical audience manipulation. Gus Van Sant, who once was capable of directing a superb and original film (*Drugstore Cowboy* [1989]), has completely abandoned his outlaw vision with the relentlessly mainstream *Good Will Hunting* (1997), and his by-the-numbers remake of *Psycho*, featuring Vince Vaughn as Norman Bates. In both cases, these filmmakers have pursued a bottom-line vision of commercial success with a series of increasingly bland, compromised entertainments, as opposed to other, more marginalized *cinéastes* who continue to create work that operates on the margins of cinema, whether superficially packaged as mainstream productions or independent efforts. But, as Benoît Jacquot observed, film is an "impure art form" (Jones 106). What drives the production and reception of the Dominant Cinema to accept, even embrace, the widest possible audience at the expense of all other considerations? The answer, in a few words, is the expense of production. With costs spiraling, a pre-sold commodity like a remake of *Psycho* (with a fresh cast) seemed appealing to exhibitors and producers. Audiences that attended the cinema in 1960 to see Hitchcock's original film are either dead, or home watching HBO; besides, Hitchcock's film was shot in black and white. A new version, commissioned for today's audience, would theoretically bring in not only a new generation of viewers, but also a few older audience members, curious to see what Van Sant has done with the original film's structure and iconographic concerns. Yet the film was a commercial and critical failure, as were the new versions of *Godzilla* and *The Mask of Zorro* (both 1998). The producers hoped that all these films would be simultaneously familiar and yet, through the use of digital sound and state-of-the-art digitized imagery, somehow fresh and original, but remakes remain a "spotty" enterprise. Certain films seem, for the moment, to be resistent to recreation.

If it's a classic in twenty years, all well and good. But, as always with the Dominant Cinema, there is one overriding concern that governs all production and exhibition enterprises, particularly in the last days of the twentieth century. Good, bad, or indifferent, the film has got to sell *now*. Films must reach an audience immediately upon their initial release; within days of a film's first screening, industry experts are able to calculate the domestic theatrical gross of any given feature film to within several hundred thousand dollars. There is no second chance, no prolonged shelf life. This is increasingly true in publishing, television production, the recording industry, cable production, and other allied fields. Where once a television series would have a season (at least) to prove itself, now instant non-performers are unceremoniously dumped from viewing schedules in a matter of weeks. Books are increasingly celebrity driven, as gigantic chains such as Barnes and Noble and Borders monopolize the retail landscape, driving smaller bookstores out of existence and imposing a "best seller" mentality on both seller and buyer. Amazon.com has successfully proven that one can even do without retail space. Books, videos, cars, plane tickets, real estate—all can be sold over the Internet with a minimum of staff and inventory. Computer programs allow Amazon.com to track reader demand for certain books, and then cross-suggest related volumes; they also allow Amazon.com to rank their entire inventory by reader popularity in depth, so that when one orders a particularly marginalized book from Amazon.com, one is informed that of all the books available in the Amazon.com cyberstore, your choice is, say, number 1,420,354th out of a possible 2 to 3 million books. Nothing like numerical superiority to enforce consensus thinking! Do you really want to read such a manifestly unpopular book? Or wouldn't you feel more at home with a book that others are reading, so that you can discuss it later over the Internet chat lines?

A look at the current landscape of cinema exhibition and distribution demonstrates how "enforced consensus" has become the driving force behind film booking in the late 1990s. Where in 1929, *four-fifths* of the American populace went to the motion picture theaters of the nation every week, in 1998, "slightly less than ten percent of the population" attended the movies each week (Epstein 34). There are more theatre screens today than there were in 1929, "over thirty thousand" of them, but they are clustered together in increasingly large multiplexes, which now house up to 24 "screens" per unit (Epstein 34). Edward Jay Epstein accompanied the head of one major theatre chain, Hollywood Theaters, to ShoWest, an annual convention where theatre owners and distributors meet to bargain over which films will be mass-marketed to audiences in the coming year. With seventy-seven theaters, or multiplexes, housing 474 screens in the Midwest and Southwest United States, Hollywood Theaters hopes to build an additional 500 screens in the next five years, making it one of the biggest chains in the country (Epstein 34).

The CEO of Hollywood Theaters, one Thomas W. Stephenson, is a former investment banker who collects abstract art as a hobby, and who entered the film exhibition business in 1995. As Epstein accompanied him, he discovered that Stephenson had no illusions about the cinema exhibition process, and was easily able to compartmentalize business and artistic concerns into widely disparate areas. Like all theatre owners, Stephenson relies on the concession stand to bolster revenue margins that would otherwise force his company into bankruptcy. While Hollywood Theaters actually loses money on the films it screens, with more than fifty percent of its gross revenue going directly to film distributors, it makes up for this with a lucrative concession stand business, where heavily salted popcorn coerces viewers into purchasing additional soft drinks to slake their thirst (Epstein 34–35). And while Thomas Stephenson may collect abstract art, he is decidedly uninterested in screening any independent films in the theaters he controls. As Epstein recounts,

> When we arrived [at ShoWest, Stephenson] decided to skip the reception hosted by independent distributors. "I personally enjoy watching many of the low-budget films that come from independents," he said, "but they are not a significant part of our business." In fact, according to Stephenson, ninety-eight percent of the admission revenues of his theaters in 1997 came from principal Hollywood studios—Sony, Disney, Fox, Universal, Paramount, and Warner . . . (35)

Such a figure is hardly surprising, given the fact that Hollywood Theaters book no independent films for playdates. How on earth can they account for a significant portion of the revenue stream if they aren't even considered for exhibition? But the majors supply marketing campaigns, posters, commercial product tie-ins, glossy one-sheet posters, and trailers, as well as massive television and radio advertisement campaigns to help sell the pictures they distribute. Such national promotion is essential for success in today's market, with hundreds of films competing for key playdates. The independent distributors can't compete with this, and relies on word of mouth and critical reviews to bring viewers into the theaters. While this may work in major metropolitan centers, such as New York, Los Angeles, San Francisco, and even Kansas City, such a prospect is hopeless in most suburban and rural markets, where televisual supply and demand drives the public consciousness. This explains why, in many twenty-four–screen multiplexes, one film will play on two or more screens at the same location: audience demand has been spurred by incessant television advertising. New exhibition strategies, such as "stadium seating," in which theatre seats are heavily raked on a downward sweep towards the screen, like bleacher seats at a football game, and cup holders that are attached to each seat so that viewers won't spill their overpriced soft drinks (Epstein 35), are touted as major advances in theatrical exhibition, while the majors put on glitzy shows designed to lure distributors into handling their product as opposed to that of their competitors. Epstein recounts one particularly tacky display of corporate largesse at ShoWest by Sony Pictures, who displayed clips from their forthcoming films for the assembled theatre owners in a ghastly pageant which, apparently, appealed dramatically to those in attendance. At the Sony presentation,

Jeff Blake, the president of Sony's distribution arm, said that last year Sony films had brought a new record gross into North American theaters: $1.27 billion. Indeed, Sony accounted for nearly one out of every four dollars spent on movie tickets in 1997. Vanna White, the television personality, then conducted a mock "Wheel of Fortune" game in which every clue referred to films coming from Sony this year, including *Godzilla* and *The Mask of Zorro*. As Vanna White announced each title, actors from the film in question rushed onto the stage—among them such stars as Michelle Pfeiffer, Julia Roberts, Nicolas Cage, and Antonio Banderas. All of this was followed by excerpts from the films. A highlight of sorts came when the stage suddenly filled with dancers costumed as characters from Sony's movies. Robert Goulet played the part of Jeff Blake and sang, to the tune of "The Impossible Dream":

This is our quest,
To be king of the box . . .
there'll be lines round the block
When that big hunk Godzilla is finally here
And you'll know what we've done for you lately
When we beat the unbeatable year. (36)

In an atmosphere such as this, what chance can a small, thoughtful film possibly have? True, Sony itself has entered the independent distribution business with its subsidiary Fineline, but the films Fineline handle are never afforded any real level of support from national advertising. As Sony obviously feels, these smaller films can only make so much money at the box office, and so why expend time, effort, and financial resources on a film whose rentals can be predictably described as marginal? With this preordained partitioning of the audience dominating current cinema exhibition practice, the chances for a breakout hit like *The Full Monty* are very slim indeed. If no one knows that these smaller films exist, and if they are never booked by the larger film chains around the country, what possible hope can they have of achieving any measure of their potential critical and commercial success? In an earlier era, before video and cable, when all films *required* a theatrical release in order to recoup their investment, these films would have had a chance at reaching a mass audiences. Now, after a few desultory bookings in specialized theaters in major markets, they will vanish to the limbo of the back shelves at Blockbuster, while a hundred copies of *Mulan* (1998) confront the potential renter at the front door of the store.

If it is difficult to get the African-American vision on the screen even in the late 1990s, in such films as Kasi Lemmons's *Eve's Bayou*, what was it like for Paul Robeson, one of the pioneering forces for African-American self-actualization in cinema and the related arts? In the next few pages of this volume, I will explore the various filmic projects that Paul Robeson appeared in, such as *King Solomon's Mines* (1937), *Sanders of the River* (1935), *Show Boat* (1936), *Tales of Manhattan* (1942) and other works, and demonstrate how these projects failed to explore the true talents of Robeson by holding him to a rigid social and racial stereotype, one in which he continually refused to participate. This led Robeson to explore the possibility of work with Sergei Eisenstein, and others who worked in less conventional cinematic forms, and finally convinced Robeson that in Hollywood (or in Britain) he would never have the opportunity to give full freedom to his gifts as a singer, actor, and social activist. In his rejection of the conventional Hollywood cinema, then, Robeson emerges as a figure of triumph, despite the numerous films he made that failed to live up to their potential.

Paul Robeson was born on April 9, 1898, in Princeton, New Jersey. Robeson's father was a Presbyterian minister who had escaped slavery as a child; his mother was a school teacher. Paul Robeson grew up with the desire to excel in all he undertook; thus, it was not particularly surprising that he won a full scholarship to Rutgers University at the age of seventeen (Duberman, *Robeson* 20), distinguished himself as a football player at the university, and graduated Phi Beta Kappa. Graduate school in law at Columbia University followed, while Robeson courted Eslanda Cardozo Goode, or "Essie," the woman he would marry. Although his primary interest during this period was the possibility of a law career, Robeson's brief stint with the Amateur Players in 1920, and subsequently in the Harlem YWCA's production of Ridgely Torrence's *Simon the Cyrenian* (43) encouraged his interest to shift to the theatre, concerts, and films. The theatrical production of *Simon the Cyrenian* was followed by Robeson's first commercial appearance in the short-lived play *Taboo*, at the Sam Harris Theatre.

Although the play received generally abysmal notices, Robeson's stage presence was duly noticed, and, with Essie's encouragement, he continued his theatrical work by joining the cast of the Broadway show *Shuffle Along*, all the while maintaining his studies at Columbia. But Robeson began to feel, more and more, that he was destined to be a performer. *Taboo* was reworked into a play titled *Voodoo*, and Robeson went to England to tour with the production. Essie, meanwhile, was forced to enter the hospital for a difficult operation. Worried about his wife's condition, and discouraged by *Voodoo*'s mostly indifferent notices, Robeson cut short his British tour and returned to America ostensibly to complete his law degree at Columbia (Duberman 1988, 51). Robeson received his law degree in February, 1923, but although he was immediately offered work, Robeson quickly perceived that the strained atmosphere at the Stotesbury and Miner Law Office would never really allow him to advance. Robeson resigned his position, and refused to take his bar exam. Now, more than ever, with law practice denied to him because of his race, Robeson set his sights on a career on the theatre (Duberman, *Robeson* 54–55).

In 1923, Robeson was asked by Kenneth Macgowan, director of the Provincetown Players, to appear in Eugene O'Neill's new play, *All God's Chillun Got Wings* (Duberman, *Robeson* 55). Robeson had been campaigning to work with O'Neill ever since the playwright's *The Emperor Jones* had opened in 1920, and now Robeson's career seemed truly launched. In addition to his work in *All God's Chillun Got Wings*, Robeson appeared in a revival of Nan Bagby Stevens's *Roseanne* and sang at the Brooklyn YWCA. But public sentiment against Robeson's participation in *All God's Chillun Got Wings* was growing. Racist letters, bomb threats, inflammatory newspaper articles, and the like created a climate of fear in which Robeson and his fellow thespians found it difficult to function (59). Despite this interference, right before the opening of *All God's Chillun*, the playhouse decided to mount a revival of *The Emperor Jones* to fill an unexpected gap in their schedule. With a scant two weeks of rehearsal, Robeson opened in *The Emperor Jones* to extremely favorable reviews. *All God's Chillun Got Wings* followed *The Emperor Jones's* limited run and fared less well with the critics. No matter. Paul Robeson was at last attracting attention and moving forward in his new career. In addition to his theatrical and stage work, movies seemed to offer a distinct opportunity for Robeson's talents (61–63).

Robeson's first film was *Body and Soul*, a 1925 production by pioneer black filmmaker Oscar Micheaux. It is actually one of Micheaux's better efforts. (When forced to switch to "talkies" with *The Exile* in 1931, and with his subsequent films such as *The Veiled Aristocrats* [1932], *Ten Minutes to Live* [1932], *God's Stepchildren* [1938], and *Lying Lips* [1940], Micheaux's production quality slipped drastically, due to the cumbersomeness of early sound recording equipment, coupled with Micheaux's already minuscule budgets.) *Body and Soul* offered Robeson one of his most interesting roles, as the Reverend Isaiah T. Jenkins, who is actually a lecherous ne'er-do-well seeking to evade the forces of authority. While ostensibly ministering to a group of devoted followers in the town of Tatesville, Georgia, the reverend drinks, gambles, and finally rapes one of his most ardent parishioners, while stealing and extorting money from the members of his congregation. Micheaux's silent camera moves with fluidity and assurance in the unfolding of the film's narrative, although too many intertitles interrupt the film's action. Nevertheless, Robeson's performance is both daring and resourceful, and the film gives one a glimpse of the range and depth that Robeson was capable of, if only his subsequent roles had given him the opportunity to display his talents. *Variety* gave the project a favorable review, finding that it had "power for both black and white audiences," and contemporary critic Donald Bogle feels that the silence of the film was in Robeson's favor. "Robeson without his voice," notes Bogle, "[is] merely beautiful and mysterious" (in Gilliam 40).

Robeson's next project was also an ambitious and unusual project for the actor. *Borderline* (1930) is an experimental silent film created by the Pool Group, a collective of artists who made several short films before completing *Borderline*, the group's only feature film. Shot for a total budget of less than two thousand dollars (Duberman, *Robeson* 131), Robeson and Essie both acted in the film for a mere nine days, under the direction of Kenneth Macpherson, who also functioned as director of photography, editor, and screenwriter for the film. The film's budget was so low that according to Winifred Ellerman (also known as Bryher), Kenneth Macpherson's wife, "the only paid member of the group was an electrician" (in Gilliam 62). The poet H. D. (Hilda Doolittle) appeared in the film under the alias of Helga Doorn (Duberman, *Robeson* 130), and the film's plot centered around the conflict caused by a black couple, Pete and Adah (Paul Robeson and Essie Robeson). The lives of another couple, Astrid and Thorne (H. D. and Gavin Arthur), are thrown into disarray by Adah's arrival in a small town in Switzerland to meet her fiancé, Pete. The film seems most deeply influenced by the cinematic techniques of Dimitri Kirsanoff, a Russian filmmaker best known for his superb silent half-hour film *Menilmontant* (1926). Actions are chopped into tiny fragments of film, scenes are broken into numerous close-ups and inserts, and whatever narrative line the film possesses is almost wholly sacrificed to the visual aspect of the production. The film is frankly an artistic rather than a commercial venture, akin to Jean Cocteau's *Blood of a Poet* (1930), and it enjoyed a limited commercial run.

Robeson's first sound film is not one of his more distinguished efforts; the O'Neill play *The Emperor Jones* was finally being transferred to the screen. Shot at Paramount's Astoria Studios on Long Island in 1933, the film earned Robeson a substantial salary but indifferent reviews under Dudley Murphy's direction. Shot quickly in a mere thirty-eight days on a budget of $280,000 (Duberman, *Robeson* 168), the film was a modest "A" effort rather than a full-scale Hollywood enterprise. The producers were John Krimsky and Gifford Cochran, who had imported Leontine Sagan's brilliant film *Maedchen in Uniform* (1931) to the United States. Krimsky originally wanted to shoot the production in Haiti, but Robeson noted that the primitive sets on the Astoria sound stages were already quite hot enough: "Bring the trees right here; if this June weather holds out, we've got plenty of tropic atmosphere right in the studio" (Gilliam 68). Robeson was good-natured about the intolerable shooting conditions, but the heat was stifling. Robeson spent his time in between takes lying down in his dressing room, trying to conserve his energy. The *Amsterdam News* gave Robeson a favorable review within the film as a performer, but denigrated the film itself as yet more racist propaganda; and the Philadelphia *Tribune* noted *The Emperor Jones* did little more than perpetuate existing racial stereotypes. Clarence Muse, another black actor whose talents were never fully appreciated by Hollywood, noted in a private letter that Robeson "gave a great performance but story and direction [were] poor . . . I think it a damn shame to use such an excellent actor to put over damaging propaganda against the Negro" (in Duberman, *Robeson* 168). Robeson himself was suspicious of what the Dominant Cinema might offer him; he rightly suggested that "Hollywood can only realize the plantation type of Negro . . ." (in Duberman, *Robeson* 168), a dire prediction that would prove sadly true by the time of his last film, *Tales of Manhattan* (1942).

But Robeson's next film, *Sanders of the River* (1935) may be the worst film of his entire career. Based on Edgar Wallace's ultraracist novel of the same name, *Sanders of the River* unfortunately belongs with D. W. Griffith's *Birth of a Nation* (1915) and Leni Riefenstahl's *Triumph of the Will* (1934) as one of the most appalling evil and racist feature films ever produced. As an African nationalist, Robeson was impressed when producer Alexander Korda screened some 160,000 feet of film that Korda's brother, Zoltan, had shot during a five-month sojourn in Africa. Most of it was in sync sound, highlighting the "music, speech, dancing, rituals," and cultural heritage of African civilization (Duberman, *Robeson* 178). Feeling that Korda's London Films (a prestigious production house that had produced the international hit film *The Private Life of Henry VIII* [1933] with Charles Laughton, among other projects) would finally offer him a chance to project his vision on the screen, Robeson enthusiastically accepted the role of Bosambo, and principal photography of *Sanders of the River* began in earnest.

In retrospect, it is difficult to understand how Robeson agreed to become involved in the film's production, even after Korda screened him the location footage from Africa. Wallace's novel, as critic David Glover, among others, have noted, is an ultracolonialist text in which the character of Mr. Commissioner Sanders, or "Lord Sandi" as he is invariably referred to by his unwilling subjects, governs by brute force and nothing else. He uses lynchings, the gatling gun, and a network of spies to enforce his reign of terror. When Sanders is forced to return to England for a short time, Robeson, as Bosambo, is required to deliver the line, "Lord Sandi, it fills our hearts with sorrow to see you go away from us." Sanders responds, "Thank you, Bosambo. And in my place Lord Ferguson will stay here and give the law to all the peoples of the River. I want you to obey him as if you were his own children" (in Gilliam 82). Even the most cursory reading of the books in the *Sanders* series reveals this as precisely the sort of project that Robeson should never have been associated with. The normally sympathetic Ben Davis of the *Sunday Worker* took Robeson to task over the finished film, accurately noting that the film constituted "a slanderous attack on African natives who were pictured as being well-satisfied with the 'benevolent' oppression of English imperialism" (in Foner, 107). Robeson's repeated response to such criticisms was to suggest that the ultraracist tone of the film was accomplished after the fact, in the cutting room, and that "the imperialist angle [was introduced] during the last five days of shooting" (Duberman, *Robeson* 179). But this can hardly be the case. Nearly every scene in the film is offensive, and Leslie Banks's portrayal of Commissioner Sanders is both vicious and condescending. Banks is perhaps most famous for his portrayal of the Mad Count Zaroff in *The Most Dangerous Game* (1932), a white Russian aristocrat who hunts human beings for sport. Though Robeson would later denounce the film in no uncertain terms—in 1950 he told a newspaper reporter flatly "I hate the picture" (Duberman, *Robeson* 182)—a great deal of damage had been done. Indeed, Robeson knew from the very first time he saw the completed film that it was a cultural and artistic disaster. At the premiere, Robeson sat "seething" in the audience, and refused to speak after the screening, abruptly walking out of the theatre (Gilliam 82). Yet subsequently, despite the rigid social confines of the era, Robeson made some interesting, socially innovative films in England (particularly *Song of Freedom*, produced in 1936). However, *Sanders of the River* remains one of Robeson's most commercially successful and popular films, even today. This in itself is deeply disturbing, and demonstrates once again the pervasive hold that racism continues to exert on motion picture history and/or criticism.

After a proposed project on Haiti with Sergei Eisenstein failed to get off the ground, Robeson agreed to appear in the 1936 version of *Show Boat* for forty thousand dollars (Duberman, *Robeson* 194). It was an experience that he found, on the whole, agreeable. James Whale, one of Universal's most renowned directors, handled the film with great efficiency and care. More famous as a horror director (*Frankenstein* in 1932; *The Bride of Frankenstein* in 1935), Whale shot 200,000 feet of film for *Show Boat* in six weeks, using a cast of thousands and atypically lavish sets for a Universal production (Duberman, *Robeson* 196). The film's budget was in fact two million dollars, an extremely large figure for the period (Gilliam 85), but the racism of the project was overpowering. Although new material was put into the script at Robeson's request, the standout number was undoubtedly "Ole Man River," which featured Robeson with a choral background seemingly defending the social inequities of the Old South. While *Variety* and other mainstream newspapers praised the film, the black press excoriated the film, as did other thoughtful observers (Gilliam 85).

In the aftermath of the production's generally successful release, Whale, Jerome Kern, and Oscar Hammerstein II seriously considered the idea of producing a musical film version of C. L. R. James's play *Black Majesty*, but Hammerstein lost interest, and the project never materialized (Duberman, *Robeson* 196–197). As for the final version of *Show Boat*, once again Robeson's part was reduced to more simplistic lines in the editing room, and Robeson vowed that the same would not happen with *Song of Freedom* (1936) or *King Solomon's Mines* (1937), his next two filmic projects. One of *Show Boat's* most perceptive critics was none other than Sergei Eisenstein who noted that "only in two or three shots is his face, figure and personality treated in the way it ought to [be] . . . would prefer realistic treatment of Paul singing" (in Duberman, *Robeson* 203–204).

Song of Freedom was directed by J. Elder Wills for Hammer Films, the studio that two decades later would become known for its horror films, especially Terence Fisher's *Curse of Frankenstein* (1957) and *Dracula* (1958). Although the film has been dismissed in some quarters as simplistic, I would argue that, despite its inherent commercialism and modest budget the film comes the closest of any of his films to projecting Robeson's ideals on the screen. In the film, Robeson plays the role of John Zinga, a dock hand catapulted from obscurity to mainstream commercial concert-hall success as a popular singer. As long as he can remember, Zinga has worn an unidentified amulet around his neck, and he is haunted by a tune whose precise words and music he somehow cannot fully recall. Eventually, Zinga discovers that he is the King of Casanga, and he gives up his concerts to return to Africa and provide leadership for his constituents. In his effort to upgrade agricultural and medical facilities in his native land, he is opposed by the local witch doctor (Arthur Williams), who not only denigrates Zinga's attempts to aid Casanga's citizens, but also contrives to throw Zinga's wife (Elisabeth Welch) into a pit of snakes at the film's climax, much like a Republic serial of that era. At the last possible moment, John Zinga realizes that the song he has been struggling to remember is the King's Song, and his spirited rendition of the melody saves his wife, disgraces the witch doctor, and brings home to his constituents the realization that John Zinga really is the King of Casanga. At the film's end, we see Zinga once again singing on a concert stage in London, but we learn that he now alternates his singing engagements with regularly scheduled trips back to Africa, where the bulk of his salary goes towards improvements in his kingdom.

While the plot of the film can be dismissed as preposterous, Robeson for the first time was given a role that was neither demeaning nor one-dimensional, a role in which he is treated as a formidable protagonist both in the scenes in London, and in the studio back-lot empire of Casanga. Robeson commented that *Song of Freedom* was "the first film to give a true picture of many aspects of the life of the colored man in the West . . . a real man" (Gilliam 85). J. Elder Wills's direction, in complete contrast to the stagebound, declamatory style used by Zoltan Korda in *Sanders of the River*, is marvelously kinetic, replete with rapid shifts in narrative, flashbacks, and a dazzling variety of wipes that recalls the construction of Thornton Freeland's *Flying Down to Rio* (1933). (In a curious coincidence, Thornton Freeland would direct Robeson in *Jericho* in 1937.) The film thus moves rapidly and efficiently along, and the script depicts Robeson as a relaxed and assured man of authority. In one particularly effective scene, John Zinga intervenes when a group of feverish villagers are left to die in a hut without food, water, or medical attention. Zinga orders that some rations of quinine be given to the sick men, and also obtains fresh water for them. When one of Zinga's aides brings him a large vat of polluted water, Zinga immediately comments that the water is so filthy that giving it to the unfortunate fever victims would "finish them off" by itself. Instead, he orders his assistants to obtain some fresh running river water, and then boil it to kill the impurities before allowing anyone to drink it. Despite Zinga's ministrations, the fever victims die, an event that triggers the climax of the film and the ultimate challenge to Zinga's authority. All in all, *Song of Freedom* offered Robeson a role of dignity and stature, and the Pittsburgh *Courier* hailed it as "the finest story of colored folks yet brought to the screen . . . a story of triumph." Poet Langston Hughes also admired the film, writing to Robeson's wife Essie that "Harlem liked *Song of Freedom*." Robeson himself felt that, of his entire filmic career, the only two roles he could take any real satisfaction in came with *Song of Freedom* and 1939's *The Proud Valley* (Duberman, *Robeson* 204).

Almost immediately after the completion of *Song of Freedom*, Paul Robeson and his wife separated for a time. Essie took a brief sojourn to Africa, while Robeson toured Russia as yet another indication of his increasing commitment to the Communist cause. Tensions between Paul and Essie had escalated to a serious level, with Essie intent on slowing down Robeson's increasing political activism, and Robeson himself more than ever devoted to the ideals espoused by the Soviet regime. Finding a refreshing absence of racism, coupled with his enthusiasm for the "collective" lifestyle, Robeson determined to move to the USSR permanently as soon as matters permitted (Duberman, *Robeson* 206–207). When Robeson returned to England, he plunged directly into the production of *King Solomon's Mines* (1937) under the direction of Robert Stevenson, another project that would turn out to be an artistic and personal disappointment. Sir H. Rider Haggard's source novel, first published in the nineteenth century at the height of the Victorian era, was yet another embarrassingly racist paean to British colonial rule, although Robeson had expressed a seemingly inexplicable desire to appear in a film version of Haggard's novel *Allan Quartermain* some years earlier (Duberman, *Robeson* 169). In any event, *King Solomon's Mines*, with its story of Umbopa (Robeson), an African servant to colonial explorer Allan Quartermain who is eventually revealed to be an African chieftain, is every bit as jingoistic and offensive as *Sanders of the River*, and perhaps even more patronizing in its construction of Umbopa's character.

Subsequently filmed four more times (in 1950, 1973, 1985, and 1987), *King Solomon's Mines* depicts Umbopa in a simplistic, one-dimensional manner, an African chieftain in exile motivated solely to regain his throne, while saving the lives of a group of White interlopers intent on looting a booty of lost treasure. With Sir Cedric Hardwicke, Roland Young, Anna Lee, and John Loder holding high the torch of the British empire, the film soon degenerates into yet another trek into the fantasyland of colonial Africa, and as in *Sanders*, Robeson is called upon to sing a variety of inauthentic hymns to the seeming inevitability of colonial rule. Again, one is amazed that Robeson undertook the role at all, particularly given the obvious racism of the source material, already ferociously outdated even in the mid 1930s, and seemingly at direct odds with Robeson's own political beliefs. Parenthetically, it is also worth noting that this ultracolonialist fable continues to have a hold on the public's imagination, as does *Sanders*—a nostalgia for the lost days of White supremacist rule in Africa. The most recent (1987) version of *King Solomon's Mines* stars Richard Chamberlain, Sharon Stone, Herbert Lom, John Rhys-Davies, and Ken Gampu appearing as Umbopa. One wonders when this odious franchise will at last be laid to rest.

Big Fella (1937) was another misfire, although this time for a different series of reasons. *Big Fella* was hammered out from a novel by

Claude McKay originally titled *Banjo,* which Robeson initially turned down flat. However, with rewrites, and perhaps as a gesture of appreciation to Hammer for producing *Song of Freedom,* Robeson went ahead with the project. He was reunited with J. Elder Wills and Elisabeth Welch from *Song of Freedom,* and the film also featured Essie in a small role as the French-speaking owner of a café given to wearing wigs worthy of Madame Pompadour (Duberman, *Robeson* 207). Nevertheless, the film suffers from the fact that the original source material is compromised to begin with, and *Big Fella*'s sentimental tale of a Marseilles dock worker who helps a lost boy return home, but who ultimately prefers to return to the docks (romanticized in the film as a phantom zone of perpetual rest and relaxation), is extremely slight material for a full-length feature. Less than a month later, after a brief trip to Russia for a series of concerts in Moscow, Leningrad, Kiev, and Odessa (Duberman, *Robeson* 208), Robeson was rushed into production of *Jericho* (1937), also known as *Dark Sands,* much of which was shot on location in the outskirts of Cairo, Egypt.

Robeson was attracted to Cairo, and even expressed a desire to make a film with Um Kalthuum, perhaps the most beloved singer in the Middle East, as the female lead (Duberman, *Robeson* 209). *Jericho* offered Robeson a change of pace in his role as Jericho Jackson, who abandons life in the army after a series of heroic deeds result in a trumped-up court martial. Escaping through Northern Africa, Robeson comes upon the beautiful Gara, played by the Taureg Princess Kouaka, and eventually opts to remain as the leader of his adopted people rather than returning to face military injustice (210). Despite the film's adventurous locale and Robeson's box office appeal, the film did poorly at the box office, and did little to improve Robeson's star status within the industry. Even in such a mildly adventurous production, Robeson was still required to sing offensively racist songs at the apparent behest of the producers; for no discernible reason at all, Robeson at one point in *Jericho* sings "Mammy's Little Baby Loves Shortnin' Bread" (Gilliam 88). Such incidents would continue to plague him for the rest of his film career.

In 1938, caught up in the events of the Spanish Civil War, Robeson and Essie visited Spain, where on a single day, January 29, 1938 (Duberman, *Robeson* 219), Robeson was filmed for a short propaganda/documentary/musical film *Canciones de Madrid* (1938), a ten-minute film directed by Juan Mañuel Plaza documenting Robeson singing to soldiers on the battle lines in the war against Franco. Robeson astutely understood that the conflict in Spain was merely a prelude to the conflagration to come. Robeson called Franco's bombing raids "absolute savagery" and noted that he could not "understand how the democracies of Britain, France and America [could] . . . stand by inactive" (in Duberman, *Robeson* 216).

Robeson's next film project would be far more ambitious: the Ealing Studios production of *The Proud Valley* (1939), directed by Pen Tennyson. Best known for their wartime comedies, Ealing also produced a series of gritty and inspirational dramas, and *The Proud Valley*, with its tale of Robeson as David Goliath, an expatriate American who eventually finds work in the Welsh coal mines and becomes involved in the fight for better job and housing conditions on behalf of the miners, was clearly a prestige project for the studio. After checking into a reducing spa to lose some unwanted pounds, Robeson reported for work on *The Proud Valley*, which began production in August of 1939. By September of that year, Britain was involved in the battle against the Nazis, and *The Proud Valley* was shot quickly and efficiently, wrapping on September 25th, 1939. Robeson saw a rough cut of the film only three days later, on the 28th of September; by September 30th, the Robesons had left England for New York. Robeson seemed deeply satisfied with the rough cut of *The Proud Valley* (Duberman, *Robeson* 233), and despite Robeson's increasingly unpopular stance in defense of the Soviet Union's actions in the deepening conflict, *The Proud Valley* opened to generally favorable reviews in 1940. While some reviewers found the basic premise of the film improbable, Robeson's own work was singled out for conspicuous praise, despite the controversial political opinions he was now openly declaiming to all and sundry. However, it was noted by a number of critics that the organizing "threat" David Goliath represented could easily be contained by the Dominant Cinema, as epitomized by the ending of *The Proud Valley*, in which Robeson's character sacrifices himself in order to save the Welsh miners during a climactic cave-in (Gilliam 94). So long as Robeson's character (and by extension, Robeson himself) was consigned to a martyr's death in the defense of White privilege, a film like *The Proud Valley* could be countenanced.

Robeson's film work was shortly to come to an ignominious conclusion with the production of Julien Duvivier's multi-part anthology film, *Tales of Manhattan* (1942), the movie that finally soured Robeson on ever again working in Hollywood. Robeson appeared in the final vignette of the film, as one of a group of sharecroppers (the other performers in this section of the film included Eddie "Rochester" Anderson as a minister, and Ethel Waters as a devout parishioner). At the production's outset, he truly believed that the film would accurately depict the problems of poor rural Blacks who invest a cache of money, literally fell from the sky, into a variety of worthy community improvement projects, rather than squandering it on momentary pleasures. However, Robeson's role in the film is cut to shreds, and although he has one brief shot where he announces triumphantly that because the found money will be distributed equitably, there will be "no more rich and no more poor," the film perpetuates the worst sort of stereotypes, so much so that Robeson himself joined those demonstrating against the film, promising to appear on picket lines wherever the film was shown during its initial New York run (Duberman, *Robeson* 260). "I wanted to pose the problem of the Negro sharecropper, but not in this way. [The producer] and I argued all through the film . . . I wasn't satisfied." Films like *Tales of Manhattan* decisively proved to Robeson that "[producers won't] offer me worthy roles to play . . . I don't want to be a noble savage" (in Gilliam 184). Indeed, Robeson was so thoroughly disgusted with the finished project that he announced his retirement from films, and, feeling that he had tried every possible avenue of artistic expression available to Blacks within the cinema of that era to no avail, he decided to return to the concert hall and the theatrical stage. Apart from his off-screen narration of Leo Hurwitz and Paul Strand's 1942 docudrama *Native Land,* which Robeson performed for the minimum fee (Duberman, *Robeson* 261), and some voiceover singing on the soundtrack of the 1954 East German documentary *Das Lied der Ströme* (*Song of the Rivers*), Robeson never worked in the commercial cinema again. *Native Land*—a film that would shortly come under attack as Communist propaganda for its realistic portrayal of the hardships of a sharecropper's existence—took five years to produce, from 1939 to 1942, and was always a "fringe" project as far as Hollywood was concerned; Robeson's participation in *Song of the Rivers* is little more than a gesture. This is a sad ending to a career of such brilliant promise. Although Robeson kept up an untiring career of concerts and public appearances for many years after his forced retirement from the screen, as a figure of cinema, a medium he instinctively embraced, his career was abruptly and unjustly truncated.

It is our loss. As the Robeson Centennial Exhibition curated by Ed Guerrero, Charles Musser, and Mark Reid aptly demonstrates, even the best of these heavily compromised films (a distinction I would give to *Song of Freedom*) gives a distinctly incomplete and inaccurate vision of Robeson's consummate power as an artist and performer. Guerrero, Musser, and Reid assiduously searched through a variety of archival sources to retrieve footage of Robeson "performing in concerts, giving interviews, addressing political gatherings" (Duberman, *Robeson* 38) to give a more accurate picture of the overall legacy that Robeson has left us. And yet the picture is still incomplete. What wouldn't one give for even a filmed newsreel record of Robeson's performance in *Othello* opposite Peggy Ashcroft in 1930, a document that would have been technically possible even then, in the early, clumsy days of sound recording? Or even a filmic record of Robeson's 1944 Broadway version of *Othello*, co-starring José Ferrer and Uta Hagen (a version of this production is preserved, imperfectly, in a series of sound recordings)? And what work might Robeson have accomplished if only he had come along in the mid 1950s, or the 1960s, or today, when stars such as Denzel Washington, and directors like Spike Lee, Darnell Martin, Julie Dash, John Singleton, Kasi Lemmons, and others can find support (albeit not enthusiastic mainstream support, even in the present era) for their projects? Robeson's triumph, and his ultimate victory, is that of the artist working upstream, against all social and political odds, to achieve work of lasting resonance and value. Continually thwarted and compromised, Robeson refused to buckle under and appear in film roles that he found demeaning or insubstantial. One might sadly argue, in the context of 1930s Hollywood and British dominant film production, that all of Robeson's cinema projects were inherently compromised by a cultural ideology that was frankly afraid of espousing, or disseminating, the true image of egalitarian cosmopolitanism that Robeson projected.

Yet simultaneously, as fleeting moments in Robeson's theatrical films, and in sustained sections of the newsreel records of his life before the public eye, one can discern the triumph of Paul Robeson over the overtly racist cinematic apparatus that sought to contain him. At length, it simply *couldn't* contain him, and Robeson's personality spilled out beyond the boundaries of his compromised screen appearances to captivate and instruct Robeson's public, who continued to celebrate his life and work. As Robeson himself commented, "my problem is not to counteract the white man's prejudice against the Negro. That does matter. I have set myself to educate my brother to believe in himself" (in Graham 234). This, finally, is the task that Paul Robeson set himself as an artist, an activist, and a figure of social conscience, a task that he admirably discharged with the greatest distinction.

CHAPTER FIVE

※

*The Past and the Future
of the Moving Image*

While the mainstream cinema can effectively challenge these stereotypes
when it wishes to, all too often such films as Steven Spielberg's *Amistad*
(1997) rely upon White protagonists to dramatize the challenges faced by
Blacks who are moved from the center of the film's narrative discourse to
the periphery of the film's syntactical structure, so that White audiences
might better identify (or so it is falsely argued) with the effects of prejudice against African-Americans in contemporary social discourse. Occasionally, however, there are some mainstream films that effectively inter-
rogate existing social constructs in a meaningful manner, although even
in these cases, the end result bears the unmistakable stamp of compromise. Jon Avnet's *Fried Green Tomatoes* chronicles the relationship
between Ruth Jamison (Mary-Louise Parker) and Idgie Threadgoode
(Mary Stuart Masterson), two women living in the 1930s in Whistle
Stop, Georgia, who become and remain close friends despite the various
obstacles that come between them, not the least of which is Ruth's abusive husband, Frank Bennett (Nick Searcy). The entire story is told in
flashbacks, and is narrated by Ninny Threadgoode (Jessica Tandy), an old
woman who lives in a nursing home, to the rapt audience of Evelyn
Couch (Kathy Bates), who happens upon Ninny through a chance
encounter. Long sections of the film are thus framed through Ninny's
monologue, although the film continually returns to the present to pick
up a framing story involving Evelyn and her husband, Ed (Gailard Sar-

tain), as Evelyn struggles to redefine herself as a woman, as a result of Ninny's compelling oral testimony. In the end of the film, it is revealed that Ninny is Idgie, and that she has has been reciting the story of her own life and relationships through the years, and particularly the aborted love relationship between herself and Ruth.

The central objection felt by many to the film was the strongly implied but never directly indicated lesbian relationship between Ruth and Idgie. Idgie is aggressive, refuses to take abuse from anyone, and serves as a role model for the more retiring Ruth. The two women meet during a wedding party, and together witness the horrific death of Idgie's younger brother, Buddy Threadgoode (Chris O'Donnell), who gets his foot caught in a train track. As a result of this, Idgie becomes desperate and cynically world-weary, trying to drown her sorrows in alcohol and cards. Idgie's mother (played by Lois Smith) brings Ruth into the Threadgoode home in the hope that the calmer, more pacific Ruth will have something of a civilizing influence on Idgie, but the two women soon become fast friends, and create their own mutuality of understanding outside the bounds of conventional society. The years pass, and the two women are separated. Then, at a key point in the film, Idgie rescues a pregnant Ruth from the brutality of her husband, and takes Ruth to Whistle Stop, Georgia, where the two women prosper as the owners of the Whistle Stop Cafe. It is during this brief idyll that the two women seem happiest, and many observers of the film felt that *Fried Green Tomatoes* was in fact depicting a happy and successful lesbian relationship in a none-too-hidden cinematic code, and were infuriated by the fact that the film refused to commit itself to this interpretation.

As the film's narrative concludes, Frank Bennett comes to the Whistle Stop Cafe and makes a clumsy attempt to kidnap his infant son. Frank is about to drive away from the café when he is killed by an anonymous assailant. Idgie immediately becomes a suspect, inasmuch as she had long hated Frank for his abuse of Ruth, but the real murderer is finally revealed as the hired hand Sipsey (Cicely Tyson), a minor character in the film who commits the crime simply to protect the child. Frank's body is never found, despite the repeated inquisitions of a persistent detective, as Idgie and Big George (Stan Shaw) cut up Frank's body (off-screen, thankfully) and make it into barbecue for the customers of the Whistle Stop Cafe. The film ends with a final return to the present, the revelation that Ninny is Idgie, and the culmination of the framing story between Evelyn and Ninny, in which the two women become fast friends despite their age differences. As with Ruth, Idgie has had a salutary effect on Evelyn, causing her to reexamine her life, and her relationship with both her husband and the world in general. No longer the meek follower, Evelyn at the end of the film emerges as a person in her own right, fully capable and desirous of pursuing her own destiny.

To say that *Fried Green Tomatoes* is a beautiful film is perhaps to put it too simply, and there are some plot contrivances toward the second half of the film that occasionally threaten to overpower the film. But in its depiction of the relationship between Idgie and Ruth, the film showcases the two masterful performances of Mary Stuart Masterson and Mary-Louise Parker with grace and intelligence, and director Jon Avnet effectively evokes both the elegiac flavor and the harsher realities of the Depression-era Southland with a rich and illustrative directorial style. Geoffrey Simpson's cinematography is muted and deliberate, and the film as a whole is dark and gently brooding, particularly within the flashbacks. Thomas Newman's music is also a considerable asset, using one main theme in a seemingly endless series of repetitions and variations, deepening the tragedy and scope of the film in the manner of Georges Delerue's evocative score for Jean-Luc Godard's film *Le Mepris* (*Contempt*, 1963).

In one sense, the film is somewhat clumsily constructed, inasmuch as the narrative told by Ninny to Evelyn seems grafted on to the film, and the flash forwards and flashbacks occasionally intrude upon the intensity of the work. If we never really believe Evelyn's character, it is perhaps because Bates is so deferential throughout the film to Tandy's incandescent presence; yet because Tandy is such a marvel of precision as an actor, we believe her incarnation of Ninny/Idgie completely. Watching the film, one is impatient to leave the present, represented by the dingy nursing home and Evelyn's unhappy marriage, and return to the past, which is full of the sights and sounds of Idgie and Ruth's shared life. Avnet's camera-work comes alive in these recreations of the old South, gliding effortlessly through a world of rundown shacks, night-time baseball games, and the homey yet businesslike interior of the Whistle Stop Cafe. But above all, it is the performances of Masterson and Parker that dominate the film, bracketed by the framing story work of Bates and Tandy. *Fried Green Tomatoes* is an actor's film, and Avnet wisely makes his camera-work and *mise-en-scène* subsidiary to the talents of these gifted performers.

As a less successful example of literary adaptation, we can consider *The Loved One*. Perhaps the most interesting version of Evelyn Waugh's novel *The Loved One* is the one that never made it to the screen. In the early 1950s, director Luis Buñuel held an option on the work, and hoped to make it into a feature film that would have undoubtedly been a typically iconoclastic work for the filmmaker. But Buñuel's project never got off the ground for a number of reasons, and so, in the early 1960s, director Tony Richardson, then relatively fresh from his success with Henry Fielding's *Tom Jones* (1963), and his earlier hit film *The Loneliness of the Long Distance Runner* (1962), took over the option from Buñuel, and assembled an international cast for a big-budget, MGM version, created as an American-British coproduction.

This 1965 film, clocking in at 116 minutes in the final cut, boasted a cast that included Robert Morse, Robert Morley, Liberace, Ed Reimers (then famous as a pitchman for Allstate insurance), Roddy McDowall, Anjanette Comer, Rod Steiger, Dana Andrews, Margaret Leighton, Milton Berle, James Coburn, Lionel Stander, Tab Hunter, and Jonathan Winters in a dual role. This richness of performing talent masks, to a certain degree, the structural uncertainty of Richardson's adaptation of the Waugh novel, as we wait expectantly to see where each instantly recognizable face will pop up: here is Tab Hunter as a cemetery attendant; now we see Roddy McDowall as a tyrannical and insincere studio boss. The list goes on and on. Money, for this film, was certainly not a problem.

Shot in seductive black and white, Richardson's version of the film takes considerable liberties with Waugh's text, and often lays on parodic effects with a sledgehammer style reminiscent of Oliver Stone, rather than allowing the Hollywood milieu which Waugh's novel so deftly satirizes to indict itself. Several sequences and performers still stand out: Steiger's performance as the embalmer Mr. Joyboy is a wonder of artifice and restraint in an otherwise overblown film; Liberace is so dead-on as an unctuous coffin salesman that he hardly needs to exert any effort beyond that of creating his typical on-stage persona. Jonathan Winters, left pretty much to his own devices, goes completely over the top as the Blessed Reverend, and Reimers, as a hurried priest alternately performing funerals and weddings on a split-second schedule, is memorable as he casually smokes a cigarette between services. On the whole, the seemingly endless chain of cameos works rather well to divert audience attention from the essential hollowness of the film.

But Robert Morse, in the title role of Dennis Barlow, mugs his ways through the proceedings shamelessly, sporting a rather unconvincing British accent at best, and Anjanette Comer is both bland and colorless as his ostensible love interest. The film is ultimately sprawling and unfocussed, and aims at too many targets to be cohesive as a completed work. One gets the distinct impression that Richardson was overwhelmed with the mechanics of so many egos at work in his widely varied cast of performers, and simply contented himself with keeping the enormous enterprise moving on time and on budget. The lurid lushness of *The Loved One*'s visual style perfectly fits the macabre vision of Waugh's novel, but Richardson's overlong and ultimately over-lavish film speaks of nothing so much as bloatedness, something notably absent from Waugh's spare and unsentimental text. Worth seeing for the gallery of splendid cameos, *The Loved One* must be still be judged as an interesting misfire. Seen from the viewpoint of the late 1990s, only the performances of Liberace and Steiger retain the power to amuse and/or shock contemporary audiences. One still wonders what Buñuel would have done with the material at hand. I suspect that Buñuel's vision of Waugh's novel would have been considerably (and appropriately) more vicious, in addition to adhering more closely to the narrative diegesis of the novel. In both *The Loved One* and *Fried Green Tomatoes*, potentially disruptive projects are continued within the boundaries of Dominant Cinematic discourse, in the service of distributors who are motivated more by a desire to supply product (even in the 1960s) than to foster the creation of a genuinely compelling, aberrant imagistic vision.

FROM TEXT TO SCREEN

When Shakespeare's work is translated to the screen, as in Kenneth Branagh's *Hamlet* (1997) or other contemporary productions, what happens is doubly intriguing. Shakespeare, the ultimate populist, who sought to appeal to all factions of the gallery, is now transformed into a theatre piece photographed and staged for an "absent" audience, although Baz Luhrman's *Romeo and Juliet* (1997) does make an attempt to break through to contemporary audiences—mostly through the expedient of a great deal of contemporary music on the soundtrack, grandiose costumes and spectacularly rundown sets, and rapid fire, MTV-styled cutting. Yet, for most Shakespearean adaptation for cinema, the inherent distancing involved in the filmmaking process is, in itself, a coefficient of the "performing self" in Shakespearean drama. Although there is something lost in any filmic translation of a staged dramatic piece, in Shakespeare's case there is also something to be gained. The framing of every film allows for final formalizing of the actor-audience relationship. In the best of the filmed Shakespearean plays, this formalizing aspect is enhanced by judicious production design, lighting, cinematography, and a peculiar style of acting that acknowledges the gap between the performer and the audience but also treats the camera as if it itself were the audience, which, of course, it is.

Laurence Olivier's 1955 production of *Richard III* is a perfect example of this vigorously exact visual style. The film is composed of long, involved takes, many using a dolly-mounted camera, in which the actors direct the camera movements, much as an audience's collective gaze is controlled by the movements of the performers on a stage. Richard's opening soliloquy, in particular, makes spectacular use of the camera's ability to "become" the audience. When Olivier beckons the camera closer to him, it comes at his bidding, lending a private but collective eye and ear to Richard's ambitious plans. That Olivier's performance is a "putting on of an aspect" is certainly never in question: in a traditional film, his work would be called overacting. On stage, the performer must raise his voice and calculate his inflection to reach even the back row of the theatre. In a film, the camera brings the audience equidistant to the performer, and no projection is necessary. But here, Olivier realizes, as part of the performance in a Shakespearean play, the actor *must* adopt a certain rigidity of stance which is closely aligned to the concerns of Elizabethan acting.

Dramatic convention in Shakespeare embraces artificiality, the act of acknowledging that what one is witnessing is a staged re-creation. In Olivier's film of *Richard III*, Olivier as Richard reminds the audience that they are about to see a pageant unfold before their eyes, in which he will be the director. He underlines this by directing the camera's gaze and thus the gaze of the audience. Further, the lighting in the production is tinged with color: reds for moments of dramatic intensity, blues for melancholic reflections. The sets themselves are stylized in the manner of Robert Wiene's *The Cabinet of Dr. Caligari* (1919): the perspectives are foreshortened, the backgrounds transparently theatrical. Because the film makes no attempt to mime reality, this artificiality works in concert with the production rather than against it. The stylization of acting and setting reminds the viewers that what they are witnessing relates to reality but is not directly part of it.

Moreover, the filmic rendering here brings a sense of timelessness to the proceedings. *Richard III* is altogether more effective on film than it would be on videotape. Indeed, one of the central faults of the videotaped BBC productions (many of them directed by Jonathan Miller) is that the plays are shot on tape rather than film, and tape has an "immediate" look to it that works against the intent of the staging. These indifferently mounted productions have the look of a hastily blocked newsreel of events rather than the stately pavanne originally intended.

The other Olivier Shakespeare films adopt much the same technique as *Richard*, although not with the same intensely stylized success. *Hamlet* (1948) is staged, but not in the best sense of the word, for the camera: what comes across is a filmed reproduction of the play, not a cinematic interpretation. The audience is distanced, but this distancing is never formally recognized by the film. *Henry V* (1945) is more open in its interpretation of the play, but again, by taking the production out-of-doors and utilizing the power of the camera to transport us, without the use of our collective theatrical imagination, to anywhere in the twinkling of an eye, the film simultaneously caters to and cheats us out of the interpretational experience Shakespeare's strategy affords. Kenneth Branagh's 1989 production of *Henry V* is perhaps the finest adaptation of Shakespeare the cinema has yet given us. In the title role, Branagh is mesmerizing, and his direction and staging of the piece (he was only twenty-eight when he directed and starred in the film) is remarkably adroit and assumed. Branagh has continued his work with Shakespeare in *Much Ado About Nothing* (1993), which offered a choice role to Denzel Washington, and in his 1997 *Hamlet*, which, though faithful to the original text, seems overproduced and ultimately collapses under the weight of an overstylized production, much like George Cukor's 1964 adaptation of Shaw's *Pygmalion*, and *My Fair Lady*, which Branagh's *Hamlet* visually resembles.

Olivier's precise delivery of dialogue is the centerpiece of all of Olivier's filmic adaptations of Shakespeare's works, along with his commanding presence as an actor. The visualization of events within the Olivier films is resolutely locked into the direct representationalism of physical existence. *Richard III* is self-contained in its approach to the physical realities of the play; it acknowledges its staging, and, therefore, transcends the limitations it sets for itself by formalizing them. Olivier's performance remains one of the most formal aspects of the piece, and Claire Bloom matches him perfectly. Olivier's production of *Richard III* is, then, one of the few filmed Shakespearean dramas that confronts the issue of performance locked into the theatrical, performing self and uses that aspect of the piece as a complement to its presentation.

The other great filmic formalizer of Shakespearean cinema is Orson Welles, in his much underrated Mercury Theatre production of *Macbeth* for Republic Pictures in 1948. Forced to make the film in a very short time for very little money, Welles had to rely on extremely long takes, stylized and spare sets, and performances that distanced the audience in two ways simultaneously. First, Welles and his troupe were ill-rehearsed for the production, and the performing aspect was firmly acknowledged in each take, as Welles rehearsed the actors scene by scene and then immediately photographed the scene, in one take, intact, before it fled from the memory of his troupe. Second, in the original production of the film (before it was altered by the studio's president, Herbert J. Yates), Welles and his performers speak in a stylized brogue which Welles thought was more accurate in its enunciation of Shakespeare's language than other traditional approaches to the piece. Then, too, Welles himself was an extremely self-conscious actor, and his performances always had an uneasy edge about them. In all of his films, it seems as if Welles may at any point throw off his acting persona, and allow his own personality alone to dominate the role. Stalking about the starkly lit sets of this minuscule but resonant production, Welles offers a prototype for a style of filmic acting which may, in fact, have influenced Olivier's later productions.

Everything in Welles's production of *Macbeth* is suggested. Physical reality is clearly secondary to Welles's vision of the play. The language of the play is mediated by the dialect he imposes upon it, and his performers are seemingly conscious of every cue, every "mark." They acknowledge this formalization transparently. Aware that he had few physical resources, Welles made the spare production values an asset to the film, and his own performance is designed to complement this spareness. The mask of the actor is everywhere evident in the finished film. Thankfully, Welles's original version of the film was not destroyed, and Republic Home Video has released Welles's uncut and undubbed version on home video. The results are indeed a revelation, and confirm the film as one of Welles's finest efforts, along with the director's later film *Chimes at Midnight* (1966), a compilation of no less than five Shakespearean texts, in which Welles plays the role of Falstaff.

Since the time of these two productions, newer Shakespearean adaptations have fallen short of achieving this interesting mix of formalized distancing and stylistic exactness. Roman Polanski's production of *Macbeth* (1969) is a sloppy, self-indulgent disaster, which attempts to impose newsreel techniques on a period piece that is rightly, and highly resistant to such a cavalier interpretation. Polanski is also obviously much too interested in the violent aspects of the play for their own sake, and he unbalances the film in favor of Gothic sensationalism. Stuart Burge's production of *Julius Caesar* in 1970, while deeply flawed, is far more interesting. Jason Robards's performance as Brutus is certainly one of the most rigorously schematic interpretations the role has ever been given. His interpretation is so world-weary and seemingly oblivious to the demands of any audience, filmic or otherwise, that it practically becomes a new form of acting, as if his lines were being fed to him telepathically during the production. One could almost call Burge's film a series of disconnected performances in search of a central uniting force: Charlton Heston's Marc Antony is a creation of artifice and bombast, but nothing more, and Christopher Lee's Artemidoris is simply a recitation of lines. Still, the film never attempts to undermine the innate theatricality of the play, and, at least in that respect, it is an honorable misfire.

Several productions of *Hamlet* represent intriguing attempts at visual and textual formalization. Richard Burton's 1964 version was hastily videotaped for presentation during its Broadway run. Within the context of an uneven performance and an undeniably marred conception of the play, Burton manages to distance Hamlet's character through the use of incongruous modern street dress and yet to make the character one with whom the audience can sympathize. Tony Richardson's 1969 film of *Hamlet* adopts a different approach. Nicol Williamson reads the part in the tired, flat monotone of an overextended businessman, as though he were bored with it before the play begins. Devoid of inflection or emotion, his Hamlet is doubly dead: he is encased by the photographic image (as Jean Cocteau once noted, "Film photographs death at work"), and he is cut off from the audience's concern by his own attitude-within-the-play towards the staged events. Franco Zeffirelli's 1990 version of *Hamlet*, starring Mel Gibson, was trounced by most critics for its extensive cuts in the play's text, yet Gibson, Glenn Close, Alan Bates, and Paul Scofield all do superb work in what I would argue is an atmospheric and essentially faithful rendition of the source text. As previously mentioned, Baz Luhrman's 1997 *Romeo and Juliet* is an interesting update of Shakespeare's play, starring Leonardo DiCaprio, Clare Danes, and John Leguizamo, transforming the rival Montagues and Capulets into warring crime families bent on the domination of a sleazy seaside resort. Of Kenneth Branagh's 1997 *Hamlet*, famously using the uncut text of the play, the less said the better. Although the stylized, Cecil Beaton-esque sets and the

70mm cinematograph are eye-catching, the overall impression is one of ponderousness and calculation.

These last approaches to the problem of formalizing the actor's role in Shakespearean drama are, however, clearly aberrational. Of all the films cited here, only the Welles's production of *Macbeth*, Olivier's *Richard III*, and Branagh's *Henry V* truly succeed in adopting a convincing strategy of conventional representation that effectively enhances the text of the plays. The question of the performing self in filmed Shakespearean drama is but a microcosmic concern in the larger question of whether or not this formalized enhancement of performance is to be desired in all Shakespearean productions. However, the doubly removed nature of filmic representation is an interestingly complex problem within the context of this inquiry. Those productions of Shakespeare's plays that strive for a kind of synthetic naturalism clearly work against the grain of the text, but does this mode of production bring anything to the piece, or does it take away more than it brings?

The naturalism implicitly sought in Polanski's film *Macbeth* or Peter Brook's film *King Lear* (much of which is also staged on natural locations) is, it seems, not to be desired in productions of Elizabethan drama. Removing all the limits of theatrical space supposedly frees the play of artificial constraints. But, in fact, so-called natural staging and an unposed performance style neutralize the collective function of the audience's interpretive imagination, and perhaps this is the final proof that the formalizing element is, indeed, required. Film staging operates with two sets of blocking, one for the actors and one for the camera. Therefore, it is inherently and consistently formalized, demanding a third level of interpretation in the interlocutory gaze of the film audience. Does this circumstance work for or against the stylized self in Shakespeare? Surely, for it. The camera eye, if properly used, can lend added credence to the measured steps and well-defined stance of the classical style of acting employed in Shakespearean drama.

AN INDUSTRIAL WORLD OF MOVING IMAGES

This text has discussed numerous cases of cinematic marginalization, racial, social, economic, and transactional, in which the potential viewer, through a variety of strategies, is literally denied access to a completed work. No group of films is perhaps more ephemeral than the "sponsored" or "industrial" film, which flourished in the 1930s to 1970s as a series of phantom, 16mm and 35mm shorts shown in schools, theaters, places of business, and other non-theatrical situations. In 1988, Rick Prelinger began saving the films that other people were throwing away: industrial films, commercials, instructional films, sponsored films, the entire gamut of "educational" films produced by various universities, corporations, and government agencies from the 1920s onward. Amazingly, none of these films were being preserved; Prelinger began hauling them literally out of the trash cans and taking them home with him, until his collection reached its present size of over thirty-three thousand titles. Prelinger is obviously in love with these films and the vision of American society they present, a vision directly at odds with the packaged gloss of Hollywood escapism, even at its most modishly *noirish* extremes.

Sixteen millimeter is pretty much a dead format. One could release these films on VHS tape or on Laserdisc (this second option might not be a bad idea), but for now, Prelinger has provided cinema scholars and cultural historians with a signal service with the release of six CD-ROMs culled from his collection, collectively titled *Our Secret Century: Archival Films from the Darker Side of the American Dream*. Distributed by the Voyager Company, the six CDs offer a compelling vision of an America not seen in theaters or, later, on television—a cinema of moralistic instruction and persuasion, in which the viewer is a target for both social and civil discipline.

The CD-ROM format allows one to skip around from film to film at will, stopping or reversing as one wishes; the disc also has a "large picture" format, which instantly doubles the image size to nearly full-screen playback. In these discs, Prelinger offers us not excerpts from the films, but the entire films, complete with opening titles and end credits, in addition to considerable critical commentary on each work. In addition, Prelinger provides "hidden" films (not shown in the table of contents) in the "From the Archives" section of some of the discs, as well as advertisements from magazines of the period, newspaper articles, and other documentation to give one a full idea of the cultural project undertaken by these ambitious and influential short films.

For a time, as noted, these "instructional" films were omnipresent. No one who grew up in the 1950s or '60s could avoid them. They were run in churches, schools, factories, and wherever groups of people congregated as part of the American social fabric. On rainy days, they were screened to "baby-sit" YWCA or YMCA campers who weren't able to play outside; schools showed them as a regular part of their assembly diet; factories screened them during lunch breaks. They run the gamut from outright advertising to social instruction, from corporate propaganda to highway safety. Prelinger has collected some of the most interesting of these films in the first four CDs, and the assortment of themes and approaches demonstrated is truly astonishing.

The first CD, *The Rainbow Is Yours*, deals mostly with glitzy advertising films, such as the General Motors 1956 musical promotional film *Design for Dreaming* and *American Look*, and demonstrates how much of the culture of 1950s America was based on conspicuous consumption and surface glamour. Volume two, *Capitalist Realism*, deals mostly with black and white 1930s industrial films, offering a grimy, anti-Capraesque vision of the struggle to survive during the Depression years. Volume three, *The Behavior Offensive*, showcases 1940s and '50s "social guidance" films, such as *Shy Guy* (starring a pre-*Bewitched* Dick York), *Are You Popular?* and *Habit Patterns*.

Volume four, *Menace and Jeopardy*, is in many ways the creepiest CD of the group, focusing on safety films which actually revel in the disaster and destruction they supposedly warn us against, particularly *Time Out for Trouble* (in which a haunted antique clock causes the various members of an average Iowa family to have a series of near-fatal accidents), *More Dangerous than Dynamite* (a film that cautions against the use of gasoline [!!] as a home dry-cleaning solvent, and features a series of graphic and grisly accidents to drive home this message), *Days of Our Years* (carelessness on the job leads to a series of fatal accidents, all of which are entirely the fault of the workers involved, never management), and *A Safety Belt for Susie* (which climaxes in a series of more than a dozen staged car wrecks, during which safety dummies are tossed through windshields and otherwise mangled for a battery of slow-motion cameras). As Prelinger notes, this last group of films almost defeats its purpose. Each film asks us to be more careful and thus avoid the accidents we see; yet as viewers, we keep waiting for the next grisly incident to inevitably occur (much like watching a film in the *Friday the 13th* series), since this is the syntactical structure the film establishes from the outset.

As cultural texts, as social artifacts, and as an examination of the "dark side" of American culture, *Our Secret Century* is an eye-opening and fascinating look at the "other movies" produced around the United States during the first one hundred years of cinema. Watching these films is an instant passport back to a culture which was simultaneously repressive and yet buoyantly optimistic; a culture in which manners, appearance, social status, and the acquisition of consumer goods counted for one's social standing within the community; a period in which video, laserdisc, and internet technology was nascent or nonexistent, and film alone was the dominant medium of imagistic exchange; a time in American society when we were forming our visual construction of our own identities both for ourselves, and for the posterity we assumed would embrace us. Hollywood did part of the job, but these films completed it. Apparently, as a society, we wanted to consign these films to the scrap heap, precisely because they tell us so much about ourselves.

THE SAFETY OF THE PAST;
THE LURE OF THE FUTURE

Conventional entertainments such as the 1998 remake of *The Parent Trap*, directed by Nancy Meyers, offer us a fantasy version of a world awash in privilege, luxury, and wealth, in stark contrast to the vision presented in the industrial films collected by Prelinger. As a heterotopic fantasy of a broken home reconstituted by the efforts of twin girls who had been separated by warring parents at birth, *The Parent Trap* has gone through numerous German, British, and American versions, all based on the novel by Erich Kästner. The first screen translation of the work was produced in the former West Germany in 1950, under the direction of Josef von Báky, and was entitled *Das Doppelle Lottchen* (*Two Times Lotte*). Next came a 1953 British adaptation, directed by Emeric Pressburger, with the title *Twice Upon a Time*. In 1961, Walt Disney bought the rights to remake the film a third time as *The Parent Trap*, directed by David Swift, and starring a photographically "doubled" Hayley Mills as the scheming twin sisters. This version, starring Mills, Brian Keith, Maureen O'Hara and Leo G. Carroll, was a worldwide hit, and provides one of the earliest instances of a popular foreign film being remade in an Americanized version rather than allowing the original film to be released to the international box-office. In addition to spawning a top ten pop hit, *Let's Get Together* (sung by a double-tracked Hayley Mills), the film also inextricably identified Mills with the role of the twins, and led to the production of the 1986 TV film *Parent Trap II*, directed by Robert F. Maxwell for the Disney studios. In 1989, two more versions of the film were produced; *Parent Trap III* and *Parent Trap Hawaiian Honeymoon* (aka *Parent Trap IV: Hawaiian Honeymoon*), both directed by Mollie Miller.

In 1993, Joseph Vilsmaier directed a new German version of the work as *Charlie and Louise: Das Doppelte Lottchen*, with Isabelle Carlson as the "doubled" twin. The overseas success of this project convinced the Disney organization that there was still some potential mileage in the property, and thus led to the 1998 version, directed by Nancy Meyers, which brought the property back to the American big screen. Amazingly, Hayley Mills appeared in all of the first four American films as progressively aging identical twins, while the script varied little from the original formula that inaugurated the series. As Mills became an adult, the plot of the *Parent Trap* films shifted from the misadventures of twin girls switching identities after an accidental meeting at summer camp to reunite their estranged parents, into the misadventures of two adult twin women who switch identities to further their own romantic machinations. In *Parent Trap III*, for example, Hayley Mills plays twins Susan and Sharon Evers, who each have romantic designs on Barry Bostwick, the unattached father of triplets. All the films rely on progressively more complex trick cinematography, which by the 1998 version is fully digitized, making the earlier versions seem visually static indeed. Yet for all the increasing technical sophistication, the plot remains essentially the same, recycled with new cast members and slightly variant situations. The film's narrative structure is merely an excuse for the ersatz spectacle of synthetic twins conjured up for the amazement of the viewer—twins who exist only within the realm of the cinematographic apparatus.

In contrast to the 1961 version, and the relatively impoverished TV movies in between, the 1998 version is hyperspectacular, a land of multi-million-dollar homes, hundred-acre vineyards, mothers who are internationally known fashion designers, fathers who make millions selling and collecting wine. Director Nancy Meyers, who co-produced the 1998 version with her husband Charles Shyer, is no stranger to domestic opulence in the service of generic fiction. Meyers's other credits include (as a producer) Charles Shyer's *Father of the Bride II* (1995) and *Father of the Bride* (1991), both remakes themselves. Natasha Richardson, who usually finds herself in less mainstream projects, had to be persuaded to tackle the role of Elizabeth James, the mother of the twins in the new version of *The Parent Trap* (her leading man in the film is Dennis Quaid, as Nick Parker, father of the twins). As she commented in an interview before the film was released,

What kind of a mother FedExes one of the twins off to Napa and says, "It's okay; I'll never see you again"? . . . You'll never see a bead of sweat in [Meyers-Shyer] movies, either. Everything has to be— even the sheets on the bed, the flowers—every little detail is sort of your dream of what life should be like. At first I was a little resistant to it. (Daly 34)

Indeed, while the 1998 version of *The Parent Trap* may echo the thematic and narrative structure of the earlier versions, what distinguishes Nancy Meyers's version from the previous ones is the lavish overproduction of the piece, in which every car is a Rolls Royce, all families have servants, and no one is poor (or, for that matter, anything other than Caucasian). While Meyers is comfortable describing her version of *The Parent Trap* as "a fable" (Daly 34), one is left to speculate as to exactly what sort of a fable the 1998 version presents its audience. Indeed, in all of Meyers-Shyer films, it seems that poverty is a crime, and that only opulence and conventional "good looks" permit one entrée into this world of conspicuous consumption. What sort of a message does this send to an audience, particularly if the children who view it come from broken homes themselves, or from families who can't afford a twenty-room mansion in the Napa Valley wine country? If this is a fable or a fairy tale, it is one that operates by rules of exclusion rather than inclusion, and seeks to offer the promise of wealth and power to its audience while simultaneously withholding it.

In contrast, the vision of America offered by the multi-media musical *Hedwig and the Angry Inch* is much more in tune with the lowered expectations and shattered dreams that dot the landscape of the late twentieth century. Created by John Cameron Mitchell, who also stars in the title role, with music and lyrics by Stephen Trask of the rock band Cheater, *Hedwig* tells the story of a young cross-dressing boy growing up in East Germany who wants to escape to the West. To do this, he agrees to a botched sex-change operation that leaves an "angry inch" of his penis still attached, but which is good enough to allow him to marry, pass for a woman, and emigrate to the United States. All this, only to land in a trailer park in Kansas. There s/he meets a young military brat, Tommy Gnosis, whom s/he molds into a major rock star, while Hedwig her/himself sinks into ever-greater obscurity, becoming, in her/his words, an "internationally ignored" cabaret star.

On the night the action of the play unfolds, we see Hedwig, with his/her supremely bored and diffident backup band, grinding through yet another forgettable one-night stand at a down-and-out rock club, in this case the Jane Street Theatre (where the production was actually staged). Hedwig treats the theatre audience as if they were paying customers at the gig, which just happens to be playing across the street from Tommy Gnosis's latest sold out concert. Throughout the play, Hedwig and/or members of the backup band open a door to the right rear of the shabby stage, to let in a blast of light and noise from the adjacent stadium concert; it is clear that the musicians in Hedwig's band would much rather be working for Tommy, who has essentially stolen Hedwig's act. As the seventy-five minute show progresses, Hedwig becomes angrier and angrier with the audience, berating his/her band and those who have come to see them for not being more attractive and appreciative of her/his efforts. Tracing the arc of his/her life for an audience of increasingly uncomfortable patrons, Hedwig simultaneously threatens, charms, and confronts the crowd, as s/he pouts and struts through a series of memorable songs that chart the major crisis points in his/her bizarre career. By the end of the performance, Hedwig has stripped off all of his/her drag gear to reveal a triumphantly re-gendered being desperately crying out for attention and approval, a woman/man who asks for little from life and receives precisely that. Infuriating and engaging, *Hedwig and the Angry Inch* offers a truer vision of the American dream, or lack of it, than most other theatrical narrative constructs. So successful is the play that by the time this book appears, the film rights will no doubt have been optioned. Whether or not *Hedwig and the Angry Inch* will make it intact to the screen, in a cinematic universe populated for the most part by disaster movies and grossout comedies, is another matter altogether.

THE FILM DIRECTOR AS OUTLAW

Conforming to a completely different set of rules, the films of the late director Al Adamson also comprise a unique testament created by an artist working on his own terms. In Adamson's case, his vision of America was more bleak and despairing than even that offered by *Hedwig and the Angry Inch*. The son of actor/writer/director Denver Dixon, whose real name was Victor Adamson, Al Adamson followed in the ultra low-budget footsteps of his father to create a series of violent, defiantly cheap films for the marginal distribution company Independent-International, before he was murdered in 1995 under mysterious circumstances. Adamson's films include *Satan's Sadists* (1969), perhaps the bleakest motorcycle drama ever made; *Five Bloody Graves* (1970), a western in which even an itinerant preacher (played by John Carradine) eventually becomes involved in a murderous rampage of destruction; *Dracula vs. Frankenstein* (1972), perhaps the most impoverished horror film ever produced; and *Brain of Blood* (1972), another Dystopian science fiction horror film. In his work, Adamson was emulating the production tactics of his father, who produced such program westerns as *Desert Vultures* (1930), *Ridin' Speed* (1931), *Desert Mesa* (1936), and his final film, *Halfway to Hell* (1961), in which his son Al made his screen debut as an actor. Victor Adamson early on decided that he could save money by performing a variety of different functions on his films, under different names. As Victor Adamson he was a producer; as Art Mix he starred in his films; as Denver Dixon he directed the sixteen films that comprised his thirty-one-year career as an independent producer/director.

Halfway to Hell was actually Al Adamson's baptism of fire as a director, as well as his acting debut. The film was begun in 1955, but the production ran short on funding, and was only completed after a number of re-shoots, hastily arranged by whatever crew was available. Al Adamson was ashamed of *Halfway to Hell*, which he thought was "very bad," but he learned one major lesson from the making of *Halfway to Hell*: "When you ran out of money, whatever you got was done. You could use it" (Konow 23).

With this methodology as his guiding principle of production, Adamson launched into a series of lurid, low-budget films, astonishingly photographed by the likes of Laszlo Kovacs and Vilmos Zsigmond, who later went onto major careers in Hollywood. As David Konow recounts,

> Zsigmond won an Academy Award for [the cinematography] on *Close Encounters of the Third Kind* [1977, directed by Steven Spielberg] and shot such films as *McCabe and Mrs. Miller* [1971, directed by Robert Altman], *Sugarland Express* [1974, directed by Steven Spielberg] and *The Deer Hunter* [1978, directed by Michael Cimino]. Kovacs shot such critically acclaimed films as *Easy Rider* [1969, directed by Dennis Hopper], *Five Easy Pieces* [1979, directed by Bob Rafelson], *What's Up Doc?* [1972, directed by Peter Bogdanovich] and *Shampoo* [1975, directed by Hal Ashby]. (25)

But at the time they were working with Adamson, both Kovacs and Zsigmond were struggling to gain a foothold in Hollywood, having recently emigrated to the United States, and were willing to work for practically nothing. Zsigmond recalled, "Al paid me $100 per day, including my equipment—lights, camera and myself. What a deal that was!" (Konow 25). Shooting in 35mm Techniscope to save money, Adamson financed an early production by delivering newspapers in the evenings, and once paid Zsigmond his day's wages in one hundred one dollar bills he had collected along his delivery route—a testament to Al Adamson's absolute tenacity of purpose (24). Using such veteran actors as Broderick Crawford, J. Carrol Naish, John Carradine, Lon Chaney, Jr., Russ Tamblyn, and other performers looking for a few days' work, Adamson shot as many as seventy set-ups (a complete change of camera and lighting) per day, and pushed his cast and crew beyond the limits of their endurance to get his films completed on time and under budget. No one can say that Adamson's films are in any way uncompromised by the speed and poverty of their execution. Yet *Satan's Sadists* and other of Adamson's exploitation films revel in a side of American culture that the Dominant Cinema scorned, and Independent-International's distribution method of simply taking the film from theatre to theatre to secure bookings also operated at the absolute fringe of the industry. In *Satan's Sadists*, as director Fred Olen Ray notes,

> The villains [a demented bunch of outlaw motorcyclists] are literally the center of attention. The heroes are just a perfunctory thing you have to have to make the story resolve itself. In most of Al's films, what I've found is that the evildoers are totally unredeemable. They're just evil and they never see the error of their ways . . . and Al always lets them off easy. . . . *Satan's Sadists* was a strong picture. It's so mean-spirited. It's such a cruel film, it's almost like *Natural Born Killers* [1994, directed by Oliver Stone]. (Konow 52–53)

When the film was completed in June, 1969, Independent-International's president, Sam Sherman, flew around the country and secured five hundred bookings for the film throughout the country (mostly at drive-ins) by the sheer persistence of his sales presentation (Konow 53, 55). The film was a resounding success, and Adamson and Sherman cranked out eighteen more features between 1969 and 1982, when the collapse of the drive-in circuit and the rise of videocassette rentals put an end to active production. Yet though Adamson's films are cheap, shoddy, violent, and often difficult to endure, the brutal tenacity of Adamson's maverick vision and his ability to complete his films for next to nothing marks him as a true, independent original. As Gary Kent, one of Adamson's co-workers, commented after the director's death, "I didn't think Al was, nor was he trying to be, Ingmar Bergman. He just wanted to make films that entertained" (Konow 148). Adamson's peculiar vision marks him as a folk artist of the cinema, self-taught, working entirely outside the established industry. His dark, brooding, disturbing films are the work of a deeply independent filmmaker who preferred to work in poverty, and make the films he chose to, rather than compromise his control over his films by working for the majors.

ROSSELLINI IN INDIA

Another fiercely independent filmmaker who often worked without the safety net of conventional distribution or production facilities was the director Roberto Rossellini, although his vision was far more polished and refined than the bleakly violent nihilism embraced by Adamson. One of Rossellini's most intriguing projects was his docudrama *India* (1958), a four-part meditation on the world's most populous democracy as it emerged from the shadow of British colonial rule. As in many of his other films, such as *Roma Citta Aperta* (*Opera City*, 1945) and *Germania Anno Zero* (*Germany Year Zero*, 1947), Rossellini used the services of non-professional actors to create India, and, as was his method, shot the film on location whenever possible. Photographed in Gevacolor and Kodachrome by the great cinematographer Aldo Tonti, and for many years considered lost, *India* has been restored by the Cinémathèque Française, and presented in archival screenings throughout the world. *India* presents four different stories, tied together only by montage, which depict a country and its citizens in personal and societal crisis, moving out of the past toward an uncertain future. In the first segment, a peasant marries the daughter of an itinerant salesman, intercut with scenes of elephants laboring to bring felled timber from the forest to nearby construction sites. The second segment documents the interior thoughts of a laborer who has worked on a dam at Hirakud for five years, and must now move on to a new job. In the third segment, an elderly man does his best to protect a tiger from a group of hunters who seek to destroy it. In the last portion of the film, a monkey whose owner has died of thirst and exhaustion tries desperately to escape from the chains that bind it to its master, while waiting vultures circle the corpse of the man, anxious to feed on his rapidly decomposing body. The monkey manages to escape at the last possible moment, and fleeing to the next town, finds a new place within the fabric of Indian social discourse. When *India* was presented at Anthology Film Archives in the summer of 1998, Fereydown Hoveyda, one of the film's scenarists, provided this account of *India*'s genesis.

> I met Rossellini in 1954 at a time when he had just finished the shooting of *La Paura* [aka *Die Angst/Fear*, 1954], after Stefan Aweig's short story. Like his previous movies with his wife Ingrid Bergman, this was a failure at the box-office as well as among most film critics. He deeply felt the need for a change both in his private life and artistic undertakings. He had always been attracted to the "East." He decided to travel to India by car through Turkey, Iran and Pakistan, and to make films about these countries. We spent many nights in 1955 and 1956 exchanging ideas about them. Several story outlines emerged from our discussions. In late 1956, he had to limit his project to India because of financial shortcomings.
>
> Rossellini envisaged a *Paisan* type of feature with four or more vignettes and a series of "Cine-oeil" (Dziga Vertov) documentaries. He was interested in what he used to call "actual and real India," not in exoticism and western-invented myths such as "spiritualism" and other tourist attractions: yoga, "serpent charming" or "rope climbing." He intended to debunk all the commonplaces and platitudes the media spilled about India. I worked with him on several story lines for the feature. He liked very much one on monkeys.
>
> Hiding with his cameraman, Aldo Tonti, in the streets or on apartment balconies of many cities, he accumulated hundreds of hours of images, while working at the same time on the feature. In Bombay he met his "future" wife Sonali Das Gupta, a married woman who helped him develop vignettes for the film. As she changed many of our previously agreed stories, Rossellini used to call me over the telephone to discuss some points about the scripts. His relationship with Sonali, who asked for a divorce and abandoned her family, erupted into a scandal which forced Roberto to leave India hurriedly before completing his feature. Additional scenes had to be shot in studios in Italy and in France. He himself edited most of the documentaries in a small makeshift editing room given by Henri Langlois at the French Cinémathèque. (Hoveyda 16)

India is thus a mixture of memory, fantasy, fiction, and documentary observation that blends the personal with the spectacular in a manner unknown to the creators of big-budget hyperspectaculars. The elephants patiently engrossed in their labors; the worker departing from the dam construction site where he has labored for so long; the monkey desperate to survive despite the death of his master; the old man, conscious of his mortality, yet determined to preserve the life of a tiger from poachers—all of these are faces of an India in transition, an enormous tapestry of humans and their works at midpoint in the twentieth century. Rossellini's humanist vision always reduces the overwhelming (the dam site, for one example) to the realm of human experience, and he is less interested in narrative than in observation, and the documentation of human emotion. With its pastel tones and gently droning soundtrack (the film was one of the first Western films to use authentic India musical accompaniment for much of the film's score), Rossellini's *India* is a testament of one film-maker's personal voyage of discovery, in which the commonplace becomes extraordinary, and the position of humankind in an uncertain universe is seen as both precarious and transcendent. From this project, Rossellini went on to make a gorgeous series of historical dramas for RAI, Italian television, including my own personal favorite, *Blaise Pascal* (1975). In all of his work, Rossellini eschews Hollywood's desire for narrative closure and momentary sensation in favor of introspection and meditation on that which one sees. As Baudrillard notes, "We must not reconcile our-selves with nature" (*End* 82); rather, we must become one with it.

STAGED REALITIES: THE WORKS OF TRACEY MOFFAT

Tracey Moffat is a late twentieth-century visual artist who has worked in a variety of mediums: cinema, video, and still photographs. Born on November 12, 1960, in Brisbane, Australia, Moffat's first major success was her short film, *Night Cries: A Rural Tragedy* (1989), which was screened at the 1990 Cannes Film Festival. Technically adroit, *Night Cries* was shot in 35mm color, and uses such distancing techniques as back pro-jection and black and white and color cinematography interspersed within the same frame, to tell the story of a young child's abandonment by its mother. It is set to the beat of the Australian pop song hit, *Royal Telephone*, as performed by the Aboriginal singing star Jimmy Little, one of Australia's first aboriginal stars to break through on the White-dominated pop charts. Moffat has also created a series of photos entitled *GUAPA* (*Good Looking*) (1995), documenting the world of roller derby in San Antonio, Texas; and *Heaven* (1997), a simple video installation in which Moffat trails a group of "extreme surfers" in Australia, admiring their physiques, and encouraging them to pose and "vogue" before her small video camera, even to momentarily drop their bathing suits to display their genitalia. *Up in the Sky* (1997) is another photographic installation, in which Moffat creates a series of mystic tableaux documenting the trials of a poor pregnant woman who is pursued by a troupe of ominous nuns, who seek to judge the woman without any regard for the social milieu in which she must survive. Set in a desolate landscape of shacks, dead animals, bare trees, and industrial garbage, *Up in the Sky* evokes a cultural crisis in late twentieth-century social discourse, in which all interventions become accusations, and words are rendered transparent.

In one photograph, number fourteen in the series, a pregnant woman holds her stomach in pain to the left of the frame, standing in front of a tumble-down lean-to, while an older man in the right foreground cradles a chicken, perhaps his only food for the day. The sky is harsh and flat; Moffat's protagonists are dressed in dirty, cast-off clothing. In number twenty-four of the series, we see the same woman from number fourteen, clutching her aboriginal child, running desperately towards the camera, pursued by an angry mob armed with sticks and clubs, obviously intent on inflicting injury. Nothing is specific in these photographs, and nothing needs to be. The aura of menace and sinister uncertainty that pervades these images is more than sufficient to engage the viewer. As with *Night Cries*, there is no linear narrative to tie the images together, but rather the *suggestion* of one. Perhaps Moffat is saying that in late twentieth-century imagistic discourse, we have outgrown the need for narrative structure, and need only the outlines of a story to perceive the inner truth of the situation being created for our visual consumption. In an interview with Coco Fusco, Moffat described how she created these haunting, evocative, yet ultimately evanescent images.

> COCO FUSCO: You work with non-professionals. How do you get them to behave the way you want? I look at some of these pictures—like the one I've got in my hand now where everybody's in their bathrobe on the street as if somebody's woken them up at five o'clock in the morning—and they're all performing in unison. What did you say? . . .

TRACEY MOFFAT: I work with actors exactly the way a film director works: Look a certain way, stand there, shift your arm, move to the background . . . I can rope people in. It's sheer force of personality and enthusiasm and getting people excited about being in art. . . . I look for the right face . . .

CF: And what sort of equipment did you work with?

TM: A 6x7 centimeter Fuji camera. The camera is very simple, it has a lens that you can't remove, it doesn't even have a light meter. I don't have any fancy equipment. I'm technically very stupid. I had a technician take the light meter readings. I don't even know how to take a reading . . . I supervise. I don't do a thing. I don't even load the film, darling. Often I required extra light, so my technician would plug in the generator and throw more light on the subjects. It's very hard when you work in the desert because you get extreme shadows and eyes become dark sockets. In photography class the first thing you learn is you must have a perfect black, a gray and a white. There's got to be that range. But I was going for just a gray really, a tone. It had to be completely tonal so that you could see into the shadows. It is important to look into the shadows in these pictures. (49, 50)

As Moffat's retrospective at the Dia Center for the Arts amply demonstrates, it is precisely this rejection of technique for its own sake that gives her images the rough-hewn beauty that she seeks. With *Night Cries*, Moffat embraced a very slick visual sensibility, and in many ways, the 35mm short film is her most traditional work, with carefully composed frames, studio lighting, and a carefully controlled use of space, color, and image density. In her newer work, Moffat seems to be moving away from the cumbersomeness of the cinematographic apparatus as it is used in the traditional studio atmosphere, towards a more direct vision using non-professional actors, the barest outline of a story, and a rawness of execution that results in a series of images that seem simultaneously documentary, and yet staged according to a carefully surreal logic. *Heaven*, in ways Moffat's simplest work, was created using only a portable, autoexposure digital camcorder, as she prowls the beaches of Australia in search of willing participants. The surfers who appear in the video piece seem to accept Moffat's presence utterly; even as she pursues them with the intensity of a stalker, Moffat's subjects delight in her obsessive documentation.

Although the surfers speak, we never hear their words, or any of the sounds recorded during the actual taping of the piece. Rather, Moffat creates an aural backdrop of gently pounding surf as a complement to these handheld, low-tech images, and thus with a single stroke isolates image from sound in a bold and decisive manner. Moffat's use of stills, home video, and other low-cost formats has only sharpened her sensibility. More than ever before, in her new work, Tracey Moffat concentrates on that which is essential in the world she creates and records. This studied primitivism may well be a useful way to undermine the suffocating slickness of the mainstream cinema. In her utilization of formats generally accessible to all, Tracey Moffat effectively demonstrates that less is indeed more compelling than the processed vision offered to the public by the Dominant image production system.

CINEMA AT THE MARGINS
IN THE NEW MILLENNIUM

Other contemporary artists, working in a variety of media, are creating equally compelling images using increasingly minimal resources. Tracey Baran, a young woman whose work has attracted great attention in New York, documents her suburban family life in a series of deceptively artless "candid" photos that feature Tracey, her mother, father, and brother in a variety of domestic poses, almost always bordering on the chaotic. Christmas is seen as a bewildering freeze-frame of opened packages, spoiled wrapping, uneaten food, and isolated gazes, as the family members inhabit the space of one room but seem otherwise utterly disconnected. A close-up of curtains reveals them to be decorated with the bodies of dead flies, untouched for months, perhaps years. When Tracey tries to relax on the lawn outside her suburban home, she seems transfixed in a pose of agony and relief—relief that she has momentarily escaped from her suburban milieu, but agony in that she knows she must, of necessity, return to her house as a matter of course. Shot in garish color, Tracey Baran's photographs are, as with Moffat's work, deceptively offhand, yet each image captures in microcosm the perils of everyday existence.

The director Masashi Yamamoto similarly covers the darker side of Japanese popular culture. His 1998 film *Junk Food* depicts Japanese society in complete crisis. As Eve Claxton describes the film,

Like the brutal black and white [stills] of photographer Nobuyoshi Araki (which blew the lid off Tokyo's S/M scene), director Masashi Yamomoto's frequently gruesome film will be all the more shocking initially to Western viewers due to its Japanese context. Of course, we like to think of Tokyo as the futuristic paradigm of efficiency, where men in gray suits run corporations peopled by obedient workers in more gray suits. Yamamoto doesn't just seek to expose the city's seamy underside; he revels in it.

The movie, which is made up of loosely interlocking stories and vignettes, opens with the tale of a heroin-addicted office worker (Ijima) who asphyxiates her lover with a plastic bag before heading out for a day at the office. Other characters include a Mexican female wrestler, a Chinese-American hooker, a Pakistani delivery man who slits his girlfriend's throat and a Tokyo gang leader who models himself and his crew on American homeboys.

Yamamoto used nonprofessional actors in the film (including Onimaru, a real-life Tokyo gang leader). . . . There's a voyeuristic edge to the way Yamamoto directs, and it will no doubt disturb some viewers. But despite its flaws, the rough, edgy and affecting *Junk Food* is a heartfelt portrait of a city and a society in a state of serious psychosis. (88)

This nonstop roller coaster of violence and chaotic countersignification, where everyday life is meaningless, violent, rife with random cruelty and bizarre disruptions echoes nothing so much, it seems to me, as the work of director Lucio Fulci, whose Gothic horror films rely on the same dreamlike plotlessness to induce a trance-like state in the viewer. Yamamoto's films have always been non-specific, but with the passage of time they have become increasingly obsessed with brutality and gore. In contrast, the director's 1987 *Robinson No Niwa* (*Robinson's Garden*), while similarly free form, seems positively idyllic. *Robinson's Garden* centers on Kumi, a young woman living in Tokyo who forsakes the fast lifestyle of her companions, and by accident, moves into an abandoned building in the center of town. As she fixes up her newfound habitat, her former acquaintances drift back into her life, threatening to turn her newfound domestic paradise into a maelstrom of drugs, sex, and petty acts of spiteful cruelty. Still, the conflicts within *Robinson's Garden* are nothing compared to the viciousness of the world depicted in *Junk Food*. As Claxton notes, Yamamoto "revels" in the brutal society he documents/creates in

Junk Food; in contrast, the relatively peaceful disputations in *Robinson's Garden* seem like the minor squabbles of an overextended family. In *Robinson's Garden*, Yamamoto holds out some hope for the regeneration of society through individual work and enterprise; in *Junk Food*, he seems to view all such efforts as futile. Yamamoto's anarchic vision depicts a world in which sensation is all, and context nothing. The domain of the protagonists of *Junk Food* is the realm of immediate gratification; all else is meaningless. Tomorrow is an abstraction, only the present is real.

STAGING THE "REAL": TRANSGRESSION AND MEMORY

In Tracey Moffat's work, in Masashi Yamamoto's work, and even in the films of Steven Spielberg, it seems as if narrative, staging, and the normal cause and effect functions of conventional linear narrative are being abrogated in favor of a desire to obtain, above other concerns, the correct *image* to convey the sensation of events as they unfold within the imagistic construct of the works in question. Steven Spielberg has stated that in staging the opening battle sequences in *Saving Private Ryan*, his intuition was first to create the battleground and choreograph the actors; and only then to place the cameras throughout the action, to document his staged conflict as though it were an event being captured by newsreel cameras. The actor Stellan Skarsgård appeared in Spielberg's *Amistad* (1997), which he found was shot in much the same manner, almost as if Spielberg was driven to complete each scene as quickly as possible, before the events he staged for the film "evaporated" in front of the camera. Skarsgård recalls that the shooting of *Amistad*

> was tough, but also it was the way the film was shot. Spielberg was doing forty set-ups a day, which means that the tempo was astonishing. It's twice as many set-ups [per day] as you usually do in a movie. And with a lot of actors and a lot of extras so there wasn't much time to try the scenes out and try to develop them, it was more or less just get there, action, and the camera was rolling immediately. (Gross 41–42)

This desire to move as quickly as possible, in direct contrast to what one would expect on a major Hollywood film, may also offer us a vision of the future of the cinema, in which speed is of the essence, not only for production and cost considerations, but also because with so many stories to tell, so many images to capture, one gets the very real sense that time is limited, and one can only accomplish so much. Spielberg's rate of production is an indicator of how the Hollywood of the twenty-first century *must* operate if it hopes to compete with the industry of its independent counterparts. Stellan Skarsgård also appears in more edgy contemporary fare, such as Erik Skjoldbjærg's *Insomnia* (1998), a Norwegian *policier* of indescribable grimness, which was shot with one-tenth the resources (if that) of *Amistad.* In its depiction of a homicide detective sinking deeper and deeper into a life of despair and corruption, *Insomnia* is also a film in a hurry, desirous of competing for our attention with all the other cinematic offerings currently being presented for public favor. Yet sadly, *Insomnia* will never receive the distribution that *Amistad* enjoyed, in part because subtitles still pose a seemingly impenetrable barrier for a great portion of the moviegoing audience, and in part because the uncompromisingly downbeat arc of *Insomnia's* narrative does not lend itself to conventional mainstream strategies of marketing and exploitation.

Major directors who have emerged since the late 1960s are also finding themselves at home in more modest productions as the century draws to a close. David Lynch, who shot to fame with his independently produced *Eraserhead* (1977), and went on to make *The Elephant Man* (1980), *Dune* (1984), *Blue Velvet* (1986), the cult television series *Twin Peaks* (1990), and *Lost Highway* (1997), has most recently made a small, offbeat film entitled *The Straight Story* (1999). I was able to watch a small portion of this project being filmed on location, thanks to the kindness of the director of cinematography, Freddie Francis. Freddie Francis had also shot *Dune* and *The Elephant Man* for Lynch, so the film was something of a reunion for the two men, and I jumped at the chance to watch the two collaborators in action. As luck would have it, I caught up with the crew at Prairie du Chien, Wisconsin, where the thirty-one-day film was entering its last day of shooting.

The Straight Story takes its name from the true story of a local farmer without a driver's license who one day hopped on his sit-down lawn-mower and drove off "to see America" at four miles per hour. He traveled through three states until the police finally pulled him off the road. The story is something of a local legend in Wisconsin and Iowa. Lynch's crew had been filming in Claremont and Mt. Zion, Iowa, for several days prior to my arrival, shooting on many of the actual locations where the story took place and working double shifts when necessary to keep on schedule. As I walked onto the set on the early morning of October 19th, I was welcomed with a bear hug from Freddie, who introduced me to David Lynch and his assistant, John Churchill. I told David I was sorry that I looked so exhausted, but that I'd just spent the night in a terrible motel where I was unable to sleep. "Welcome to the club," David replied with a laugh. "We've been staying in terrible hotels for weeks!" Indeed, both cast and crew were anxious for filming to end. "I hear you're four days ahead of schedule. That's great," I ventured to Lynch. "Well, that's okay if it looks all right," David responded somewhat dourly. "Well, that's why you have Freddie, right?" I reminded him, and David smiled broadly. "You're quite right," he said. "We couldn't do it without him."

Most of the other conversations swirling around the set dealt with the uninspiring local cuisine ("When I get back to LA, I'm going to order three plates of sushi *delivered!*" swore one crew member), horror tales centering on the series of Spartan motels the company had been billeted in, and how to file Iowa income tax forms once the company was safely back in Los Angeles. Only the catering crew's excellent meals kept the company on their feet. Oblivious to the rugged beauty surrounding them, everyone was more than anxious to get home.

It was a beautiful, crisp fall day, with sunshine pouring through the clouds. Nevertheless, the atmosphere was a mixture of elation and tension. Although this was to be the final day of the shoot, the crew still had two major sequences to complete, including the climax of the film, which was (somewhat unusually) being shot roughly in narrative sequence. Though the film was described by Lynch's assistant as "a nice small picture, and an interesting change for David," it was nevertheless a fully unionized shoot, with IATSE crews driving camera trucks emblazoned with "HOFFA IN 98" bumper stickers, and a fairly large crew. The stars were Richard Farnsworth, Sissy Spacek, and Harry Dean Stanton; the film was being partially financed by Canal +, the French production/distribution organization, who sent along two young Parisians to make a video documentary of the shooting.

What impressed everyone connected with the production was how quickly David and Freddie were moving, even though the film was being shot in CinemaScope, which takes more time to frame for each new setup. There was also the weather to be considered. Gordon Hayman, Freddie's camera operator on the film, gestured towards the fall foliage that surrounded us, and told me, "When we arrived here, these trees were just starting to turn. Now, look at them. They're almost stripped. That's fall in the Midwest for you . . . fifteen minutes long, and that's it. Winter." In addition, a snowstorm was forecast for the day after next, so shooting, for a variety of reasons, simply had to be finished that day. Fueled by coffee, steak, salad, and lemon meringue pie, Freddie and Gordon were pushing the crew with their customary brilliance through a myriad variety of shots. The morning's first major sequence took place on a small road not far from base camp: a long tracking shot following Richard Farnsworth's progress on the sit-down lawnmower he used to travel through several states.

After a technical rehearsal that lasted all of thirty seconds ("Let's just make sure this rig is hooked together, shall we?" Lynch asked politely), Farnsworth's stand-in was replaced by the actor himself. Just as the scene was about to start, a burst of brilliant sunlight shot through the gray over-hanging clouds, illuminating the scene as if on cue. Gordon and Freddie laughed, adjusted the exposure, and started filming. Obediently, the camera truck started drifting slowly down the barely paved road, towing the lawnmower behind it. Meanwhile, a number of second unit crews were busy filming various barns, weathervanes, and other cutaway footage, pretty much under their own direction. As we watched, the crane truck vanished over the hilltop, and everyone else went back to base camp. Typically, Lynch and Francis accomplished the rather complicated set-up in one take, making a shot that was both elegant and technically compli-cated look breathtakingly simple.

Back at base camp, a huge lunch was being served: shrimp, new pota-toes, asparagus, broccoli, and three different kinds of pie. Harry Dean Stanton moved forlornly through the buffet line in make-up, looking for all the world like a dustbowl transient, picking at the food experimentally. I sat next to Freddie and Gordon, talking about the shoot. Freddie was pleased with the film's progress, but Gordon remained wary. It was nearly two o'clock, and the crew still had the film's climax, a sort of wordless con-frontation between the film's protagonists, to film at a location known as Lyle's House, about fifty yards up the road. There was no way they could go into another day, and Gordon was anxious to get on with it.

Still, Lynch and Francis seemed sanguine about the film's progress; they'd just pulled a marathon shoot on Saturday in Mt. Zion, Iowa, film-ing throughout the night in a torrential rainstorm. By sunrise, they had two scheduled days of filming in the can, and all of it looked gorgeous. Freddie was pleased that he had taken on the assignment. "When David called me up and told me he was making this movie, I said 'Of course I'll do it, simply as a friend,'" he said. "We didn't even discuss money. I only work for friends now; I have no time for people who are messing about. But working with David is always a pleasure. Everyday, when we finish a set-up, we walk off the floor and say, 'Okay, that's the stuff that's going in the movie.' It's as simple as that. That's what makes working on a film like this much more interesting that a big-budget spectacle." Finally, Gordon stood up from the table. It was time to go back to work. He drained the last bit of coffee from his cup and looked up at the sky. "Come on, Freddie. We've still got three shots to finish. The light's going." Someone yelled out, "Okay, we're back!" And the crew started walking up the road to the house, to finish the last day's work on the film. It is the production of personal, small-scale films such as this that gives one hope for the future of cinema. The film recently opened to excellent reviews.

Another director who is working with even smaller crews, shooting in small-format digital video and then blowing up the results to 35mm, is the Danish director Thomas Vinterberg, whose film *Celebration* (originally titled *Festen*, 1998) is one of the wonders of the current digital film renaissance. In 1995, feeling that films had become both too commercial and too dependent on sensation and huge budgets to preserve any semblance of artistic or intellectual integrity, Vinterberg and director Lars von Trier drafted a document that became known as Dogma 95, in which they resolved to produce only those films that accurately reflected the human condition at the turn of the century, using the most utilitarian and democratic means available. The full document has become a rallying cry for a new generation of filmmakers, making it possible for even the most impoverished artists to create feature-length films for the price of several videocassettes and a small-format digital video camera. I reproduce it here as a call to arms for a new generation of *cinéastes*.

I swear to submit to the following set of rules drawn up and confirmed by DOGMA 95:

1. Shooting must be done on location. Props and sets must not be brought in (if a particular prop is necessary for the story, a location must be chosen where this prop is to be found).
2. The sound must never be produced apart from the images or vice versa. (Music must not be used unless it occurs where the scene is being shot.)

3. The camera must be hand-held. Any movement or immobility attainable in the hand is permitted. (The film must not take place where the camera is standing; shooting must take place where the film takes place.)
4. The film must be in color. Special lighting is not acceptable. (If there is too little light for exposure, the scene must be cut or a single lamp be attached to the camera.)
5. Optical work and filters are forbidden.
6. The film must not contain superficial action. (Murders, weapons, etc. must not occur.)
7. Temporal and geographical alienation are forbidden. (That is to say that the film takes place here and now.)
8. Genre movies are not acceptable.
9. The film format must be Academy 35mm.
10. The director must not be credited.

Furthermore, I swear as a director to refrain from personal taste! I am no longer an artist. I swear to refrain from creating a "work," as I regard the instant as more important than the whole. My supreme goal is to force the truth out of my characters and settings. I swear to do so by all the means available and at the cost of any good taste and aesthetic considerations.
Thus I make my VOW OF CHASTITY.
Copenhagen, Monday 13 March, 1995
On behalf of DOGMA 95
(Signed) Lars von Trier   Thomas Vinterberg (51)

Though the document is intentionally ironic, at base its purpose is absolutely serious. Vinterberg is justifiably disturbed by the onslaught of mindless action/genre films that currently dominate the world's cinema screens, and with these strict rules, he seeks a return to a more democratic era of image production.

Celebration documents a harrowing family reunion at a large country hotel, which has been owned and operated by the patriarch of the family, Helge (Henning Moritzen), who is celebrating his sixtieth birthday. As the members of Helge's extended family gather around him at a huge dinner table, one of Helge's sons, Christian (Ulrich Thomsen), raises his glass in a toast that unexpectedly turns the festivities into a brutal battle for individual survival. Christian accuses Helge of systematically sexually abusing not only himself, but also his brother Michael (Thomas Bo Larsen) and his sister Helene (Paprika Steen). Further, Christian contends, it was Helge's systematic sexual abuse of Christian's twin sister, Linda (Lene Laub Oksen), which caused Linda to take her own life. Superbly scripted by Mogens Rukov and Vinterberg himself, *Celebration* is continually inventive not only in terms of its plot and the way in which the various other family members present at the gathering strive until the final moments of the work to deny the reality of the situation that confronts them, but also in terms of Vinterberg's restlessly roving camera, which darts behind banisters, glides through hallways, and effortlessly captures the forced cheer and pandemonium of this horrific event. As the nameless master of ceremonies, Klaus Bondam strives to keep the gathering light and non-confrontational, even as all family barriers collapse around him. Bjarne Henriksen, as the chef, conspires to help Christian in his endeavor by stealing all the car keys of the various guests so that none may depart before the final reckoning, and even goes so far as to lock a particularly contentious guest in the wine cellar. By using only natural light and existing sets, Vinterberg creates a near-newsreel actuality of a staged event, and in his giddy handheld camerawork, creates an entire new repertoire of visual compositions and camera movements which mimic body language, and the darting glance of the human eye. *Celebration* stands as one of the key films of the late 1990s, and points directly towards the new digital future. Shot on digital video, then transferred to 35mm Academy ratio for projection, the film opens the door for numerous others to follow in Vinterberg's footsteps to create stripped-down, directly accessible feature films of their own.

Other films that emulate *Celebration*'s minimalist intensity include Amos Kollek's *Sue* (1997), which documents in neorealist style the last fifteen days in the life of a young woman living in Manhattan, who is unable to find a new job when her employer of twelve years abruptly goes bankrupt. Kollek, the son of Teddy Kollek, the former mayor of Jerusalem, directed and scripted the film, shooting it entirely on location in New York City in a bleak succession of diners, movie theatres, barren apartments and dead-end bars. The film starts and ends with Sue, and never leaves her. The camerawork throughout is handheld, and there are no opticals, special effects, or gratuitous scenes of violence, exactly as required by Dogma 95. Drifting from one meaningless affair to the next, drinking too much, haunting movie theatres and bars for companionship, Sue (deftly portrayed by Anna Levine) is the embodiment of all our urban fears and desires as she threads her lonely way through the metropolis in search of friends, a stable relationship, or a job—something to hold onto in her increasingly insulated life. At length, evicted from her apartment, Sue dies on a bench in Union Square Park, unnoticed by the group of young boys who skateboard by, oblivious to her plight. The intensity of the film is almost unbearable. At its finest, *Sue* recalls the insistent honesty of Cassavetes or Bresson, and makes its protagonist's plight both realistic and harrowing for the members of the audience.

In an entirely different vein, yet still shot with only the barest of physical materials, Janaf Panahi's *The Mirror* (1997) follows a fictional young girl named Mina (played by Mina Mohammad-Khani) as she searches through the streets of Tehran for her home and mother, lost in the great jungle of the city. Her arm in a cast, Mina hitches rides from one bus and then another and commandeers taxi drivers for assistance. She seems on the verge of finding her fictional mother when suddenly, stepping out of character, the real Mina suddenly takes off the prop cast and walks off the set in disgust, complaining, "All they want me to do is cry all the time," and refuses to go any further with the day's filming. Members of the crew make various attempts to coax her back to work, but the real Mina is resolute; she will find her mother on her own, and get home from the set without any assistance. This decisive, rupturing moment is captured by a 16mm crew filming a documentary on the making of the film.

Momentarily, director Panahi seems at a loss to deal with the situation, but he suddenly realizes that Mina is still outfitted with a wireless microphone. As Mina wanders off on her own, Panahi instructs the crew to follow at a distance. Using their telephoto lenses for maximum surveillance capability, they capture the real Mina's journey through the streets of the metropolis as she continues to badger passersby for assistance. Abruptly, all traditional cinematic cutting ceases, as Panahi simply loads one ten-minute 35mm magazine of film after another into his camera, and relentlessly pursues Mina through an urban landscape of wrecked cars, semi-sympathetic bystanders, bewildered policemen, and unceasing pollution and noise. When the wireless microphone that Mina is wearing shorts out, the film becomes silent; when it cuts back in again, we are allowed to hear the real-time sounds of the city. We realize that the filmmakers themselves have no idea what will happen next, and have completely abandoned any fictive framework; what we are seeing and witnessing now is real and relatively unmediated. The first half of the film is a remarkable achievement, but the second, near-documentary section of the film becomes a trance-like meditation on the mechanics of reality and role playing, in which the camera's insistent and impassive gaze recalls the early films of Andy Warhol.

Panahi, Kollek, and Vinterberg are all avatars of the new generation of filmmakers who prize the honesty of the moment above all other considerations, and who are disinterested in spectacle for the sake of audience entertainment. Together with other contemporary film artists, these filmmakers seek to elevate the humanist concerns of the cinema above the mechanisms of genre and disaster which pervade much recent commercial filmmaking, and in doing so, to reclaim the cinema for the new millennium.

THE DAWN OF THE DIGITAL OPERA

Philip Glass's new 3-D digital opera, *Monsters of Grace*, is a stunning achievement in every respect, and signals the dawn of a new era in interactive multimedia presentation while serving as a millennial antidote to the overstuffed, Franco Zeffirelli productions currently in vogue at Joseph Volpe's Metropolitan Opera House in New York City. Using a spare ensemble of perhaps a dozen musicians, complemented by an enormous, panoramic projection screen hanging overhead, *Monsters of Grace* presents the audience with the spectacle of the first truly "portable opera," in which all the sets, costumes, and "actors" are digitally generated, and then pre-recorded on 70mm film for playback by a high-intensity 3-D projection system. As with many of his other works, Glass's visual designer on *Monsters of Grace* is the gifted Robert Wilson, who collaborated with Glass on the epic *Einstein on the Beach*. *Einstein on the Beach* is one of the signal events in modern performance history, an enormously long (four and one-half hours) and ambitious spectacle that required the talents of numerous musicians and performers, and a wide variety of spectacular props for each presentation. With *Monsters of Grace*, both Glass and Wilson have stripped down their emphasis on the epic to create a work that requires only seventy-three minutes to perform, and needs only the musicians and an unexceptionally adroit projection staff to present their combined vision to the public gaze.

Monsters of Grace contains many signature characteristics of Glass and Wilson's past collaboration: as always, Wilson's digital sets and simulacric performers move through their paces at an almost imperceptible pace, creating an ever-changing landscape of humanist and spatial configuration that perfectly complements Glass's insistent, pulsating score. The unifying element of *Monsters of Grace* is in the libretto, which ties together concerns of memory, love, desire, and human frailty with a series of brief and elegiac passages, sung by the members of Glass's ensemble. But the scale of the completed opera would be impossible, or impracticably expensive, to perform with human actors and full-scale props. As Glass told writer Jeff Brown,

> When Robert [Wilson] and I conceived this piece back in 1993, we soon came to the realization that, without artistic assistance and financial backing, we could not stage the production conventionally. It was just too broad and ambitious. So we shelved it until we could find a better way to conceive it live . . . that's when we hooked up with Jeff Kleiser and Diana Walczak, our 3-D computer firm, to create our performance using stereoscopic animation. And so the *Monster* was born. (53)

Above the singers, an enormous screen (perhaps a hundred feet long and thirty feet high) vibrates with a series of disparate and haunting images, faultlessly projected in stereoscopic verisimilitude. In a mountainous terrain, a series of helicopters flies through the skies aimlessly, as if engaged in a reconnaissance mission without any concrete objective. A series of attenuated tendrils, or sinews, lead to a decapitated hand, which turns and gestures towards the audience, its fingers extending out into space over the heads of the crowd, as a small knife traces the lifelines of the disembodied hand in minuscule rivulets of blood. A house drifts out to sea, past a dense and lushly populated jungle, then past a distant, monolithic metropolis, and finally past an enormous iceberg, while a sea serpent threatens to devour the house and its inhabitants, who glide towards each other in a trance, on the rooftop of the derelict abode. Notes Glass, creating "the animation was fun. I've always loved Robert's work, and to see it jump out of the screen at you is really exhilarating. It is truly something that has to be seen to be believed" (in Brown 53).

At other points in *Monsters of Grace*, the images become even more abstract, as when a series of glowing lines stretch across the screen in ethereal slow motion, creating a series of luminescent Mandarin paintings in the simulacric 3-D performance space. What is most impressive about *Monsters of Grace*, as I have previously suggested, is that it can easily be taken out on tour in its "original" form, with the original performers, rather than in an inferior "road company" version that dilutes and vitiates both the quality and intensity of the work. While traditional opera relies upon hyperspectacle, with enormous sets and ornate costumes, and a company of performers, *Monsters of Grace* signals the dawn of a new operatic performance style in which economy of presentation is not allowed to affect the emotional impact of the work. When the Metropolitan Opera presents *La Traviata*, for example, in Central Park, as part of their annual summer series of free presentations, the visual aspect of the work is almost entirely sacrificed in order to transport the performance into the public sphere. Sets, costumes, even stage directions, are almost entirely eliminated. What results is only an approximation of the actual experience of witnessing *La Traviata* on stage at the Met. The performers must carry both the burden of the spectacle and the rituals of presentation, without any aid from the imposing physical sets they are used to inhabiting and relying upon. By contrast, one could easily imagine an outdoor evening presentation of *Monsters of Grace* being every bit as effective as one witnessed on stage; as long as the 3-D image projection quality is maintained, nothing would be sacrificed.

To better understand the impact on, and the prescient example that *Monsters of Grace* presents for, contemporary audiences, a bit of history on the performance piece itself and the careers of those involved in its production is both instructive and necessary. Philip Glass was born in Baltimore, Maryland, and as a child, received a rather unorthodox but engaging education in the classics. As his biography on the *Monsters of Grace* web site notes,

> Glass discovered music in his father's radio repair shop. In addition to servicing radios, Ben Glass carried a line of records and, when certain ones sold poorly, he would take them home and play them for his three children, trying to discover why they didn't appeal to customers. These happened to be recordings of the great chamber works, and the future composer rapidly became familiar with Beethoven quartets, Schubert sonatas, Shostakovich symphonies and other music then considered "offbeat." It was not until he was in his upper teens did Glass begin to encounter more "standard" classics. (Glass and Wilson)

Glass practiced the flute and violin as a child and budding teenager, but soon grew bored with the repertoire at his disposal, and the lack of opportunities for advancement in Baltimore. Glass graduated from the University of Chicago at the precocious age of nineteen, and moved to New York City to attend the Juilliard School. After study with such notables as composer Darius Milhand and Nadia Boulanger, Glass garnered as an assignment, the transcription of Ravi Shankar's music into Western notation as part of a film project. Immediately overwhelmed by the impact of Shankar's music, Glass embarked on an extended trip through India, North Africa, and the Himalayas, gathering additional knowledge which he would later incorporate into his own works.

By 1974, Glass had written a large amount of music for the Mabou Mines (a group he co-founded), and also started the Philip Glass Ensemble, which exists to this day, to perform his new work. In 1976, Glass and Robert Wilson co-created *Einstein on the Beach*, merging Wilson's slow-motion theatrical spectacle with Glass's trance-like musical score and creating one of the key artifacts of performance art in the process. Since that time, Philip Glass has engaged in a wide variety of projects, including the operas *The Fall of the House of Usher*, *Satyagraha*, and *Hydrogen Jukebox*, as well as film scores for *The Thin Blue Line*, *Kundun*, *Koyaanisqatsi*, *Mishima*, and *A Brief History of Time*. In addition, Glass has composed three operas based on the works of Jean Cocteau, and is working at this writing on a new project, *White Raven*, which will be yet another collaboration with Robert Wilson. This outline is the merest sketch of Glass's work as a composer for opera, theatre, and film; his prolificity is matched only by the high degree of quality he brings to each new project (for more details, see Glass and Wilson, *Monsters of Grace* web site).

Robert Wilson, born in Waco, Texas, received his education at the University of Texas and the Pratt Institute in New York City, where he was granted a B.F.A. in 1966. Almost immediately, Wilson propelled himself to the forefront of the avant-garde with his experimental theatrical works *Deafman Glance* (1970) and *The Life and Times of Joseph Stalin* (1973). As noted in the *Monsters of Grace* web site,

> In June 1971, following the Paris debut of Wilson's *Deafman Glance*, French Surrealist Louis Aragon wrote to André Breton, "I have never seen anything more beautiful in the world." Hailed as "a revolution of the plastic arts one sees only once or twice in a generation," *Deafman Glance* evolved from many workshops and impromptu performances that Wilson held with his New York-based Byrd Hoffman School of Byrds. (Glass and Wilson)

After this auspicious debut, Wilson's international reputation was assured, and he went on to stage a variety of personal and classical works, including *Death, Destruction and Detroit* (1979), *The Golden Windows* (1982), and productions of *Salomé, Parsifal, The Magic Flute*, and *Madame Butterfly* throughout the world in the 1980s and 1990s. He has collaborated on various projects with such diverse talents as William S. Burroughs, David Byrne, Susan Sontag, Jessye Norman, and Lou Reed, and continues to operate on the cutting edge of contemporary theatrical discourse at the dawn of the new millennium (see *Monsters of Grace* web site for further details).

The lyrics for *Monsters of Grace*, far from being contemporary, are the work of Jelaluddin Rumi, a thirteenth-century Turkish mystic who is generally credited with the distinction of being the originator of the "whirling dervishes." Rumi, who lived from 1207 to 1273, composed a series of meditations on human existence that comprise the entire text of the libretto for *Monsters of Grace*, as translated into English by Coleman Barks. Using this exquisite text as the backbone of the opera, Philip Glass composed a haunting, trance-like score that accentuates the mystic and ephemeral qualities of Rumi's text. These qualities are exemplified by this brief excerpt, which forms the entirety of the text for an extended section of *Monsters of Grace*, subtitled *Don't Go Back to Sleep*:

> The breeze at dawn has secrets to tell you.
> Don't go back to sleep.
> You must ask for what you really want.
> Don't go back to sleep.
> People are going back and forth across the doorsill
> Where the two worlds touch.
> The door is round and open.
> Don't go back to sleep.

As the musicians and vocalists of Philip Glass's ensemble repeat these evocative phrases with controlled intensity, the screen above the live performers fills with a forest of digitally generated trees, which gradually, as we move through the foliage, reveals a group of inviting, doll-like houses, with illuminated windows. It is the fantasy landscape of childhood brought to life, a place of peaceful sanctuary. Because the images we watch are rendered in faultlessly effective 3-D, it seems as if the distance between this bucolic scene and the audience has been dissolved: we are *in* the for-

est, gliding through the trees, slowly and with a certain inexorably deliberate grace. As we watch, a young computer-generated boy on a bicycle
appears on a road that runs between the houses, far in the distance, slowly
pedaling towards us. It takes perhaps five minutes for the young boy to
reach the center of the performance space in front of us; just as he dominates the center of the 3-D frame, the view cuts to an out-of-focus side
angle of the houses in the distance. As we watch, disoriented by this
change in perspective and spatial differentiation, an enormous child's shoe
(seen in close-up) drops from the top to the bottom of the frame, resting
in front of our collective gaze, an ominous talisman of disaster. What has
happened to the image of domestic serenity and safety? Disaster has
befallen the young boy, but the accident, observed only through the
agency of his falling sneaker, remains obscured from our view, and thus
becomes more sinister, less defined.

The non-specificity of Robert Wilson's images is inextricably intertwined with Rumi's text, creating a sense of mystery and evocative sadness
which is no less tangible for being, in a certain sense, undefined. Then,
too, it should be noted that all of the 3-D digital images in *Monsters of
Grace* are determinedly "constructed," that is, no attempt at verisimilitude
(with perhaps one exception, the "stereoscopic couple" sequence [actually
titled "Stereo Gram"]) in the creation of Wilson's glyphic universe.
Rather, under Wilson's guidance, visual artists Jeff Kleiser and Diana Walczak have created a series of storybook images that seem remote yet accessible, reminding one of the brightly colored world of children's story-
books, coupled with the surrealist bent of Magritte. Kleiser and Walczak
have used digital special effects (computer generated imagery, or CGI) to
create such recent projects as the Columbia Pictures logo, as well as special effects for the feature films *Stargate* (directed by Roland Emmerich,
1994) and *Clear and Present Danger* (directed by Philip Noyce, 1994),
and numerous other assignments. Given the current capability of CGIs to
produce near-perfect copies of human, animal, or objectificational models, it would easily have been possible for Wilson, working with Kleiser
and Walczak, to create more "realistic" performers for *Monsters of Grace*.
But it is the absolute transparency of Wilson's creations in *Monsters of
Grace* that transfixes us; like the nascent pod-people in *Invasion of the
Body Snatchers* (directed by Don Siegel, 1956), the figures and locations
of Wilson's landscapes are vaguely familiar, and yet indistinct, featureless,
as if waiting for a final stroke of definition to individuate them. Because
of this, the dreamlike locale of the visuals in *Monsters of Grace* is simulta-

neously universal and distant, becoming to us even as it withholds from us the final seal of significatory identification.

This is entirely in keeping with Glass's score for *Monsters of Grace*, which, as Glass notes,

> incorporates samples of Persian and other Middle-Eastern or similar-sounding string and percussion instruments in the design of the keyboard sounds. Among the stringed instruments sampled are: jubus, saz, tzouras, baglamas, Ethiopian double harp, psaltery, ukelin, Renaissance lute, archlute, and Chinese zheng; percussion instruments include the dumbeq (Persian drum), gomé (African drum), and Iranian zill (finger cymbal) . . . [computer] samples have also been created of Persian instruments of ancient origin including: the santur, a hammered dulcimer with a lovely ringing tone; the tar, a banjo-type instrument with a skin head and adjustable gut frets; its relative, the sitar, a lute with a small oval laminated wood body, also with moveable gut frets; and the oud, a large lute with a teardrop-shaped laminated wood body, more closely resembling [the] Western lute, with an unfretted neck and a tuning peg block at a 90 degree angle to the neck. (Glass and Wilson)

These "samples" are fed through a complex variety of Macintosh computers utilizing sample cell II playback cards, although all the "'samples" used are manually performed by members in the ensemble during each performance—no automatic sequencing is used. Yamaha synthesizers power the entire performance of *Monsters of Grace*, and so the resultant sound mix is simultaneously electronic-edged and yet derived from natural sound sources. The musical score, grounded in the past and in the humanist concerns of Jelaluddin Rumi's poetry, is nevertheless very much a contemporary electronic construct, just as the images that accompany the score are entirely the product of a CGI digital imaging processor.

Once Robert Wilson storyboarded one of the sections of *Monsters of Grace*, Jeff Kleiser and Diana Walczak were faced with the formidable task of concretizing these images into real-time 70mm film for 3-D stereoscopic projection, a task significantly more difficult than merely enhancing existing imagery in a conventional theatrical motion picture. In *Monsters of Grace*, each scene was created from the drawings alone, as in a conventional animated cartoon, but with considerable additional difficulty. The process of creating the visual environment for the opera was both labor and equipment intensive:

Monsters of Grace breaks barriers in technical innovation and production for digital stereoscopic film. Each scene is animated, mod-
eled and lit . . . using the full spectrum of Alias/Wavefront software:
Maya, Alias, TAV, Explore, Dynamation, Kinemation and Composer running on O2 graphics workstations . . . [This] specialized . . . hardware can perform perspective and shade polygons in
real time, essential for rapid creation of 3-D environment, . . . [cre-
ating] images for over two hours of 70mm film. . . . Every scene created . . . for *Monsters of Grace* has a team of at least three people
working on it. Once the art department finalizes the story boards
originally designed by Robert Wilson, a modeler is assigned to
"build" the elements of the scene using the computer software tools
most suited for the task. The completed models are then handed
over to an animator who choreographs and executes the desired
action within the scene again within the parameters of computer
technology. The final member of the team must light the scene just
as though it were a traditionally stated scene, with the added challenge of creating the depth, colors and textures which would occur
naturally in the real world. Depending upon the complexity of the
scene, the entire process can take anywhere from four to 12 weeks.
Ultimately plans call for *Monsters of Grace* to exist in purely digital
form as a CD-ROM, DVD, three-dimensional enhanced website or
VR installation. (Glass and Wilson)

In short, a complete synthetic, virtual landscape is created through the use
of contemporary computer technology, one in which all is fabricated—
real and tangible, but still not derived from nature.

All of this technology would be of no purpose if the completed work
was lacking in a human aspect, however, and this is where *Monsters of
Grace* succeeds as a combined live performance/simulated action performance piece. Indeed, I am deeply suspicious of the announced plans for
the work to exist ultimately "in purely digital form as a CD-ROM, DVD,
three-dimensional enhanced web site or VR installation," precisely because
it is this mixture of human agency and digital technology that makes the
resultant work so compelling. Remove the members of the musical ensemble from the performance of the work, and you would have only the
"record" of their voices and instruments, accompanied by the visuals Wilson has designed. It is the contributions of the ensemble members, including Glass as keyboardist/conductor, Michael Riesman as musical direc-

tor/keyboardist, Jon Gibson on flute, bass flute, clarinet and soprano sax-ophone, and the vocal performers Marie Mascari (soprano), Alexandra Montano (mezzo-soprano), Richard E. Peck, Jr. (tenor/soprano/alto saxo-phone), Gregory Purnhagen (baritone), and Peter Stewart (baritone) who make *Monsters of Grace* such a compelling site of mediation between the real and the simulated, the actual and the projected. Even with the creation of an entirely digital universe, what renders *Monsters of Grace* ineffably human is the element of chance and mortal frailty that both intrinsically archaic film projection (an extension of the ancient magic lantern device, or light thrown on a screen, shadow-play) and the incorporation of live performance (both the keyboard and wind instrumentalists, but especially the singers) bring to the work, making each performance individual and unique.

As the opening words of Jelaluddin Rumi's meditations remind us,

> Don't worry about saving these songs!
> And if one of our instruments breaks,
>   it doesn't matter.
> We have fallen into the place
> Where everything is music . . .
> Stop the words now.
> Open the window in the center of your chest,
> And let the spirits fly in and out.

Even in an age driven by technology, and one that necessarily embraces that technology as an extension of human vision, if we erase that which is intrinsically mortal in our works, they cease to be a part of our experience and become instead markers that stand outside the domain of humanis-tic commerce. In short, these are tricky shoals to navigate. *Monsters of Grace* succeeds because it uses digital imaging, stereoscopic projection, and synthesized "samples" in the service of the performer, who controls the spectacle she/he creates, but is never dominated by it. As each vocal-ist performs her/his part, a keylight illuminates his/her face, reminding us that it is human agency that made this entire construct possible.

Conventional opera performance is equally a creature of artifice and synthetic creation; if a backdrop quivers and collapses, or a singer misses a note, the illusion of perfection (which is what all performance strives for) is marred—but this is part of the fabric of the creative act. Towards the end of *Monsters of Grace*, an enormous Chinese tea set is displayed in the space above the performers' heads, extending out into the audience space through the medium of 70mm stereoscopic film projection. As we watch, the image begins to disintegrate into a series of lines and pixels, as if acknowledging the ephemerality of its phantom existence. Similarly, in the sequence in which a series of digital helicopters roam a phantasmal mountain terrain and gigantic birds fly over the heads of the audience, these images, too, are allowed to evanesce into video oblivion, relinquishing their tenuous hold on the real, authenticating the truth of their constructed, synthetic origins. If *Monsters of Grace* succeeds so brilliantly as a work of art, and as the operatic spectacle of the future, it is because of this alliance between the real and the manufactured which Glass and Wilson continually reaffirm, and transgress upon. Indeed, the title itself restates this pull between the mortal and that which survives mortality—we are monsters who strive for grace, and enlightenment, in an increasingly technological environment that seeks (at its worst) to replace the humanist instinct with synthetic visions alone: witness "point and kill" video games, television programs where spectacle *becomes* content and violence supersedes any human intercession, such as the recent spate of Fox television "specials" involving high-speed automobile chases, crashes, and other disasters.

Monsters of Grace thus occupies a site of contested ground between the real and the hyperreal, and mediates this merging of the simulacric and the simulacra through the ineluctable modality of visible human intervention—a merging of performer and performance, in which emotion is not denied. Having now seen the opera performed several times, I can attest to the passion and commitment that Glass and his ensemble bring to the proceedings, presenting a concert in one city after the next in an exhausting road tour that many other artists would have avoided. After all, Glass is quite profitably employed creating, among other pieces, film soundtracks, and it would be easy for Glass to simply sit back in Hollywood and create music for *The Truman Show* (as he did). He could send out a road company of assistants to perform the work, or even stage the work solely in major metropolitan centers and leave the rest of the country with videodiscs and second-hand accounts of the actual performance. That he has not done this is a tribute both to Glass's own tenacity and commitment, but also to the inherent construction of the piece. Designed for easy transport from one location to the next, *Monsters of Grace* has been performed at numerous sites around the world since its world premiere on April 15, 1998, at Royce Hall, on the campus of the University of California–Los Angeles.

Monsters of Grace thus signals toward the possible future of operatic presentation, because the "spectacle" inherent in all operatic presentation resides, for this production, within the confines of a film can, ready to be re-projected and re-experienced with each successive performance. But without the random operations of chance inherent in all live performances, and without the *visible proof* of human agency provided by the members of the ensemble during each presentation, much of the power of the work would be lost. Thus, even as we beckon towards the digital future, we must remember that we are the beings who devised that future, and those who must necessarily bear ultimate witness to all its creations. *Monsters of Grace* may be either a "springboard into the void," as Cocteau characterized all works that challenge contemporary norms, or it may be a harbinger of the future of "portable" spectacle, opera for a new post-digital public. In its linkage of the mechanistic and the real, Robert Wilson and Philip Glass have devised an entirely new sort of work, yet one which certainly has links to La Scala and the Met. As we cross into the next century, it will be fascinating to see how this new hybridized medium continues to evolve.

THE DIGITAL HORIZON

As the cinema ends its first century of active development and gestation, we can see that it has always been in a process of becoming something new, changing and adapting with each new circumstance and shift in society. From silent flickering images thrown on a screen, the cinema formed a voice through the efforts of Alice Guy and Léon Gaumont, then Thomas Edison, Lee de Forest, Vitaphone, and other allied processes that have brought us into the Dolby stereo age of digital sound and image processing. From black and white paper negatives, the cinema has moved swiftly through silver nitrate film, safety film, 3-strip Technicolor, Eastman monopack film, moveable mattes, and split-screen "doubling," until it now stands on the threshold of the final video transformation, where the film camera ceases to exist, and is replaced by an entirely digital imaging system that will soon replace conventional 35mm production and exhibition process. The moving image, while still controlled as a commercial medium by a few conglomerate organizations, has become, with the use of inexpensive camcorders and the like, a truly democratic medium, as has been proven by the Rodney King tape, footage of the events at Tiananmen Square, and other documentary videotapes that have altered the public perception of the formerly illimitable dominion of authoritarian regimes. It is impossible to hold back the flood of images created by these new technologies, and in the coming century, these images will both inform and enlighten our social discourse. The surveillance cameras now used in New York night clubs to provide low-cost entertainment for web browsers can only proliferate; there is no surcease from the domain of images which shape and transform our lives. In these pages, I have tried to suggest not only where we are going with these new technologies, but where we have been. While big-screen spectacle will continue to flourish, a plethora of new image constructs now compete for our attention, often with a significant measure of success.

The monopoly of the television networks is a thing of the past. Who is to say that theatrical distribution as we know it will not also collapse, to be replaced by a different sort of experience altogether? IMAX films and other large-format image storage and retrieval systems mimic reality, but in the future, holographic laser displays, in which seemingly three-dimensional characters hold forth from a phantom staging area, may well become the preferred medium of presentation, signaling a return to the proscenium arch—but in this case, a staging space with infinite possibilities for transformation. Powered by high-intensity lasers, this technology could present performances by artists who would no longer have to physically tour to present their faces and voices to the public. Indeed, as the twenty-first century dawns, it seems that video projection of feature films will rapidly replace conventional 35mm and/or 70mm projection, as James Sterngold recently noted:

> Within two years, movie theatres are expected to begin installing the first generation of digital projectors. And reels of 35-millimeter film—which are several feet in diameter and very heavy—would, at long last, disappear, to be replaced with electronic projectors that use magnetic tape or discs. (C1)

Using a "light valve" projector, Texas Instruments has created a new projector that uses digital video imagery exclusively to throw the image on to the theater screen, and exhibitors, as a group, are enthusiastically awaiting the change. Said the president of one large chain of multiplex theatres, "We can't wait for the day we're unshackled from the 35-millimeter prints" (Sterngold C2). The advantages for studios and distribution companies are also obvious. No more shipping of prints, no more theft of prints, and perhaps, with the use of satellite technology, the "movie" to be screened can be directly downloaded from space, eliminating the need for any copy of the original at all. While films will still originate on 35mm film for a short time in the future, it seems inevitable that we are headed for a fully digitized future in the area of moving image production, reception, and distribution. And the quality of the new "light valve" projection image is being enthusiastically embraced by filmmakers, as well. Notes Martin Cohen, the director of post-production at Dreamworks SKG, "I went into one demonstration where the only way I could tell the difference between the film and the electronic version was that the film one had that jittery movement and the electronic one didn't" (Sterngold C2). This new technology, which has been looming on the horizon for some time now, will represent as much of a revolution to motion pictures as the coming of sound, or color: the elimination of film itself from the process. Films will now be digitized immediately after post-production, and then disseminated in the cheapest way possible to an audience that probably won't even notice the difference.

Heralding this new development in digital cinema, George Lucas has decided to open his new film, *Star Wars: Episode I-The Phantom Menace*, in four theatres on June 18, 1999, in an entirely digital format. Although there are still some technical bugs to be ironed out, Lucasfilm is going ahead with their all-digital presentation plans because, as they see it, the shift from film to digital video is right around the corner, and not surprisingly, Lucas and his compatriots want to be first in line. "It's show time!" exclaims Rick McCallum, who served as co-producer on *The Phantom Menace*. "The quality is going to get better, but we're doing it now because, as George says, 'Why not push it now?' It's inevitable anyway" (Mathews 2). And the aesthetic and commercial stakes in this experiment are considerable, inasmuch as the studios and their distribution arms stand to save $1.2 billion each year by embracing digital distribution, which will effectively do away with striking 35mm film prints for exhibition, and shipping them to the thirty-four thousand movie theatres in the United States, to say nothing of the global total of ninety thousand cinema screens worldwide (Mathews 2). "The whole industry is going to be keying on what happens at those four theaters" notes Paul Dergarabedian, the president of Exhibitor Relations Inc, a firm that tracks new technological developments within the motion picture industry. "Digital is a technology whose time has come, but how fast it happens is going to depend a lot on what people see . . ." (Mathews 2).

Lucas presented a demonstration of the new digital process at the 1999 ShoWest Convention in Las Vegas, in which 35mm film and digital projection were shown side-by-side, to offer a direct comparison between the two mediums. As Michael Fleeman noted, the demonstration "revealed digital movie quality is now as good—and in some respects better—than film, with a cleaner, sharper image that won't show wear and tear with repeated showings. The only problem with digital (projection) appeared to be color, with white tones taking on a yellow tint, the blues becoming purplish, and skin tones giving actresses in the demonstration an artificial almost mannequin-like complexion" (50). Nevertheless, most audience members were favorably disposed towards the idea. "I was very impressed with the quality" said one large theater chain owner. "It's almost to the point that it's ready" (Fleeman 50).

Said Lucas, "I'm very dedicated and very enthusiastic about the digital cinema," as he stressed the "quality, the savings in cost, and the ability to do things that just aren't possible today" with dully digitized video projection (Fleeman 50). Using the Texas Instruments digital projector, which "creates a screen image by bouncing light off 1.3 million microscopic mirrors squeezed onto a square-inch chip" (Fleeman 50), Lucas's four-theatre presentation of *The Phantom Menace* in fully digital format serves as the forerunner of Lucas's plans to photograph and produce the next two *Star Wars* films entirely with digital imaging, completely eliminating conventional 35mm film as part of the production, post-production, and distribution process. Using a new camera co-developed by Sony and Panavision, images will be shot digitally, processed digitally, and then "distributed from studio to theatres by satellite, over fiber-optic cable or on special discs" (Fleeman 50). While a number of differing digital imaging systems are being developed, most feel that the Texas Instruments light valve has the edge on the competition, simply because Lucas and his associates have already adopted it.

As Paul Breedlove, director of digital imaging systems at Texas Instruments comments, "at this point, it's not a technical issue. The technology is ready. The industry just has to make its business arrangements and figure out how it will be put together . . . there's a much smaller group of players within the movie industry that can make a decision and go forward. Lucas, Spielberg . . . people like that are going to decide the issue just by doing it" (Mathews 2). William Kartozian, president of NATO, the National Association of Theater Owners, echoed Breedlove's sentiments. "I wasn't sure how inevitable [digital] was until Lucas spoke up at

ShoWest. Now . . . it's just a matter of how we make the changeover, and who pays for it" (Mathews 2). Adds Breedlove, "it's the last frontier. They've fixed everything else . . . seating, sound, comfort. The only thing that hasn't changed in the last 100 years is how you project the movies" (Mathews 2).

Nor is the digital change over-confined to big-budget spectacles. Stefan Avalos, Lance Weiler, and Esther Robinson have recently produced a startlingly polished first feature, *The Last Broadcast*, using solely digital means (and, in particular, relying on the Sony VX 1000 camera for image capture) for a grand total of $900. Of this amount, $240 was spent on DV (Digital Video) tape stock—the largest single expenditure—and the finished digital feature was edited on a PC desktop system that the trio managed to patch together from existing equipment they already owned. They didn't even buy a digital camera to shoot *The Last Broadcast*—they borrowed one. The film has since been shown via satellite in Cannes in the spring of 1999, and is already a financial success, having grossed $18,000 in a few select theatrical play dates in Philadelphia, Minneapolis, and Portland (Conlin 168). The stunning slickness of *The Last Broadcast*—superbly acted, and edited with the style and polish that one associates with much more expensive films such as *The Matrix* (1999)—demonstrates that in the digital future, financing need not be a barrier for the completion of selected films. As Peter Broderick of Next Wave Films puts it, "filmmakers don't have to be financiers anymore" (Conlin 168).

While the new digital projectors will cost at least $100,000 apiece for each theater to install, versus $30,000 on a standard 35mm "platter" projector (Fleeman 50), theater owners will probably split the cost of the installation with a consortium of the major distributors, inasmuch as all sides will benefit, at least economically, from the changeover. While not wishing to appear apocalyptic, I feel that the changeover, once it begins, will be both swift and brutal, much like the switch from silent movies to sound in 1927. At that time, two competing methods battled for dominance in the marketplace: sound on film, and sound on disc. Sound on film, using optical sound tracks, eventually became the industry standard, but even the cost of switching from one medium to another, or of rewiring the theaters for sound was insufficient to halt the switch in the face of overwhelming public demand.

Here, we have a slightly different situation, in that demand for the switch to digital seems to be dictated more by economic concerns than any other factor, and by a handful of technologically-entranced mainstream filmmakers, who nevertheless control a significant portion of the domestic and international box-office. But aesthetic concerns—matters of film grain, contrast, the entire magic lantern process of throwing light though colored plastic onto a screen—will fade and dwindle in the public consciousness, almost as if they had never existed. Film itself will be confined not only to the era of the twentieth century; motion pictures shot and mastered on 35mm or 16mm film will now be relegated to the realm of the revival house and/or museum, curiosities from a bygone age. Indeed, in the twenty-first century, when we speak of film studies, we may well be referring to a uniquely twentieth-century art form, when moving images were actually captured on photographic stock, as opposed to being created from pixels and electron beams.

While digital imaging makes films easier and cheaper to produce, the late-century demand for spectacle (which will certainly continue for some time) ensures that only those films produced by the dominant cinema will reach a truly international audience, in stark contrast to the situation that prevailed only forty years ago, when a resolutely non-commercial film such as Michelangelo Antonioni's *L'Avventura* (1960) could still be certain of a theatrical release, if only because theatrical presentation was the only method by which producers could recoup their costs, or distribute the film at all on an international scale. The era of the low-budget film, in which Roger Corman's five-day epics could compete on the same commercial basis with more costly major studio product are also a thing of the past; commercial filmmaking at the turn of the twenty-first century relies on excess and spectacle above all other considerations, and what is left is relegated to the realm of television sitcoms, or equally formulaic mainstream films. Smaller "art films" will continue to proliferate in the major cities—New York, Paris, London—but their hold on the provinces has evaporated. Even with the ease and low cost of the digital age of production, distribution is still the most important, if not the deciding factor, in who will see precisely what films, and where, and how.

And yet even this hurdle can still be overcome by an exceptional low-budget film. In late 1999, *The Blair Witch Project* emerged as one of the most successful low-budget feature films in history. Shot on digital video and 16mm film and mastered to 35mm for conventional theatrical distribution, *The Blair Witch Project* suggests that talent, more than any other factor, remains the deciding factor in what film audiences choose to see. As Ann Hornaday notes,

The Blair Witch Project, which involves a trio of film students who become lost while searching for a legendary witch in the Maryland woods, was directed by Daniel Myrick and Eduardo Sanchez, who financed the film mostly on credit cards. When the movie opened July 16, [1999] it earned more than seven times its budget its first weekend out, even though it was shown on only a handful of screens. The movie expanded to 2,100 theaters last weekend.

Myrick and Sanchez originally filmed *The Blair Witch Project* for around $60,000. When they premiered the movie at the Sundance Film Festival last January, it was immediately bought for $1.1 million by Artisan Entertainment. The studio went on to give the filmmakers money for shooting new scenes and sweetening the sound. The film's final budget has been reported as about $350,000.

Profitability is a famously squishy concept in Hollywood, where revenues are eaten up by percentage deals with actors, deals with theaters, and the costs of prints and advertising. But any way you slice it, *Blair Witch* still stands to make a handsome return on its initial investment. Observers project grosses between $130 million to $150 million. (Hornaday 41)

With no special effects, a minimal budget, and a core cast of three performers, *The Blair Witch Project* demonstrates that even in the era of hyperspectacle, films of authentic talent and vision can still compete in the commercial marketplace.

DIGITAL AMSTERDAM

In striking contrast to the way in which computer technology has been applied in the United States, Amsterdam has become a truly "wired" city within the last few years, without sacrificing the quality of life for its citizens. Thanks to state subsidies, the arts flourish in Amsterdam, whether it be opera, painting, theatre and/or the moving image. A recent production of Wagner's *Ring Cycle*, for example, was presented live in the city's opera house for an audience of several thousand, and simultaneously recorded in digital, widescreen, high-definition television format for public projection on a huge screen in a nearby park, creating a second audience for the work, and a permanent record of the production. Libraries go in-line, but do not discard their documents from the past, specifically books which may no longer seem entirely relevant to the present digital age. Indeed, for those who forecast a "paperless" society in the digital future, where portable electronic books have replaced conventional ones, the case of Amsterdam's respect and reverence for its cultural heritage demonstrates that old and new technologies can comfortably interface, each supporting the other. Internet booths proliferate on street corners, complementing and/or replacing telephone booths, and are used regularly as a part of city life.

Nearly everyone in Amsterdam has access to a computer, and is on-line; digital cellular phones are routinely carried by members of the pop-ulace. Yet none of this embrace of the future is allowed to detract from the cultural life of Amsterdam, something which all too often happens elsewhere. Cafés are open from morning to late night, and locals sit and discuss the day's events over newspapers and coffee; debate and theatre groups abound throughout the metropolis. Libraries are superbly stocked with many thousands of books, all of which are lovingly preserved as part of the cultural record of Dutch society. Dance clubs, summer concerts in the park (particularly the Holland Festival) and a more relaxed approach to daily existence and work make Amsterdam a city that has decisively entered the future, without sacrificing the charm and allure of the past.

Far from being composed entirely of chrome, steel, and an imper-sonal approach to cultural life, Amsterdam explodes with journals, poetry magazines, "planning societies" that map the city's future, and remains faithful to the centuries of literary, theatrical and artistic tradition implicit within the fabric of Dutch society. The Society for Old and New Media, a digital imaging collective located in the Waag, near the Central Station in Amsterdam, is a perfect example of this confluence of old and new. Housed in an ancient castle that has been partially converted into a restaurant, the Society occupies the entire top floor of the building with a phalanx of Macintosh computers, creating both commercial projects (TV bumpers, ads, and rock videos), along with community service pro-jects for children and the elderly. On any given weekday morning, one can witness the members of the Waag Collective filtering into their vari-ous work stations, fueled by coffee and croissants from the café down-stairs. Suitably fortified, the collective members then embark on their tasks for the day—an Austin Powers TV ad and some animation for a BBC literary program, perhaps—before moving on to less lucrative but more socially conscious work, such as designing web sites for non-profit groups, and creating CD-ROM programs for the disabled and other marginalized members of society. In this 50/50 balance between profit and social conscience, Amsterdam's enthusiastic entry into the digital age is a model of moral and community responsibility, in that the necessary tools for creation and communication have been made available to all. As their own in-house document details,

> De Waag was built in 1488 as a city gate and, today, is the oldest secular building in Amsterdam. In the centuries that followed the building served alternatively as a weighhouse, guildhall, fire station, municipal archives and Jewish historical museum . . . today [,] De Waag is home to the Media Lab and presentation space of the Society for Old and New Media (Maatschappij Voor Oude en Nieuwe Media). . . . The Society for Old and New Media organizes lectures, workshops and exhibitions in the Theatrum Anatomicum. The hall, which is fully equipped with internet, video conferencing and presentation facilities, is available to the public to rent. The building offers a unique location for press meetings, receptions, seminars, congresses and meetings. "The hall can conveniently be set up as a virtual classroom with high-speed access to the internet." (Society for Old and New Media Pamphlet, n. pag.)

This digitization of the moving image is also a common part of the everyday process of making films, both feature films and videos, which are far more digitally sophisticated than their American counterparts. Dutch cinema has also recently created an interesting and innovative way to remove the language barrier that impedes the international distribution of all foreign films. According to Hans Pos, a principal partner in Shooting Star Films, one of the Netherlands' major film studios, digitization is making its way into homegrown Dutch cinema in an unusual way: dubbing. Subtitles traditionally alienate commercial audiences, and so Shooting Star and other production companies located in the cities of Amsterdam and Hilversum are experimenting with a relatively new technique that allows the lips of each actor to be digitally removed, and then replaced (for example) with the lips of an actor speaking in English, along with an English soundtrack. This results in a curious "disembodiment" of performance, yet makes the film consequently much easier to import for the American market. As proof of this, Shooting Star's latest production has just been acquired by Disney for several European markets, with a possible eye towards a dubbed U.S. version, utilizing the new method.

Commercial Dutch cinema operates on a very slim margin of economic viability. Each film must be a commercial success; one failure, and the company would be seriously imperiled. Because of this, Shooting Star and the four or five other film companies that make up the major portion of the Dutch film industry make only one or two features per year, each one for theatrical release rather than straight to videotape, and most Dutch films are made (somewhat surprisingly) for the family market. There is a huge underground production system for pornographic films, exploitation films, and other "fringe" product, but for mainstream Netherlands' cinema, the vast majority of films are aimed at a family audience. American films, playing in huge, multi-story multiplex cinemas such as The City Cinemas in Amsterdam, still dominate the box-office, with their predictable mixture of sex, violence, and superficially spectacular special effects. Shooting Star uses digital effects for a much more gentle effect: to recreate bombed-out cityscapes in Rotterdam, for example, or to digitally create period boats and cars for their most recent film, the story of a young boy searching for his brother and father in Holland in the 1920s. Predictably, the film has a happy ending, but this is the home-produced entertainment that Dutch audiences crave from their own production companies, even as they flock to the theatres to see the equally predictable genre films *The Matrix* and *The Phantom Menace* (both 1999).

Television in Amsterdam is also remarkably sophisticated, offering programming on demand on a number of channels, including The Box, a 24-hour "video juke box" that serves up the latest hits to its patrons on a customized basis, and The Music Factory, which offers much the same service. In both cases, the videos are far more sophisticated and adventurous both thematically and visually than their American counterparts, and offer the viewer a range of music from sheer bubblegum pop to sophisticated trance/techno hybrids. One fact is immediately apparent upon even the most casual viewing of either channel; dance music, specifically trance/dance music, fuels the Amsterdam music scene, and indeed, trance and techno form the backbeat against which all of Amsterdam operates. Accessing these videos for personal viewing is easy and inexpensive. Viewers simply phone in, request a specific video, and within a minute the song of their choice is sent via cable directly to their television set for a nominal charge.

Thus, television in The Netherlands can truly be said to be interactive, as this same "programming on demand" system is also used for movies, sports, and other programming, in addition to Teletext, a service that supplies up-to-the-minute information on news, sports and weather, arranged in hundreds of individually addressable video "pages" of text, any or all of which can be summoned by the viewer/participant. Teletext, which has been in use in various versions throughout Western Europe for more than a decade, is yet another example of the ways in which TV is being transformed from a passive experience into an interactive medium. Coupled with the superior image quality of the PAL/SECAM broadcast system, with 625 lines per image, and the pervasive use of digital cameras to create films, videos, and television programs, the visual world of contemporary Holland is both seductive and slick. This will only improve when HDTV, already in use in several specialized locations throughout the city, becomes the universal broadcast standard in the early years of the twenty-first century. It is also worth noting that nearly all programming is letterboxed, and wide-screen televisions are common throughout the Netherlands.

On the other end of the spectrum, Amsterdam, through the work of The Filmmuseum (as The Nederlands Film Museum is locally known), remains respectful of cinema's past, as evidenced not only in the some 30,000 feature films housed in the museum's collection, but also in the production of new films celebrating the archival process, such as Peter Delpeut's *Diva Dolorosa* (1999), which received its world premiere in Amsterdam on June 25, 1999. Essentially a compilation film comprising scenes from silent Italian melodramas of the early 20th century, *Diva Dolorosa* follows in the footsteps of Delpeut's *Lyrical Nitrate* (1990) and *The Forbidden Quest* (1992), both of which use existing silent archival footage to constrict narrative and/or poetic meditations on the fragility and transience of the cinematic image. As we watch the film "divas" Francesca Bertini, Pina Menichelli, Lyda Borelli and others caught up in a gorgeously contrived web of evocative romance, in films that now survive in hand-tinted and machine-colored copies only through the aggressive preservation policies of modern film archival practice (all of the footage Delpeut uses was originally shot on early, highly unstable nitrate film), we are forced to contemplate not only the ephemorality of the filmic process, but also our own fleeting mortality.

Accompanied by a live orchestral score created by Loek Dikker, *Diva Dolorosa* is a valentine to cinema's past, and simultaneously a contemporaneous work which suggests how audiences in 2100 will view the films of 2000. As the auditorium fills with the silent, flickering, carefully preserved images of *Diva Dolorosa*, silent except for the accompaniment of the orchestra, we witness for seventy-five minutes a simulacrum of cinema's past. The silent cinema has long since ceased to function as a commercial medium, and it is only in specialized situations (such as archival theatres, museums and the like) that it still can find an audience. How will such films as *The Matrix* (1999) look in one hundred years? I rather suspect that, like the fragments of human existence in *Diva Dolorosa, The Matrix* will look rather like a trick film by Georges Méliès, innocently reveling in its power to astonish, unaware that one hundred years have transformed spectacle into nostalgia. *Diva Dolorosa* does not return us to the past, but it preserves it for the present, no matter what form the cinema of the future may take.

DIGITAL ANIMATION

Sally Cruikshank is an animator with a long history of film and video production, whose animated cartoons *Ducky*, 1971 (5 minutes), *Fun on Mars*, 1972 (5 minutes), *Quasi at the Quackadero*, 1975 (10 minutes), *Make Me Psychic*, 1978 (10 minutes), *Quasi's Cabaret Trailer*, 1980 (3 minutes), *Face Like a Frog*, 1987 (10 minutes), with music by Danny Elfman, *Your Feet's Too Big*, 1994 (2 minutes) and *From Your Head*, 1996 (2 minutes), with music by Betty Carter, display an arresting and bizarre visual sense akin to the old Betty Boop cartoons of the 1930s, blended with Cruikshank's own unique sensibility. Starting out in traditional animation, Cruikshank has recently moved into digital animation on the web, pursuing her craft in a new medium with astonishing virtuosity. Cruikshank's work has been honored with a retrospective at The Museum of Modern Art, and Cruikshank received the Maya Deren Award for Independent Film and Video in 1986.

Cruikshank has also done animation and main titles for commercial films, including *Twilight Zone: The Movie* (1982), *Top Secret!* (1984), *Anijam* (1984), *Ruthless People* (1986) and numerous other films. It was during this period that Cruikshank switched from traditional "cel" animation (using multiple drawings, an overhead camera to photograph them, and single-frame photography) to digital animation, essentially teaching herself as she went along.

Using this new technology, during the 1980s and 1990s Cruikshank animated and produced many children's music videos for the long-running teleseries *Sesame Street*, and in 1997 contributed to *Elmopalooza*, a

Children's Television Workshop/CBS primetime special. For the program, Cruikshank created an animated music video using a Macintosh PC computer, featuring music by Jimmy Buffett. Starting in 1999, Cruikshank began what she considers her most ambitious project to date, an extensive animated web site for her principal characters, Anita, Quasi, Snozzy, and Rollo, starring in two adventures, *Charbucks at Sea* and *Titanic II*, at <http://www.funonmars.com/html/intro.html>. An index of Cruikshank's work can be found at <http://www.awn.com/cruikshank/index.html>. I interviewed Cruikshank on her life and work in the Spring of 1999; she began by talking about her most recent work in digital animation for the web.

SALLY CRUIKSHANK: Well, this is actually the most exciting stuff I've ever done, I feel. I don't think you can find anything like this anywhere on the web right now. And it's sort of like the first days for me of independent films, because I'm able to just do whatever I want, and tell a whole story in this case. It doesn't cost me any money, and I can do it, and then change it. I can do all these crazy things, and put it up on the web, so anybody who wants to see it can see it.

WHEELER WINSTON DIXON: Tell me a bit about your past.

SC: Well, I was born in New Jersey in 1949. My sister was an extremely talented painter who was never recognized. She was talented as a child, so I was shadowed by her as an artist growing up. She died seven years ago. Initially, I wanted to be a writer. I loved her artwork, was not jealous of her ability, but it inspired me. My father worked as an accountant in New York. He was very smart and very quiet. Phi Beta Kappa from Duke. He loved classic cars, Packards. Both my parents were Southerners. His parents had both been teachers, his mother, my grandmother, was the president of St. Mary's College in Raleigh, NC, a very old school (1842) and an unusual job for a woman, I think.

My mother is a very creative and original woman, a strong personality who brightens any situation she enters. She is very observing and funny but kind-hearted and outgoing. There were many difficult and sad situations in my family during my childhood and adolescence which pointed me to an artist's life as a way of dealing with them. My parents both encouraged me, I have always been fully confident in my abilities as a student, a writer and as an artist.

I believed (naively in retrospect) that as many opportunities were open for a woman as for a man.

I collected postcards of amusement parks for many years, in particular Coney Island at the turn of the century. Fantasy in architecture, the structures built were incredible, because it was high craft, high quality, but Melies-like in sensibility. I looked at those cards a lot in designing *Quasi at the Quackadero*. I always liked amusement parks. The tawdriness appeals to me, and the excitement.

I've always liked music from the twenties. We had a 78 RPM windup phonograph in the basement when I was little, and the family famous embarrassing story is that my little friend and I used to wind up "My Bonnie Lies Over the Ocean" and dance around naked to it while my brother and his friends watched through the window! I became quite a collector of 78s for awhile. The lonely dreamy feeling of the music, the sweetness appeals to me. I still love it. I just never really liked rock music. I was not a hippie and not a drug user either, although the dean at Smith once called me into her office, convinced I took drugs because of my art work!

My junior year in college I was chosen from many art students to go to Yale Summer Art School in Norfolk Virginia. This was significant. All the art students there were chosen based on slides and talent. It was free fun and crazy! A close friend ever since, Warner Wada is the person who suggested I try animation. I was quite a compulsive drawer and there were many ducks in my drawings. So when I got back to Smith that fall, I decided to teach myself animation. I'm entirely self-taught in animation.

On the more personal side, I met my husband Jon Davison [a Hollywood producer whose credits include *Airplane* and the more recent film *Starship Troopers*] when I was looking for a producer for *Quasi's Cabaret*. We married in 1984 and have one daughter, Dinah, who is ten.

I'm very involved in my new work on the web, and am beta-testing an extraordinary program that makes my new *Titanic Two* pages easy to make. I really feel this is breakthrough material, unlike anything anyone else is doing. I also feel this is one of the most creative periods of my life. Of course I'm always finding myself in media that have no dollar signs in their future, but I am so excited to be at the forefront of a new medium before it's been all developed.

My digital animation for the Children's Television Workshop, *From Your Head* was particularly hard to visualize, because the concept was just so abstract, with the theme that "thoughts come from your head," so I was pleased with its specificness in the end. The arrhythmic jazz track, with vocal by Betty Carter, was an intriguing challenge for me, since I usually use such pronounced rhythms.

WWD: Well, you started out on the East Coast, but then you made the jump to San Francisco in the early 1970s. Why did you move to San Francisco?

SC: Actually one of the reasons I went to San Francisco was because when I first saw R. Crumb's work, I was so stunned. It just seemed so great, and like nothing I'd seen before. And then I heard there was this underground cartoonist movement. I thought, well this has got to be the place to be. And then I fell into the most extraordinary job, working for a man named Gregg Snazelle, after I created a short film called *Chow Fun*. Snazelle looked at it, and offered me the most extraordinary job, which I had for ten years, where they paid me to do whatever I wanted.

WWD: That's just utterly amazing.

SC: I know. Once in awhile I'd do a commercial, but years would go by and I wouldn't do anything, yet he continued to keep me on salary. Oh, it was incredible. We weren't close or anything. It was a very baffling situation the whole time. He was so professionally devoted to me, and yet he didn't seem very interested in my work. And that's when I made things like *Quasi at the Quackadero* and *Make Me Psychic*. But then I got stuck, after the *Quasi's Cabaret Trailer*. I don't know what it was. I'm not a very good salesperson. But I wrote scripts, had storyboards, I had a lot of meetings and nothing ever happened. And then I wrote another script that was *really* wild. It was called *Love That Makes You Crawl*, which was "R" rated. Joe Dante was going direct the live action. But then it didn't pan out. It was at the same time as *Roger Rabbit*, and then that happened, and my project didn't.

WWD: So how long did *Quasi at the Quackadero* take to make?

SC: It took me about two years. And I worked on it all the time, sixteen hours or more every day, I worked on weekends, and I painted so many cels . . . it was really a labor of love.

WWD: So, how much was the budget on that?

SC: I added it up at the end. It may have been around ten thousand. Something like that. Today, a four minute traditional animated cartoon would cost at least fifty or sixty thousand dollars.

WWD: So how did you make the jump to *The Twilight Zone*?

SC: Well, because I came down to Hollywood, looking for work. And trying to sell these features. Everything was kind of leading this way. I met my husband, Jon Davidson, and he was producing an episode of *The Twilight Zone* movie with Joe Dante. So basically that's how I got the work for *Twilight Zone* and *Top Secret*. Then came *Ruthless People*, which was really fun to do. The filmmakers were hard to work for because they wanted every joke to be the perfect joke. So they pushed me much harder that I was ever pushed myself.

WWD: But also during this period you're working for *Sesame Street*.

SC: Yes, I'd been working for them pretty steadily since 1990. But now I've switched to computers. I'm totally digital. The funny thing is, I was very anti-computer, as are most people. But I was hired to come up with ideas for a top secret computer game a couple of years ago, because a friend of mine was president of the company for awhile. I had to learn how to use the computer overnight! So I broke into the computer world through that. And then about two years ago I got another CTW job for an animated video. They were doing *Elmopalooza*, and I animated a Jimmy Buffet music video for that, using Adobe Photoshop and Adobe Premiere, and was able to color it all in myself. It didn't take nearly as long as if I'd done it in the traditional manner. Then I did another *Sesame Street* job this fall, using all the same procedures. I really feel that I'm breaking into a new area that's never been really explored.

WWD: I thought your pages were really clean, well-designed and really beautiful. And the *Cha-Cha-Cha* page is funny as hell.

SC: You have to adopt a slightly different approach to animation, because you can't use imagery in the same way. You have to use loops, small bits of animation that repeat, and you have to think in segments, rather than in large chunks. You have to have smaller files that are switching off with other smaller files.

WWD: Where do you think your future work is headed now, in what direction?

SC: I think you often see, in retrospect, new movements in the arts predicted by things that came before, but you don't see it until you have the benefit of hindsight. And I had always felt that independent animation all occurring around the same time was an indication of something that was coming ahead. That there was a new format coming, even if I couldn't figure out what it was. And now I feel like this could be what I've always felt it was heading towards. I think animation is really key to the internet. I think it will get easier and easier for people to deal with, and animation will really explode on the web in the coming years.

WWD: So are you going to try and make a feature again?

SC: I don't think so. There's too many meetings, and too many people have to work on it, and they want to change everything that you do. With my new work on the web, I can do any darn thing I want. The characters can say anything they want, and they can do whatever they want. And I can change or alter it at any time, so it's always a work in progress. Plus, it doesn't cost me any money, so no one can tell me that "this isn't commercial" or something; it makes me the final and only authority on what will happen on the screen. And there's another factor: when I put something on the web, it gets immediate distribution, and that intrigues me. So there's a lot of things to consider; it's a whole new medium. Right now, I'm doing a digital animated video for the musical group Mannheim Steamroller; it was a pretty complicated shoot in Omaha, Nebraska, with several hundred dancers, and so that should be fun to animate.

THE NEXT WAVE

Another interesting development in the new world of digital filmmaking is the emergence of a variety of production companies dedicated to creating works in this new medium. Next Wave Films, a division of The Independent Film Channel, is one of the leaders in this new movement. Headed by Peter Broderick, Next Wave has already produced a number of interesting features, including Christopher Nolan's *Following*, a superb thriller shot in England in 16mm black and white format on a shoestring budget, reminiscent in many ways of the "B" British thrillers churned out by the Danzigers and other small producers at Merton Park and New Elstree in the 1950s and '60s. Winner of the Tiger Award at the Rotterdam International Film Festival in 1999, *Following* is a neatly contrived suspense film with a series of deftly constructed twists and turns in the course of its brief narrative. Nolan photographed, wrote and directed *Following* with smooth, even arrogant assurance, even though it took him more than a year to complete, shooting on weekends, using friends as actors, and available apartments and real-life locations for his sets. As Frank Scheck observed of *Following* in an article in *The Hollywood Reporter Weekly International Edition*,

> Christopher Nolan's noirish thriller is an uncommonly polished and assured feature debut, highly clever textually and supremely accomplished technically. This ultra-low-budget exercise marks the emergence of a significant directorial talent who should have no problem parlaying this calling card into studio work. (22)

With a cast consisting of four principal characters, Nolan creates a world as convincingly claustrophobic as any of the classic suspense thrillers of the 1940s, and the film is an auspicious debut for both Nolan and Next Wave Films. The budget of the film was a mere $7,000—proof that superb films can still be produced on the most minimal of budgets. Next Wave stepped in after principal photography had been completed, and Nolan had screened a rough cut for Broderick, who was very impressed by what he saw. As Broderick told reporter Sandy George of *Screen International*, the film stood out from the competition so strikingly that Broderick felt that Next Wave simply had to acquire the film. Although *Following* was shot on film and not on digital tape, it still fit in superbly with Next Wave's overall mission. Wrote George,

> Next Wave Films has chosen a United Kingdom film, *Following*, as the second project worthy of its support. The decision underlines Next Wave president Peter Broderick's assertions that the Los Angeles-based finishing fund for ultra-low-budget features is open to films from anywhere in the world, providing that they are shot in English.
>
>   [Said Broderick,] "when the Independent Film Channel started Next Wave, I said I wanted it to be international and they were enthu-

siastic about that, but I would have supported this film if it was from Soho or Santa Monica. . . . Although *Following* screened in the Discovery Programme of this week's Toronto Film Festival, a spot that was secured with Broderick's support, Next Wave will fund improvements to the sound mix and a 35mm print. As producer's representative, it will also help implement a marketing and festival strategy, and secure distribution, particularly in the North American market.

We hope to choose at least two more films by the end of the year. We look for exceptional talent that jumps out of the screen at you . . . and theatrical potential."

To be eligible, a film must have at least finished principal photography and the budget must be less than $200,000. Next Wave can spend up to $100,000 on as many as four films each year and has screened about 450 films since its March 1997 launch. (13)

As Broderick noted in "The Making of a Movie Movement" in *MovieMaker* magazine, *Following* is just one example of the new explosion in micro-budgeted feature films, allowing even those with the most modest means at their disposal to create a feature film. Said Broderick,

Last year the typical budget of films received by Next Wave Films was in the $40,000–$60,000 range. This January [1998], we started getting movies made on budgets of $1,000–$1,500. More remarkable than the budgets was the fact that these were well-made movies. (Broderick 46)

In another interview, Broderick told reporter George Wing about his first viewing of Scott Saunders' film *The Headhunter's Sister* (1997), a ninety-six-minute feature shot on Beta SP and then transferred to 35mm film using the Sony HDTV process.

When I first saw that film, I had to pinch myself. I knew it was shot on video, but watching the image, I was having trouble believing it . . . some of these features are being shot with two or three person crews. On one film, the director was also the cameraman[,] and the only other crew member recorded sound. (Wing 48)

Scott Saunders noted other advantages to shooting on digital video. First of all, using digital tape, Saunders could afford the luxury of a 30:1

shooting ratio, which would have been financially impossible using film. Indeed, as Christopher Nolan found when shooting *Following*, if one has no money for endless re-takes, a rigorous rehearsal period is essential if the end product is to have any sort of professional polish. But on *The Headhunter's Sister*, Scott Saunders found that,

> When you shoot video [,] you can [paradoxically] often shoot fewer takes. The actors relax because they aren't under pressure to get it right the first time. So they do. But if your budget allows only one or two takes, and the pressure is on, the work with actors is often little more than damage control. (Wing 48)

Production values are not the key to a successful film for Next Wave (although high-quality sound is essential, a failing of many low-budget films), but rather a strong script, and equally adept performances. Noted Broderick,

> You're not going to shoot *Days of Heaven* on digital video, or any project where stunning panoramic photography is critical. But I believe *Clerks*, *Go Fish*, and *The Brothers McMullen* would have been just as successful if they had been shot on video. . . . Many successful no-budget filmmakers have two things in common. First, they are compelled to make films and will make them no matter what it takes. Second, instead of writing a script and then spending years trying to find financing, they begin by analyzing the resources available to them and then write their scripts. The coming of digital video has drastically reduced the financial resources they need to get their films in the can. (Wing 49)

How drastically? George Wing sums up the incredibly low-cost world of digital feature film production by noting that,

> A sample package might include a high-end consumer grade mini-DV camera such as the Canon XL-1, a DAT recorder and some microphones and a few small lights. For desktop post-production, you need a powerful PC with video capture and playback capability, loaded with a program like Adobe Premiere and plug-ins such as Sonic Foundry's Sound Forge for audio manipulation and Adobe After Effects to give your video footage a "film look." That's it. If

you wanted to own your equipment, you could buy the whole package for less than the cost of a 16mm sound mix, and you could fit it all into a duffel bag. (Wing 49)

Perhaps the most stunning example of just how low-budget digital feature filmmaking can be is Bennett Miller's *The Cruise* (1998), which Miller shot entirely on his own, using available light, and "miking" his principal performers with a wireless microphone to eliminate the need for a "boom person" to record the sound. Using a lightweight digital camera, Miller recorded the day-to-day activities of Timothy "Speed" Levitch, a tour guide who conducts decidedly eccentric tours of Manhattan on a Gray Line bus that caters to inquisitive out-of-towners. The resulting documentary is both harrowing and heartbreaking, as Levitch fights to retain his self-respect and personal integrity in a city that he both loves and despises. Shot on digital video, then blown up to 35mm for theatrical release, *The Cruise* is a riveting example of cinema verité at its rawest, as Miller's omnipresent yet unobtrusive camera records the hours and minutes in the life of a gloriously individualistic human being who refuses to buckle under to convention. *The Cruise* is a perfect example of the kind of low-cost feature that digital video makes possible—personal, compact, incisive and intensely poetic. In short, there are no more excuses for not being able to afford to produce a feature film—all one needs is talent and the will to succeed. As Lance Weiler of *The Last Broadcast*, the digital feature film produced for $900, commented, "we made an independent feature and we don't owe anyone any money" (Wing 49).

But there is still one last problem to deal with: distribution. This is where companies such as Next Wave come in, although Broderick sees the role of the distributor changing in the future as well. *The Last Broadcast* was produced on digital video, and projected as a finished digital video feature: film never entered the project at any point in its creation. Projecting with video rather than film has some drawbacks, but also numerous advantages, as Lance Weiler discovered.

When we project we get stereo surround sound instead of the limited optical track of print film. In fact, the quality of sound is so good that we have to take special pains with it, because audiences can hear any problems more clearly. (Wing 49)

Certainly George Lucas is capitalizing on this same phenomenon with his digitally projected presentations of *Star Wars: Episode I-The*

Phantom Menace, and others will follow in the wake of these films. But whether a feature is projected on film or tape, the key issue of distribution still remains. You can use a satellite to download a digital feature to a theatre for projection, but how does one get the use of the theatre in the first place? The major Hollywood studios still control distribution and theatrical release patterns worldwide, and they certainly will not relinquish this power without a fight. Says Broderick,

> The biggest problem right now is the theatrical distribution bottleneck. It has gotten increasingly difficult for movies that are independently produced and financed to get into theaters in the United States. The volume of movies being released theatrically seems overwhelming. So many movies open most Fridays in New York and Los Angeles that it is very difficult for any film without major marketing support to capture public attention. If half of the movies are studio releases and another couple are from major indie distributors, then any remaining ones without substantial marketing support have very little chance to break out. These days a movie has to succeed not just the first week, but the first Friday night.
>
> Maybe because I'm an optimist, I believe that there are going to be alternative distribution routes that will soon emerge. Theatrical distribution may remain vital for many years, but there will be new ways for independent filmmakers to reach audiences. The internet will play a key role. In the short run, you won't be watching features on your computer, but you'll be able to learn about independent films that you can order online and receive through the mail (they may cost $10 to rent or $15 to purchase). As critics start to highlight the best features that haven't received theatrical distribution, a new system will be in place for recognizing the most talented new filmmakers. This will enable them to develop a certain level of awareness, and help them to find more resources so they can keep making movies.
>
> Independent production isn't going away. Studios will be interested in financing the subsequent films of directors who launch their careers with ultra-low-budget wonders. The thing that we at Next Wave Films are sure of, based on the filmmakers we talk to and the films we see, is that people are out there determined to make movies by any means necessary. As long as that's true, there will be great new directors coming out with exceptional movies. (Zack 49)

Thus the future of the moving image is both infinite and paradoxical, removing us further and further from our corporeal reality, even as it becomes ever more tangible and seductive. The films, videotapes, and production systems discussed in this book represent only a small fraction of contemporary moving image practice, but they point in the direction to work that will be accomplished in the next century. Far from dying, the cinema is constantly being reborn, in new configurations, capture system, and modes of display. While the need to be entertained, enlightened and/or lulled into momentary escape will always remain a human constant, the cinema as we know it today will continue to undergo unceasing growth and change. Always the same, yet constantly revising itself, the moving image in the twenty-first century promises to fulfill both our most deeply held dreams, while simultaneously submitting us to a zone of hypersurveillance that will make monitoring devices of the present day seem naive and remote. Yet no matter what new genres may arise as a result of these new technologies, and no matter what audiences the moving images of the next century address, we will continue to be enthralled by the mesmeric embrace of the phantom zone of absent signification, in which the copy increasingly approaches the verisimilitude of the original.

WORKS CITED
AND CONSULTED

Adams, Thelma. "The Inside Outlaw." *Interview* (August 1998): 32, 34.

Asher, Levi. *Notes from Underground.* CD-ROM, with liner notes. New York: Literary Kicks, 1998.

Atkinson, Michael. "*Off the Menu.*" *Village Voice* (June 23, 1998): 135.

———. "Sheer Synergy: Selling Off the Dream Factory." *Village Voice* (August 4, 1998): 106.

Balun, Charles. *Lucio Fulci: Beyond the Gates.* Key West, FL: Fantasma, 1997.

Barclay, Barry. *Our Own Image.* Auckland, New Zealand: Longman Paul, 1990.

Baudrillard, Jean. *The Illusion of the End.* Chris Turner, trans. Stanford: Stanford UP, 1994.

Blythe, Martin. *Naming the Other: Images of the Maori in New Zealand Film and Television.* Metuchen, NJ: Scarecrow, 1984.

Boxer, Sarah. "Tazio Secchiaroli, the Model for 'Paparazzo,' Dies at 73." *New York Times* (July 25, 1998): B18.

Broderick, Peter, as transcribed by Joel Bachar and Scott Noegel. "The Making of a Movie Movement." *MovieMaker* 30.5 (September 1998): 44–46.

Brown, Corie, and Joshua Hammer. "Okay, So What's the Sequel?" *Newsweek Extra: A Century at the Movies* (Summer 1998): 116–118.

Brown, Jeff. "Glass Menagerie," *Pitch Weekly* (February 25–March 3, 1999): 53–54.

Brown, Lloyd L. *Paul Robeson Rediscovered.* New York: American Institute for Marxist Studies, 1976.

———. *The Young Paul Robeson: On My Journey Now.* Boulder, CO: Westview, 1997.

Brunette, Peter. *Roberto Rossellini.* New York: Oxford UP, 1987.

Bunn, Austin. "Machine Age." *Village Voice* (August 4, 1998): 27.

Burleson, Donald R. *H. P. Lovecraft: A Critical Study.* Westport, CT: Greenwood, 1983.

———. *Lovecraft: Disturbing the Universe.* Lexington: UP of Kentucky, 1990.

Burres, Bruni, Heather Harding, and Marian Masone. Program notes for the 1998 Human Rights Watch International Film Festival, *Stagebill* (June 1998): 6–15.

Cairns, Barbara, and Helen Martin. *Shadows on the Wall: A Study of Seven New Zealand Feature Films.* Auckland, New Zealand: Longman Paul, 1994.

Cannon, Peter. *H. P. Lovecraft.* Boston: Twayne, 1989.

"Cartoons Merging TV and Web Worlds." *Omaha World Herald* (Friday March 5, 1999): 44.

Charlotte, Susan, Tom Ferguson, and Bruce Felton. *Creativity: Conversations with 28 Who Excel.* Troy, MI: Momentum, 1993.

Christian, Dionne. "Seven Years On: Ratings and Realism on *Shortland Street.*" *Southern Skies* (July 1999): 62–64.

Christoffel, Paul. *Censored: A Short History of Censorship in New Zealand.* Wellington, New Zealand: Dept. of Internal Affairs, 1989.

Churchman, Geoffrey B., ed. *Celluloid Dreams: A Century of Film in New Zealand.* Wellington, New Zealand: IPL Books, 1997.

Claxton, Eve. "*Junk Food.*" *Time Out New York* 144 (June 25–July 2, 1998): 88.

Conlin, Michelle. "Sam Goldwyn on $900." *Forbes* (December 14, 1998): 168.

Crisp, Quentin. *The Naked Civil Servant.* London: Cape, 1968.

———. *How to Go to the Movies.* New York: St. Martin's, 1985.

———. *Resident Alien: The New York Diaries.* Donald Carroll, ed. London: Harper Collins, 1996.

Crisp, Quentin, with John Hofsess. *Manners from Heaven: A Divine Guide to Good Behavior.* New York: Harper and Row, 1984.

Daly, Steve. "Don't Tell Mama." *Entertainment Weekly* 443 (July 31, 1998): 32–34.

Davis, Lenwood G., ed. *A Paul Robeson Research Guide: A Selected Annotated Bibliography.* Westport, CT: Greenwood, 1982.

Debord, Guy. *The Society of the Spectacle.* Donald Nicholson-Smith, trans. New York: Zone, 1995.

Dennis, Jonathan. *Moving Images from Aotearoa, New Zealand.* Sydney: Museum of Contemporary Art, 1992.

Dennis, Jonathan, ed. *Under the Macrocarpas: Treasures of Early European Cinema: The Aran Roberts Collection.* Wellington, New Zealand: The New Zealand Film Archive, 1996.

Dennis, Jonathan, and Jan Bieringa, eds. *Films in Aotearoa New Zealand,* 2nd edition. Wellington, New Zealand: Victoria UP, 1996.

Dennis, Jonathan, and Clive Sowry. *The Tin Shed: The Origins of the National Film Unit.* Wellington, New Zealand: The New Zealand Film Archive, 1981.

"Digital Cinematography Opens New Production Opportunities." Advertisement in *Filmmaker* 6.4 (Summer 1998): 5.

Dixon, Wheeler Winston. Interview with John O'Shea. Wellington, New Zealand, August 5, 1999. Unpublished.

———. "The Portable Opera Comes of Age: Philip Glass's *Monsters of Grace.*" *Popular Culture Review* 10.2 (August 1999): 33–42.

———. "When I'm 63: An Interview with Jonathan Miller." *Popular Culture Review* 10.1 (February 1999): 1–11.

———. *Disaster and Memory: Celebrity Culture and the Crisis of Hollywood Cinema.* New York: Columbia UP, 1999.

———. *The Transparency of Spectacle: Meditations on the Moving Image.* Albany: State University of New York Press, 1998.

———. *The Exploding Eye: A Re-Visionary History of 1960s American Experimental Cinema.* Albany: State University of New York Press, 1998.

———. *The Films of Jean-Luc Godard.* Albany: State University of New York Press, 1998.

———. *It Looks at You: The Returned Gaze of Cinema.* Albany: State University of New York Press, 1995.

———. "For Ever Godard: Notes on Godard's *For Ever Mozart.*" *Literature/Film Quarterly* 26.2 (1998): 82–88.

———. "The Commercial Instinct: New Elstree Studios and the Danziger Brothers, 1956–1961." *Popular Culture Review* 9.1 (February 1998): 31–43.

———. "An Interview with Bryan Forbes." *Classic Images* 270 (December 1997): 34–40.

———. "Moving the Center: Notes Towards the Decentering of Eurocentric and American Cinema." *Popular Culture Review* 8.1 (February 1997): 3–16.

———. "The Curious Case of John H. Collins." *Classic Images* 261 (March 1997): C8–11.

———. "Surviving the Studio System: The Films of Actor/Director Alex Nicol." *Classic Images* 255 (September 1996): 28–31.

———. "Interview with Ralph Thomas: British Film Director" *Classic Images* 249 (March 1996): 34, 36, 38, 40, 42–43.

———. "Gender Approaches to Directing the Horror Film: Women Filmmakers and the Mechanisms of the Gothic." *Popular Culture Review* 7.1 (February 1996): 121–134.

———. "Ida Lupino: In the Director's Chair." *Classic Images* 248 (February 1996): 14–16, 18, 20, 22.

———. "Maureen Blackwood, Isaac Julien and the Sankofa Collective." *Film Criticism* 20.1/2 (Fall/Winter 1995–96): 131–143.

———. "The Digital Domain: Image Mesh and Manipulation in Hyperreal Cinema/Video," *Film Criticism* 20.1/2 (Fall/Winter 1995–96): 55–66.

———. "The Site of the Body in Torture/The Sight of the Tortured Body: Contemporary Incarnations of Graphic Violence in the Cinema and the Vision of Edgar Allan Poe." *Film and Philosophy* 1.1 (1994): 62–70.

———. "*Femmes Vivantes* and the Marginalized Feminine 'Other' in the Films of Reginald LeBorg." *Cinefocus* 3 (1995): 34–41.

———. "Twilight of the Empire: The Films of Roy Ward Baker." Part One, *Classic Images* 234 (December 1994): 14–16, 18, 34; Part Two, *Classic Images* 235 (January 1995): 22, 26, 28, 30; Part Three, *Classic Images* 236 (February 1995): C12, C14, C16, C18.

———. "*Act of Violence* and the Early Films of Fred Zinnemann." *Film Criticism* 28.3/29.1 (Spring/Fall 1994): 30–45.

———. "It Looks at You: Notes on the 'Look Back' in Cinema." *Post Script* 13.1 (Fall 1993): 77–87.

———. "Alice Guy: Forgotten Pioneer of the Narrative Cinema." *New Orleans Review* 19.3/4 (Fall/Winter 1992): 7–15.

———. "The Early Films of Andy Warhol." *Classic Images* 214 (April 1993): 38–40.

———. "An Interview with John Kricfalusi." *Film Criticism* 17.1 (Fall 1992): 38–49.

———. "*The Long Day Closes*: An Interview with Terence Davies." *Cineaste* 19.2/3: 20–23.

———. "Shooting *Cape Fear*: An Interview with Freddie Francis at the National Film Theatre, London." *Classic Images* 208 (October 1992): 16–20.

———. "Program Notes for a Series of Films on Dystopian Science Fiction, Curated by Wheeler Winston Dixon." *National Film Theatre Monthly* (April 1992): 8–13.

———. "The Doubled Image: Montgomery Tully's *Boys in Brown* and the Independent Frame Process." *Film Criticism* 16.1/2 (Fall/Winter 1991–92): 18–32.

———. "Cinematic Interpretations of the Works of H. P. Lovecraft." *Lovecraft Studies* 22/23 (Fall 1990): 3–9.

———. "The Early Film Criticism of François Truffaut." *New Orleans Review* 16.1 (Spring 1989): 5–32.

———. "Urban Black Music in the Late 1980s: The 'Word' as Cultural Signifier." *Midwest Quarterly* 30.2 (Winter 1989): 229–241.

———. "An Interview with Roger Corman." *Post Script* 8.1 (Fall 1988): 2–15.

———. "William Inge as Walter Gage: *Bus Riley's Back in Town*." *Literature Film Quarterly* 16.2 (Spring 1988): 101–106.

———. "H. P. Lovecraft: A Critical Reevaluation." *West Virginia University Philological Papers* 34 (Fall 1988): 102–110.

———. "Film and Literature: The Narrative Connection." *Thousand Oaks Journal* 1.1 (Fall 1987): 35–38.

———. "Cinema History and the 'B' Tradition." *New Orleans Review* 14.2 (Summer 1987): 65–71.

———. "The Performing Self in Filmed Shakespearean Drama." *Shakespeare Bulletin* 5.4 (July/August 1987): 18–19.

————. "The Romance of Crime." *Proceedings of the Fourth Annual Kent State Conference on Film.* Ohio: Kent State University, Spring 1987, 70–74.

————. "Financing for the Independent Filmmaker: Sources and Strategies." *Journal of Film and Video* 38.1 (Winter 1986): 23–34.

————. "How Does the Independent Filmmaker Deal with Hollywood?" *International Journal of Instructional Media* 12.4 (1985): 321–330.

————. "The Child as Demon in Films Since 1961." *Films in Review* 37.2 (February 1986): 78–83.

————. "François Truffaut: A Life in Film." Part One, *Films in Review* 36.6/7 (June/July 1986): 331–336; Part Two, *Films in Review* 36.8/9 (August/September 1986): 413–417.

————. "The 'B' Film in the Societal Vanguard." *Proceedings of the Third Annual Kent State Conference on Film,* Ohio: Kent State University, Spring 1985, 10–13.

————. "The Camera Vision: Narrativity and Film." *New Orleans Review* 12.2 (Summer 1985): 57–61.

————. "PRC: The Unknown Studio," *Films in Review* 35.7 (August/September 1984): 405–410.

————. "The Cinema: An Index of Directors 1929–78." *AFTA* 1.2 (Summer 1978): 140–149.

————. "In Defense of Roger Corman." *Velvet Light Trap* 16 (Fall 1976): 11–15.

Downes, Peter. *Top of the Bill: Famous New Zealand Entertainers Through the Years.* Wellington, New Zealand: A. H. and A. W. Reed, 1979.

Duberman, Martin Bauml. *Paul Robeson.* New York: Knopf, 1988.

————. "A Giant Denied His Rightful Stature in Film." *New York Times* (Sunday, March 29, 1998), Section 2: 1,38.

Duckworth, William. *Talking Music: Conversations with John Cage, Philip Glass, Laurie Anderson and Five Generations of American Experimental Composers.* New York: Schirmer, 1995.

Eder, Klaus, and Deac Russell, eds. *Dossier 11: New Chinese Cinema.* London: NFT, 1993.

Epstein, Edward Jay. "Multiplexities." *New Yorker* 74.19 (July 13, 1998): 34–37.

Faig, Kenneth W., Jr., and S. T. Joshi. "H. P. Lovecraft: His Life and Work." *H. P. Lovecraft: Four Decades of Criticism.* S. T. Joshi, ed. Athens: Ohio UP, 1980, 1–19.

Feeney, F. X. "In Vinterberg Veritas." *LA Weekly* 20.48 (October 23–29, 1998): 51.

Finley, Karen. *Living It Up: Humorous Adventures in Hyperdomesticity.* New York: Doubleday, 1996.

Fisher, Sara. "Movies on the Cheap." *Los Angeles Business Journal* (April 19, 1999): 3, 77.

Fleeman, Michael. "Film: The End of An Era." *Classic Images* 287 (May 1999): 50.

Foner, Philip S. *Paul Robeson Speaks: Writings, Speeches, Interviews 1918–1974.* New York: Brunner/Mazel, 1978.

Foster, Gwendolyn Audrey. *Women Filmmakers of the African and Asian Diaspora.* Carbondale: Southern Illinois UP, 1997.

————. *Captive Bodies: Postcolonial Subjectivity in the Cinema.* Albany: State University of New York Press, 1999.

Fusco, Coco. "Tracey Moffat." *Bomb* 64 (Summer 1998): 44–50.

Geller, Matthew. *From Receiver to Remote Control: The TV Set.* New York: The New Museum of Contemporary Art, 1990.

George, Sandy. "*Following* Wind Speeds Up Film Finishing Fund; Next Wave Backs Toronto Discovery; Seeks Ultra-Low Pics." *Screen International* (September 25–October 1, 1998): 13.

Gilliam, Dorothy Butler. *Paul Robeson: All American.* Washington D.C.: New Republic Book Company, 1976.

Glass, Philip, and Robert T. Jones. *Music by Philip Glass.* New York: Harper and Row, 1987.

Glass, Philip, and Robert Wilson. *Monsters of Grace* web site at http://www.extremetaste.com.

Glass, Philip, Robert Wilson, and Jelaluddin Rumi. Libretto for *Monsters of Grace: A Digital Opera in Three Dimensions.* Dexter, Michigan: Thomson-Shore, 1998.

Glover, David. "Looking for Edgar Wallace: The Author as Consumer." *History Workshop Journal* 37 (Spring 1994): 143–164.

Goins, Liesa. "Crackling Crisp." *Resident* (June 23, 1998): 15.

Gomez, Edward M. "A 60s Free Spirit Whose Main Subject Was Herself." *New York Times* (Sunday, July 5, 1998): Section 2, 29, 31.

Gómez-Peña, Guillermo. Manifesto for *El Mexterminator.* New York: Creative Time/El Museo del Barrio, 1998.

Gómez-Peña, Guillermo, and Roberto Sifuentes. *Temple of Confessions: Mexican Beasts and Living Santos.* New York: Powerhouse, 1998.

Gove, Alex. "Beam Me Down: An All-Digital Movie Challenges Traditional Film Distribution Methods." *Red Herring* (April 1999): 136.

Graham, Shirley. *Paul Robeson: Citizen of the World.* New York: Julian Messner, 1948.

Grainger, Matthew. "Review of *Scarfies.*" *The Dominion* (August 6, 1999): 16.

Graser, Marc. "Digital on Tech Menu at Cannes' MITIC Pavilion." *Variety* (May 10–16, 1999): C8.

Gross, Larry. "Stellan Skarsgård." *Bomb* 64 (Summer 1998): 36–42.

Gussow, Mel. "The Whitney Cancels a Karen Finley Exhibition." *New York Times* (July 4, 1998): B12.

Haden-Guest, Anthony. "Dept. of Night Life: Clubgoers Are Seeing the Future—and the Future Is Seeing Them." *New Yorker* 74.20 (July 20, 1998): 27.

Hamburger, Aaron. "Wry Crisp: Quotable Quentin Crisp Doesn't Mince Words," *New York Blade* (June 12, 1998): 25.

Harris, Richard James. "Once-Thriving Film Business Battles the Blues." *Variety* (June 22–28, 1998): 34.

Harvey, Dennis. "A Winning Equation from Tyro Helmer." *Variety* (January 26–February 1, 1998): 67.

———. "Story Holes Keep Pic from Docu Nirvana." *Variety* (January 26–February 1, 1998): 71.

Hayward, Henry J. *Here's To Life: The Impressions, Confessions, and Garnered Thoughts of a Free-Minded Showman.* New Zealand: Oswald Sealey, 1944.

Heim, Michael. *Virtual Realism.* New York: Oxford UP, 1998.

Hernandez, Eugene. "Beam Me Up!: Using Satellite Hook-Up, *The Last Broadcast* Makes its Theatrical Premiere." *The Independent* (October 1998): 34–35.

Herskovitz, Jon. "Exploits Go to Extremes: Programs of Bizarre Are a Hit in Japan." *Variety* (June 22–28, 1998): 29.

Hoberman, Jim. "Thru a Lens Darkly." *Village Voice* (June 9, 1998): 143.

Hornaday, Ann. "Low Budget *Blair Witch Project* Earns Big Bucks." *Omaha World Herald* (August 13, 1999): 41.

Horrocks, Roger. *Meet the Filmmakers Catalogues Series.* Auckland, New Zealand: Auckland City Art Gallery, 1985.

———. *Composing Motion: Len Lye and Experimental Film-Making.* Wellington, New Zealand: National Art Gallery, 1991.

Hoveyda, Fereydoun. "Notes on Roberto Rossellini's *India.*" *Anthology Film Archive Program Notes* (May–June, 1998): 16.

Ingham, Gordon. *Everyone's Gone to the Movies: The Sixty Cinemas of Auckland.* Auckland, New Zealand: Cyclostyle, 1973.

Jacobson, Sarah. "Being and Nothingness." *Filmmaker* 6.4 (Summer 1998): 44, 47.

James, Nick, ed. *360 Classic Feature Films from the National Film and Television Archive.* Special supplement to *Sight and Sound* 8.6 (June 1998).

———. "Medium Cool." *Sight and Sound* 8.8 (August, 1998): 12–15.

Jaymanne, Laleen. "'Love Me Tender, Love Me True, Never Let Me Go . . .'; A Sri Lankan Reading of Tracey Moffat's *Night Cries: A Rural Tragedy.*" *Feminism and the Politics of Difference*, Sneja Gunew and Anna Yeatman, eds. St. Leonard, Australia: Allen and Unwin, 73–84.

Jones, Graham. *Talking Pictures: Interviews with Contemporary British Filmmakers.* Lucy Johnson, ed. London: BFI, 1997.

Jones, Kent. "Girl Crazy: Benoît Jacquot's Cinema of Seduction." *Village Voice* (August 4, 1998): 106.

Joshi, S. T. "Lovecraft Criticism: A Study." *H. P. Lovecraft: Four Decades of Criticism.* S. T. Joshi, ed. Athens: Ohio UP, 1980: 20–26.

Kaufman, Anthony. "French Film *est mort? Non!* The Next Wave." *Indie* (July–August 1998): 15, 17.

Kelly, William. "Lynn Hershman Leeson: On Conceiving Byron's Daughter." *Cover* 13.2: 32.

Kisseloff, Jeff. *The Box: An Oral History of Television, 1920–1961.* New York: Viking, 1995.

Klawans, Stuart. "Crime Most Unfoul." *The Nation* (July 27–August 3, 1998): 35–36.

Konow, David. *Schlock-O-Rama: The Films of Al Adamson.* Los Angeles: Lone Eagle, 1998.

Kostalanetz, Richard. *Writings on Glass: Essays, Interviews, and Criticism.* New York: Schirmer, 1997.

Kusama, Yayoi. *Recent Works.* New York: Robert Miller Gallery, 1996.

———. *Hustler's Grotto: Three Novellas.* Ralph F. McCarthy, trans. Berkeley: Wandering Mind, 1998.

———. *Violet Obsession.* Hisako Ifshin and Ralph F. McCarthy, trans. Berkeley: Wandering Mind, 1998.

Leguizamo, John, and David Bar Katz. *Playbill* (98.7) for *Freak,* July 1998.

Leshko, Adriana. "Voices from the Ukraine's Past Tell the Story of the Great Terros." *Ukrainian Weekly* (Sunday, June 7, 1998): 6, 21.

Levi, Asher. *Notes from Underground.* CD-ROM, with liner notes. New York: Literary Kicks, 1998.

Lévy, Maurice. *Lovecraft: A Study in the Fantastic.* S. T. Joshi, trans. Detroit: Wayne State UP, 1988.

Lewenz, Lisa. Presskit for *A Letter Without Words.* New York: 1998. Unpaginated.

Lim, Dennis. "Kino's Scope." *Village Voice* (May 12, 1998): 128.

Long, Frank Belknap. *Howard Phillips Lovecraft: Dreamer on the Nightside.* Sauk City, WI: Arkham House, 1975.

Lovecraft, H. P. *The Dunwich Horror and Others.* Selected by August Derleth, textual editing by S. T. Joshi. Introduction by Robert Bloch. Sauk City, WI: Arkham House, 1963.

———. *Selected Letters V: 1934–1937.* August Derleth and James Turner, eds. Sauk City, WI: Arkham House, 1976.

Mabbott, T. O. "H. P. Lovecraft: An Appreciation." *H. P. Lovecraft: Four Decades of Criticism.* S. T. Joshi, ed. Athens: Ohio UP, 1980, 43–45.

MacCaulay, Scott. "The Numbers Game: An Interview with Darren Aronofsky and Eric Watson." *Filmmaker* 6.4 (Summer 1998): 26–30.

MacDonald, Scott. "Raphael Montañez Ortiz." *A Critical Cinema 3: Interviews with Independent Filmmakers.* Berkeley: University of California Press, 1998, 324–346.

Markoff, John. "Fight of the (Next) Century: Converging Technologies Put Sony and Microsoft on a Collision Course." *New York Times* (Sunday, March 7, 1999): Section 3, 1, 11.

Martin, Adrian. "Tracey Moffat: The Go-Between." *World Art* 2 (1995): 24–29.

Martin, Helen, and Sam Edwards. *New Zealand Film 1912–1996.* Auckland, New Zealand: Oxford UP, 1997.

Martin, Michael T., ed. *Cinemas of the Black Diaspora: Diversity, Dependence and Oppositionality.* Detroit: Wayne State UP, 1995.

Mathews, Jack. "Movies at the Cutting Edge." *New York Daily News, New York Now* Magazine Section, Sunday, April 11, 1999: 2.

McLauchlan, Gordon, ed. *New Zealand Encyclopedia.* Auckland, New Zealand: David Bateman, 1992.

Mellencamp, Patricia. "Haunted History: Tracey Moffat and Julie Dash." *Discourse* 16.2 (Winter 1993/1994): 127–163.

Mirams, Gordon. *Speaking Candidly: Films and People in New Zealand.* Hamilton: Paul's Book Arcade, 1945.

Moffat, Tracey, and Gael Newton. *Tracey Moffat: Fever Pitch.* Sydney: Piper Press, 1996.

Morse, Margaret. *Virtualities: Television, Media Art, and Cyberculture.* Bloomington: Indiana UP, 1998.

New Zealand Film Archive Database Catalogue (computer data base). Wellington, New Zealand, 1999.

O'Shea, John. "Some Notes on Film Production in New Zealand." Unpublished report for the Department of Industries and Commerce, 1966.

———. *Don't Let It Get You! Memories—Documents.* Wellington, New Zealand: Victoria UP, 1999.

Palmer, Scott. *A Who's Who of Australian and New Zealand Film Actors: The Sound Era.* Metuchen, NJ, 1988.

Pevzner, Vadim. Manifesto on his film and video work, distributed at a screening at the Void, New York, NY, Summer, 1998.

"The Pieces of *Pi.*" *Filmmaker* 6.4 (Summer 1998): 82.

Pirie, David. "Roger Corman's Descent in the Maelstrom." *Roger Corman: The Millenic Vision.* David Will and Paul Willemen, eds. Edinburgh Film Festival: 1970, 45–67.

Pressbook for *Amor Vertical*. Paris: Pandora Distribution, 1997.

Price, Simon. *New Zealand's First Talkies: Early Filmmaking in Otago and Southland 1896–1939*. Dunedin: Otago Heritage Books, 1996.

Program notes for *Monsters of Grace*, performance Thursday, February 19, 1999, the Lied Center for the Performing Arts, Lincoln, NE. In *Lied Magazine* (February/March 1999): 13–20.

Pultz, David. Pressbook for *The Great Terror*. NY: Wellspring Films, 1997.

Rafferty, Terrence. "The Shrug of the New." *GQ* (March, 1999): 129–130, 132, 134, 136.

Reid, John F. *Some Aspects of Film Production in New Zealand: A Report Prepared for the Queen Elizabeth II Arts Council of New Zealand*, 1972. Manuscript only, held in private collection of the New Zealand Fondation.

Reid, Nicholas. *A Decade of New Zealand Film: Sleeping Dogs to Came a Hot Friday*. Dunedin: John McIndoe, 1986.

Robeson, Paul. *Here I Stand*. New York: Othello, 1958.

Rotherstein, Edward. "Class Lessons: Who's Calling Whom Tacky?" *New York Times* (July 25, 1998): A11, A13.

Sawhill, Ray. "A Talk with Pauline Kael." Newsweek Extra: A Century at the Movies (Summer 1998): 93–94.

Scheck, Frank. "Nolan Embraces a Strong Following." *The Hollywood Reporter Weekly International Edition* (April 13–19, 1999): 22.

Scher, Julia. "The House That Watches Back." *From Receiver to Remote Control: The TV Set*. Matthew Geller, ed. New York: The New Museum of Contemporary Art, 1990, 116, 117.

Schneeman, Carolee. *Up to and Including Her Limits*. New York: The New Museum of Contemporary Art, 1996.

Schnoebelen, Tyler. "Be More Than You Can Be." *Village Voice* (July 21, 1998): 42–43.

Schwartz, Stan. "*Voyage to the Beginning of the World*." *Time Out New York* 144 (June 25–July 2, 1998): 86.

Schwarz, Robert K. *Minimalists*. London: Phaidon, 1996.

Schweitzer, Darrell. *The Dream Quest of H. P. Lovecraft*. San Bernardino, CA: Borgo, 1978.

Scott, Winfield Townley. "His Most Fantastic Creation: Howard Phillips Love-craft." *Exiles and Fabrications.* Garden City, NY: Doubleday, 1961, 50–72.

Shreffler, Philip A. *The H. P. Lovecraft Companion.* Westport, CT: Greenwood, 1977.

Sigley, Simon. *The Cinema in New Zealand: A Short Survey.* Unpublished paper, held in the collections of the New Zealand Film Archive.

Sirmans, Franklin. "Tracey Moffat: So Many Stories to Tell." *Flash Art* 30.195 (Summer 1997): 118–121.

Smith, Dinitia. "Chantal Akerman and the Point of Point of View." *New York Times* (Sunday, April 26, 1998): Section 2, 15, 24.

Smith, Peter, John Reid, and Nevil Gibson. *The Moving Image: A Bulletin for Schools.* Wellington, New Zealand: School Publications Branch, Department of Education, 1974.

Smith, Roberta. "Jane and Louise Wilson: *Stasi City.*" *New York Times* (June 5, 1998): E37.

Society for Old and New Media Pamphlet, n.p., 1998.

Sowry, Clive. *Film Making in New Zealand: A ??? Historical Survey.* Wellington, New Zealand: New Zealand Film Archive, 1984.

Sterngold, James. "A Preview of Coming Attractions: Digital Projectors Could Bring Drastic Changes to Movie Industry." *New York Times* (Monday, February 22, 1999): C1–2.

Strauss, Neil. "Hong Kong Film: Exit the Dragon?" *New York Times* (Sunday, August 2, 1998): Section 2, 1, 22.

———. "Amid Decline, Some Standouts." *New York Times* (Sunday, August 2, 1998): Section 2, 23.

Streisand, Betsy. "Chris Walker: A Man and His Suit Reanimate Animation." *U.S. News and World Report* (December 28, 1998–January 4, 1999): 56–57.

Sullivan, Maureen. "Taking Stock: Economic Concerns Replace Chinese Worries on Territory's Front Burner." *Variety* (June 22–28, 1998): 33, 38.

Tashima, Chris. Production notes from *Visas and Virtue.* Los Angeles: 1996, 1997, unpaginated.

Tomkins, Calvin. "Mind Games: Charles Ray and Andrew Wyeth Collide at the Whitney." *New Yorker* 74.20 (July 20, 1998): 70–73.

Tucker, Marcia, ed. *The Art of Memory: The Loss of History.* New York: The New Museum of Contemporary Art, 1985.

Twik, John. "Digital Habitat: Lance Weiler and Stefan Avalos." *RES* 2 (Winter 1998): 46–47.

Vaigro, Wendy. *Carnival and the Grotesque Body in Contemporary Women's Art and Film.* M.A. Thesis, University of Auckland, 1992. Unpublished. Held in the collection of the New Zealand Film Archive.

Vinterberg, Thomas. "Dogma 95: The Vow of Chastity." *LA Weekly* 20.48 (October 23–29, 1998): 51.

Vita, Simon. "A Life Still Rolling." *Wellington City Voice* (August 5, 1999): 13.

Wassmann, Jung, ed. *Pacific Answers to Western Hegemony: Cultural Practices of Identity Construction.* Oxford: New York, 1998.

Watson, Chris, and Roy Shuker. *In the Public Good?: Censorship in New Zealand.* Palmerston North: Dunmore, 1998.

Watson, Russell, and Corie Brown. "The 100 Best of 100 Years." *Newsweek Extra: A Century at the Movies* (Summer 1998): 20.

Weinraub, Bernard. "Two Mediums Make Like One." *New York Times* (Sunday, July 19, 1998): Section 2, 1, 20.

Weitzman, Elizabeth. "Truth's Ally." *Interview* (August 1998): 72–73.

Wilson, Edmund. "Tales of the Marvelous and the Ridiculous." *H. P. Lovecraft: Four Decades of Criticism.* S. T. Joshi, ed. Athens: Ohio UP, 1980, 46–49.

Wing, George. "The Digital Revolution." *MovieMaker* 30.5 (September 1998): 48–49.

Wood, John, ed. *The Virtual Embodied: Presence/Practice/Technology.* London: Routledge, 1998.

Zack, Christopher. "Many Happy Returns (By Any Means Necessary)." *MoveMaker* 30.5 (September 1998): 47–49.Zelevansky, Lynn. "Driving Image: Yayoi Kusama in New York." In *Love Forever: Yayoi Kusama 1958–1968.* Lynn Zelevansky, Laura Hoptman, Akira Tatehata, and Alexandra Munroe. Los Angeles: Los Angeles County Museum of Art, 1998, 10–41.

Zelevansky, Lynn, Laura Hoptman, Akira Tatehata, and Alexandra Munroe. *Love Forever: Yayoi Kusama 1958–1968.* Los Angeles: Los Angeles County Museum of Art, 1998.

Zha, Jianying. *China Pop: How Soap Operas, Tabloids and Bestsellers Are Transforming a Culture.* New York: The New Press, 1995.

ABOUT THE AUTHOR

Wheeler Winston Dixon is Professor of English, Chairperson of the Film Studies Program at the University of Nebraska, Lincoln, and editor of the State University of New York Press series on Cultural Studies in Cinema/Video. His most recent book is *Disaster and Memory: Celebrity Culture and the Crisis of Hollywood Cinema* (Columbia University Press, 1999). Forthcoming is *Film Genre 2000: New Critical Essays* (State University of New York Press, 2000). With Gwendolyn Foster, Dixon was recently appointed editor-in-chief of the journal *Quarterly Review of Film and Video*.

INDEX